D0939043

Please return or renew by
latest date below

LOAN[illegible] MAY BE RENEWED BY PHONE
[illegible]48-5710

ECONOMETRICS

ECONOMETRICS

A VARYING COEFFICIENTS APPROACH

BALDEV RAJ AND AMAN ULLAH

WITHDRAWN
☐ DESELECTED
☐ LOST
☐ DAMAGED
☐ MISSING (INV.)
☐ OTHER________

ST. MARTINS PRESS NEW YORK

HB
139
R33

©1981 B. Raj and A. Ullah

All rights reserved. For information write:
St. Martin's Press, Inc., 175 Fifth Avenue, New York, NY 10010
Printed in Great Britain
First published in the United States of America in 1981

Library of Congress Catalog Card Number 81-50016

ISBN 0-312-22632-2

WARD CHIPMAN LIBRARY
U.N.B. IN SAINT J HN

Contents

1987(K-9835)734

List of Tables and Figures

TABLES

FIGURES

Preface

The purpose of this book, which is written for economists, is threefold: (a) To provide a simple, unified and systematic treatment of the alternative forms of varying coefficients model; (b) To illustrate various applications of the varying coefficients model; and (c) To provide an extensive bibliography of the past and ongoing research in this area. Thus, the book has two important characteristics: (a) the topics covered in most standard textbooks (and some new topics, such as the analyses of structural break and aggregation, ridge regression and the Bayesian estimation) are discussed in the context of the random coefficients model as opposed to the fixed coefficients model (an assumption which is restrictive and sometimes unnecessary); and (b) most chapters have a section on the application(s) of the model.

The book is divided into two parts: single equation and multi equations models. The first nine chapters in Part One deal with the problems of statistical inference in single equation linear models with varying coefficients. The prerequisites are first level courses in econometrics, calculus and matrix algebra. The text in Part Two is slightly more advanced. However, the entire book could easily serve as a text for a second level one-semester course in senior undergraduate and graduate econometrics.

To facilitate the students who need to refresh their knowledge of statistical concepts we have provided a brief review in Appendix A. However, no separate review appendix on matrix algebra is provided in the book since most contemporary books in econometrics contain such a review and students have easy access to at least one such text. Moreover, we have stated the necessary results in matrix algebra either in the main text or in the notes at the end of each chapter.

We gratefully acknowledge the financial assistance from the Social Science and Humanities Research Council of Canada in the form of research and leave fellowship grants, as well as the research and typing help at Wilfrid Laurier University and the University of Western Ontario.

We are especially grateful to P.A.V.B. Swamy for his helpful comments and suggestions on a number of our working papers. We also wish to thank Brian Bentley, Ralph Blackmore, Asraul Hoque and Lonnie Magee for their help in reading parts of the book at various stages of its preparation. We would also like to thank Marg Gower (Western Ontario) for typing of the first draft, Dave Kroeker for copy editing, Elsie Grogan (Wilfrid Laurier) for exceptional care in preparing the final typed copy and Margaret Dilworth for proof reading. Our special thanks to the editor, Peter Sowden, for his assistance at various stages of completion of the manuscript.

Finally, we wish sincerely to thank Balbeer Raj, Rahul Raj, and Shobha Ullah for their affection and moral support, which helped immeasurably in completion of this book.

August, 1980

Baldev Raj
Aman Ullah

Part One
Single Equation Varying Coefficient Models

1. Introduction

1.1 PREAMBLE

Econometric model building is concerned mainly with statistical inference of such behavioural economic relationships as the consumption and investment functions, wage equations and the production function. The econometric methods employed to estimate economic relationships often assume that the regression coefficients do not change from observation to observation. The assumption that the coefficients are fixed is restrictive and sometimes even unnecessary. Consider, for example, the regression of the quantity demanded of a certain commodity on its price. If time series data are used on these variables, it is quite likely that the price elasticity of demand will not remain the same over the sample period.

Similarly, in a cross-section study of the production function of firms, labour and capital elasticities might vary from small firms to large firms due to economies of scale, managerial abilities, etc. In another example of a regression relationship between savings and incomes of a sample of households, the marginal propensity to save is likely to differ for each household because of different average ages and wealth holdings. This indicates that the assumption of fixed coefficients in modelling economic relations is restrictive and that a more flexible approach to econometric modelling requires that regression coefficients vary from observation to observation.

1.2 CAUSES OF COEFFICIENT VARIATION

Essentially, an econometric model is an approximation of reality and as a result is subject to a number of misspecifications such as the exclusion of relevant variables, a wrong choice of functional form , etc. These lead to a variation in coefficients. Five of the main causes for such variation are discussed below.

(i) Coefficient Variation due to Omitted Variables

Consider an econometric relationship

(1.1) $$y=f(x_1,x_2,..,x_K)+u$$

where y is (say, linearly) related to a set of explanatory variables. The error in regression u captures the influence of the omitted explanatory variables which are normally assumed to have a minor effect on the dependent variable. However, the omitted variables may be more significant than assumed. Then it is clear that the regression relationship needs to be respecified by including the significant omitted variables. This may not always be possible, however, because of the limitation of the number of observations and hence the degrees of freedom. If so, their inclusion may actually reduce the explanatory power of the model. Variables, moreover, may have to be omitted because of problems of measurement.

Often an alternative is to assume a first order autoregressive process for u, that is, $u = \rho u_{-1} + v$, where the subscript -1 represents a lagged value of u and the v is a serially uncorrelated error. The problem with this alternative is that even though the incorporation of this may change the value of a coefficient it may not reflect the fact that the coefficient varies for different observations.

When omitted variables are changing, it may be more appropriate to add a varying intercept term to capture their effect. In econometric forecasting it has frequently been necessary to adjust the intercepts of the equation to take into account various structural changes (see Klein and Evans [1967]). It is important to note that if the behaviour of the omitted variables is subtle and fluctuating it can also lead to changes in the coefficients of the included variables. When coefficient variation is due to omitted variables that are highly significant it would be more reasonable to include them. But even where it is possible, the inclusion of omitted variables in a linear fashion may not eliminate the variability of the coefficients. Duffy (1969) has shown that changes in coefficients related to omitted variables will produce variation in the coefficients of included variables in the regression, unless the omitted variables are uncorrelated with both the dependent and independent variables.

(ii) Coefficient Variation Due to Proxy Variables

When some explanatory variables are not measurable it is a common practice to use proxy variables in their place. The use of proxy variables can be another source of coefficient variation. Consider, for example, the log linear production function

$$(1.2) \qquad y=\beta_1+\beta_2 x_2+\beta_3 x_3+u$$

where y represents the log of output, and x_2 and x_3 represent the log of the flow of capital and labour inputs. The true variable x_2 cannot be directly measured. Accordingly, the stock of capital (say x_2^*) is used as a proxy for x_2. The coefficients of the log linear model when estimated with x_2^* are subject to bias. This is because we are now estimating the model $y=\beta_1+\beta_2 x_2^*+\beta_3 x_3+w$ where $w=\beta_2(x_2-x_2^*)+u$ is correlated with x_2^*. The bias is likely to vary because of the fluctuations in the intensity of capital utilisation. Thus, output elasticities of capital and labour would vary over the business cycle. This suggests that the use of proxy variables can be a source of coefficient variation.

(iii) Coefficient Variation Due to an Incorrect Functional Form

A common practice in econometrics is to formulate linear relationship among economic variables. If this is incorrect, the estimated coefficients may be subject to variation. Suppose the functional form (1.2) for the log linear production function is incorrect and the true functional form is given as

$$y=\beta_1+\beta_2x_2+\beta_3x_3+\beta_4x_2x_3+u.$$

Then the output elasticities of capital and labour respectively are:

$$\frac{\partial y}{\partial x_2}=\beta_2+\beta_4x_3$$

$$\frac{\partial y}{\partial x_3}=\beta_3+\beta_4x_2,$$

which are not constant.

(iv) Coefficient Variation Due to Policy Variables

In many situations the economic relationships are derived from some maximisation (or minimisation) principle by economic agents taking policy variables into account. Accordingly, these policy variables are determinants of the parameters of the model.

For example, consider a firm as an economic agent which wants to maximise its profit,

$$\pi=py-wx_1-rx_2,$$

where y is output, x_1 and x_2 are the labour and capital inputs (policy variables), p is the price, w and r are the wage and interest rate. Let the output be given by:

$$y=\alpha x_1^{\beta_1}x_2^{\beta_2}$$

where α, β_1, β_2 are the parameters of this relationship. Then from the first order conditions for a maximum, that is, $\partial\pi/\partial x_1=0$ and $\partial\pi/\partial x_2=0$, we obtain

$\beta_1 = wx_1/py$ and $\beta_2 = wx_2/py$. This implies that both β_1 and β_2 are the function of policy variables and hence vary.

Lucas (1976) has argued that most long run policy evaluations based on the fixed coefficients model are meaningless. This is because the equations in an econometric model represent the optimal decision rules of the economic agents. These decision rules vary systematically with the structure of forecasting series, which are of interest to the decision makers and are a function of policy variables. Thus if policy variables change it will effect the behavioural equations, and hence the parameters. The way out is therefore to formulate the econometric model with varying coefficients.

(v) Coefficient Variation Due to Aggregation

Often econometric relationships are among macro variables which are the outcome of an aggregation over micro variables. In some situations it may be reasonable to assume that the process describing the distribution over time of these macro variables is stationary if the process generating the distribution over time of micro variables is stationary. However, over long periods of time the aggregation weights of micro economic units would change as the relative importance of micro units change. Thus, either the macro variables may not reflect the change at all, or may reflect it inaccurately, resulting in misspecification of macro model and coefficient variation.

Another source of coefficient variation may be due to the use of aggregated variables which are indexed at discrete time points. However, if these aggregated variables are obtained from an underlying process which is continuous over time, then the coefficients of such intertemporally aggregated relationships would not be constant but varying (Sims [1971]).[1]

1.3 HISTORICAL NOTE

In 1947 Wald first observed that the coefficients in a regression equation can be random. He made the statement: 'In some problems it seems reasonable to assume that the regression coefficients $\beta_1, \beta_2, .., \beta_p$ are not constants but chance variables'. (Wald (1947), p. 586). However, he did not explore this idea further. Later Hurwicz (1950) and Rubin (1950) developed this idea and suggested a maximum likelihood estimation method for some simple cases of such a model. The later work by Klein (1953), Theil and Mennes (1959), Nerlove (1965), Rao (1965), Zellner (1966) and Fisk (1967), provided further motivation and understanding of the nature of the problems of inference from the random coefficients model.

A more rigorous and fruitful study regarding the estimation problem was taken up by Hildreth and Houck in 1968. In the same year Swamy (1968) examined a model with cross-sectional time series data under the assumption that the coefficients vary across the cross-sectional units. A closely related model, based upon the Kalman filtering, was also considered by Rosenberg (1968). The work of Cooley (1971) and Cooley and Prescott (1973) with respect to the adaptive coefficients model popularised the random coefficients model with applied researchers.

Recently several researchers, including the authors of this text, have contributed in this important area. The material in this text covers most of the work done to date.[2]

1.4 BRIEF OUTLINE OF THE BOOK

The coefficient variation can be systematic and/or random. The alternative specifications for these two kinds of coefficient variations and their implications for estimation are examined in this text, which has 13 chapters divided into two parts. The first nine chapters in Part One deal with the econometrics of single equation, whereas Part Two, with four chapters, deals with multi equation varying coefficient models. Appendix A contains a brief review of the statistical concepts.

This text discusses most of the econometric topics covered in a standard econometrics text but with two important differences: (a) The topics are discussed in the context of a randomly varying coefficients model as opposed to a fixed coefficients model; and (b) Most of the chapters have a section on application(s) of the model. The material for the text is obtained from published and unpublished sources. We have attempted to cite references wherever possible without jeopardising the smooth flow of the material.

NOTES

1. Apart from these justifications for varying coefficients one may use some statistical tests to verify if the coefficients are changing or not. A number of ad hoc procedures exist for this purpose. These procedures require testing either for the statistical significance of the coefficient(s) of dummy or trend variable(s) in the regression or for the serial correlation in the error structure or break in the regression structure. More recently tests based on the princi-

ples of Lagrage-multiplier, likelihood ratio and Wald have been suggested. See Chapters 4 and 9.

2. The two topics not covered in the text are: (a) A random coefficients approach to time series models (see Liu and Tiao [1980] and Havenner and Swamy [1978]); and (b) A random coefficient Probit model (see Akin, Guilkey and Sickles [1979]).

2. Simple Linear Model with Varying Coefficients

2.1 INTRODUCTION

In Chapter 1 we discussed the causes of variation in the coefficients of a linear regression model. Now we shall consider the problem of estimation of a simple linear model with varying coefficients using alternative specifications for the varying coefficients.

Consider a linear functional relationship between two variables, y and x, with varying coefficients,

$$y_i = \beta_i x_i + \alpha_i + u_i \qquad i=1,2,...,n \tag{2.1}$$

where y_i is the ith observation on the dependent variable, x_i is the ith observation on the independent (or explanatory) variable and u_i is the ith value of the disturbance (or error) term in the regression. The α_i and β_i are the unknown regression coefficients, which take different values for different observations. The disturbance term u_i represents the influence of leftover variables and arises because all the relevant factors cannot be accounted for in the regression. We make the following simplifying assumptions regarding the disturbance term u_i:

(i) $E(u_i)=0$ for all i

(ii) $E(u_i^2)=\sigma^2$ for all i

(iii) $E(u_i u_j)=0$ for all $i \neq j$; $i,j=1,\ldots,n$

(iv) $E(u_i x_i)=0$ for all i.

In simple terms these assumptions state that the disturbances in the regression have zero mean, constant variance and they are uncorrelated. Also, they are uncorrelated with the independent variable. The objective is to obtain estimators of the unknown parameters α_i's and β_i's. For this we turn to the 'method of least squares', i.e. choose $\hat{\alpha}_i$ and $\hat{\beta}_i$ as estimators of α_i and β_i, respectively, so that

$$S = \sum_1^n (y_i - \hat{\beta}_i x_i - \hat{\alpha}_i)^2$$

is a minimum. This is done by equating the first derivatives of S with respect to α_i and β_i to zero. We get

$$\frac{\partial S}{\partial \hat{\alpha}_i} = \sum_1^n 2(y_i - \hat{\beta}_i x_i - \hat{\alpha}_i)(-1)=0,$$

or

$$(2.2) \qquad \sum_1^n y_i = \sum_1^n \hat{\beta}_i x_i + \sum_1^n \hat{\alpha}_i .$$

Similarly,

$$\frac{\partial S}{\partial \hat{\beta}_i} = \sum_1^n 2(y_i - \hat{\beta}_i x_i - \hat{\alpha}_i)(-x_i)=0,$$

or

$$(2.3) \qquad \sum_1^n y_i x_i = \sum_1^n \hat{\beta}_i x_i^2 + \sum_1^n \hat{\alpha}_i x_i .$$

It can easily be verified that it is impossible to obtain solutions for the 2n unknown $\hat{\alpha}_i$'s and $\hat{\beta}_i$'s from the two normal equations (2.2) and (2.3). Thus to achieve the objective of obtaining estimators in the linear regression model (2.1) we need to utilize some prior information about the coefficients α_i's and β_i's. Many different types of prior information are possible. These can be broadly classified as (a) Systematic priors consisting of only nonstochastic terms; and (b) Stochastic priors consisting of both systematic and random components. The model (2.1) using systematic and stochastic priors will be called, respectively, the systematically varying coefficient and the randomly varying coefficient models. We shall consider each of these two kinds of models under alternative prior information.

In general the estimation of the systematically varying coefficients model is straightforward The estimators obtained are both consistent and efficient. On the other hand, in the case of the randomly varying coefficients model the estimation problem is more difficult. The easily obtained consistent estimators of the parameters will not be as efficient as those discussed later in this chapter. The problem of efficient estimation will be taken up in the next chapter.

2.2 SYSTEMATICALLY VARYING COEFFICIENT MODELS UNDER ALTERNATIVE SPECIFICATIONS

A common prior assumption regarding the varying

α_i's and β_i's in (2.1) is that these coefficients remain fixed (or stable) over all observations. This assumption, though restrictive, produces consistent and efficient estimators of the two fixed coefficients. The best justification for this assumption is its simplicity. The estimates of fixed coefficients can also serve as initial estimates in obtaining the optimal estimators for the random coefficient models discussed in Chapter 3. The fixed coefficients assumption implies that

$$(2.4) \qquad \beta_i = \beta \text{ and } \alpha_i = \alpha \quad \text{for all } i.$$

The linear regression model (2.1) under this assumption becomes $y_i = \beta x_i + \alpha + u_i$, where α is the common intercept term and β is the common slope coefficient. Further, the normal equations (2.2) and (2.3) now become

$$(2.2a) \qquad \Sigma y_i = \hat{\beta}\, \Sigma\, x_i + \hat{\alpha}\, n$$

$$(2.3a) \qquad \Sigma y_i x_i = \hat{\beta}\, \Sigma\, x_i^2 + \hat{\alpha}\, \Sigma x_i .$$

These two normal equations in two unknowns, $\hat{\beta}$ and $\hat{\alpha}$, yield the following solutions:

$$(2.5) \qquad \hat{\beta} = \frac{\Sigma(x_i - \bar{x})(y_i - \bar{y})}{\Sigma(x_i - \bar{x})^2} = \Sigma d_i y_i = \beta + \Sigma d_i u_i ,$$

$$(2.6) \qquad \hat{\alpha} = \bar{y} - \hat{\beta}\bar{x} = \Sigma e_i y_i = \alpha + \Sigma e_i u_i ,$$

where

$$d_i = (x_i - \bar{x}) / \Sigma (x_i - \bar{x})^2,$$

$$e_i = (1/n) - \bar{x} d_i,$$

$$\bar{y} = \Sigma y_i / n,$$

$$\bar{x} = \Sigma x_i / n.$$

It is easily verified that $E\hat{\beta}=\beta$ and $E\hat{\alpha}=\alpha$, and $\operatorname{plim}_{n\to\infty} \hat{\beta}=\beta$ and $\operatorname{plim}_{n\to\infty} \hat{\alpha}=\alpha$. The estimators $\hat{\beta}$ and $\hat{\alpha}$ are known as ordinary least squares (OLS) estimators, and they are the Best Linear Unbiased Estimators (BLUE) of β and α under assumptions (i) to (iv).

Another prior assumption regarding the varying coefficients in model (2.1) could be that they vary systematically with the policy variable(s). Supposing that variations in both β_i and α_i can be explained by movements in the policy variable p_i, we write

(2.7) $\quad \beta_i = \beta + \delta p_i$ and $\alpha_i = \alpha + \gamma p_i$ for all i,

where α, β, γ and δ are unknown fixed parameters and p_i is the ith observation on the policy variable. The simple linear model (2.1) under assumption (2.7) becomes the multiple regression model:

(2.8) $\quad y_i = \beta x_i + \gamma p_i + \delta p_i x_i + \alpha + u_i.$

Now, if we assume that p_i and u_i are uncorrelated: $E(p_i u_i)=0$, then we can write the normal equations corresponding to (2.2) and (2.3) as

$$
\begin{aligned}
(2.9)\quad \Sigma y_i &= \hat{\beta}\,\Sigma x_i + \hat{\gamma}\,\Sigma p_i + \hat{\delta}\,\Sigma p_i x_i + \hat{\alpha} n, \\
\Sigma y_i x_i &= \hat{\beta}\,\Sigma x_i^2 + \hat{\gamma}\,\Sigma p_i x_i + \hat{\delta}\,\Sigma p_i x_i^2 + \hat{\alpha}\,\Sigma x_i, \\
\Sigma y_i p_i &= \hat{\beta}\,\Sigma p_i x_i + \hat{\gamma}\,\Sigma p_i^2 + \hat{\delta}\,\Sigma p_i^2 x_i + \hat{\alpha}\,\Sigma p_i, \\
\Sigma y_i p_i x_i &= \hat{\beta}\,\Sigma p_i x_i^2 + \hat{\gamma}\,\Sigma p_i^2 x_i + \hat{\delta}\,\Sigma p_i^2 x_i^2 + \hat{\alpha}\,\Sigma p_i x_i.
\end{aligned}
$$

These are four equations in four unknowns, which may be solved to obtain the OLS estimators of the fixed coefficients α, β, γ and δ, provided that p_i and x_i are not linearly related. Substituting these estimators in (2.7) one can then get $\hat{\beta}_i = \hat{\beta}+\hat{\delta}p_i$ and $\hat{\alpha}_i = \hat{\alpha}+\hat{\gamma}p_i$, the estimators of β_i and α_i, respectively. A justification for (2.7) is that econometric relations such as (2.1) are generally an outcome of maximisation (or minimisation) behaviour of the micro unit taking the policy variables into account in their decision. Policy variables as determinants of regression coefficients may enter the model in interaction with independent variables in addition to entering additively. It is interesting that the resulting linear regression model (2.8) may be used to test the hypothesis that α_i and β_i are not influenced by the policy variable p_i (or α_i's and β_i's are fixed coefficients). The hypothesis that α_i and β_i are fixed is equivalent to the hypothesis that $\gamma=\delta=0$.

Thus the systematically varying coefficients model amounts to nonlinear transformation of regressors in some cases and poses no serious problem in the efficient estimation except that the number of regressors in the model is increased and a criterion to select a specific set of policy

$V(e_i) = Ee_i^2 = \sigma^2(2+x_i^2)$ where $V(u_i)=V(\varepsilon_i)=V(\eta_i)=\sigma^2$ and $Eu_i\varepsilon_i=E\varepsilon_i\eta_i=Eu_i\eta_i=0$.

Now consider another random coefficient specification by adding the random error in the systematic specification of (2.7), viz.,

$$(2.15) \qquad \beta_i = \beta+\delta p_i+\eta_i,$$

$$\alpha_i = \alpha+\gamma p_i+\varepsilon_i.$$

Substituting (2.15) into model (2.1), we write

$$(2.16) \qquad y_i = \beta x_i+\gamma p_i+\delta p_i x_i+\alpha+e_i,$$

where $e_i=u_i+\varepsilon_i+\eta_i x_i$. Once again, the four normal equations under the OLS technique are identical to (2.9) provided u_i, ε_i and η_i are distributed with zero means and are uncorrelated with p_i and x_i. The OLS estimators of unknown coefficients from (2.9) may be used to obtain consistent estimators of variable mean responses $\beta+\delta p_i$ and $\alpha+\gamma p_i$ respectively of the random coefficients β_i and α_i. It is important to note that the error term e_i is again heteroscedastic even under the restrictive assumptions that the error terms u_i, ε_i and η_i are homoscedastic with a common variance and are mutually uncorrelated. Thus the OLS estimators of α, β, γ and δ will again be consistent and unbiased but not efficient. The efficient estimation of unknown parameters will be discussed in the next chapter.

It is not necessary to have a random coefficient specification just by adding an error in systematic components. Thus, for example, a prior assumption regarding varying coefficients in model (2.1) may be that the coefficients are random but vary sequentially over observations as

(2.17) $$\beta_i = \lambda_{11}\beta_{i-1}+\lambda_{12}\alpha_{i-1}+\eta_i,$$

$$\alpha_i = \lambda_{21}\alpha_{i-1}+\lambda_{22}\beta_{i-1}+\varepsilon_i,$$

where λ's are known transition constants and ε's and η's are random errors as before. The specification (2.17) is fairly common in control theory, engineering and applied physical sciences literature and commonly referred to as Kalman filter and adaptive filter models.[3] The prior knowledge about the transition constants reflects the prior belief of the analyst about the class of paths for the varying coefficients β_i and α_i. The problem of identifying an appropriate set of λ's in model (2.17)is similar to the problem of isolating the appropriate variable(s) to be included in the model.

An alternative way of looking at the Kalman filter type specification is given below. Suppose p_i and z_i are two economic policy variables such that according to the specification in (2.15)

$$\beta_i = \gamma p_i+\eta_i,$$

$$\alpha_i = \delta z_i+\varepsilon_i.$$

Now consider the variables p_i and z_i such that

$$p_i=\rho_{11}p_{i-1}+\rho_{12}z_{i-1},$$

$$z_i=\rho_{12}z_{i-1}+\rho_{22}p_{i-1},$$

where ρ's are the response coefficients. Then substituting these values of p_i and z_i into β_i and α_i would provide a specification similar to (2.17) where coefficients vary sequentially with a complex error structure.

A special case of sequentially varying coefficient models where $\lambda_{11}=\lambda_{22}=1$, and $\lambda_{12}=\lambda_{21}=0$ is commonly referred to as the adpative regression model. This was developed independently by Cooley (1971) and Cooley and Prescott (1973a). In this case, specification (2.17) reduces to

$$\beta_i=\beta_{i-1}+\eta_i, \tag{2.18}$$

$$\alpha_i=\alpha_{i-1}+\varepsilon_i.$$

After repeated substitutions (2.18) may be written as

$$\beta_i = \beta_o+ \sum_{s=1}^{i} \eta_s \quad \text{or } \beta_i = \beta_o+ \sum_{s=o}^{i-1} \eta_{i-s}, \tag{2.19}$$

$$\alpha_i = \alpha_o+ \sum_{s=1}^{i} \varepsilon_s \quad \text{or } \alpha_i = \alpha_o+ \sum_{s=o}^{i-1} \varepsilon_{i-s},$$

where β_o and α_o are (fixed) initial values for β_i and α_i respectively. Once again we see that formulation (2.19) decomposes the coefficients β_i and α_i into deterministic and random parts as in the case of (2.12) and (2.15). However, note that the random part is now in thc form of moving averages or the sum of the random walk of the errors. This specification is suitable provided the coefficients are believed to drift continuously from period to period. A special case, where $\beta_i=0$ and α_i is given by (2.19), was considered by Muth (1960) for economic predictions from (2.1).

Model (2.1) under assumption (2.19) becomes

$$y_i = \beta_o x_i + \alpha_o + e_i^*, \tag{2.20}$$

where $e_i^* = u_i + \sum_{s=1}^{i} \varepsilon_s + x_i \sum_{s=1}^{i} \eta_s$ for all i. Assuming ε_i and η_i have zero mean and are uncorrelated with u_i and x_i, we can write the consistent and unbiased OLS estimators of β_o and α_o from the normal equations

$$(2.21) \qquad \Sigma y_i = \hat{\beta}_o \Sigma x_i + \hat{\alpha}_o n,$$

$$\Sigma y_i x_i = \hat{\beta}_o \Sigma x_i^2 + \hat{\alpha}_o \Sigma x_i.$$

These estimators will be identical to the estimators of β and α under the specification of (2.12). The error e_i^* in (2.20) has, however, a more complex variance-covariance structure than e_i in the model (2.13). Thus the efficient estimators incorporating error structures in the respective models will be different.

Another special case of sequentially varying coefficient models is commonly referred to as stochastically convergent coefficient models introduced by Rosenberg (1968 and 1973c). The prior specification for this type of model requires that the adaptive process converges to the fixed and unknown population (norm) value. The tendency of the varying coefficients to converge to respective population values results from the interdependency of individual responses to similar environments. Social interaction among community members tends to preserve similarity among individuals playing the same role. Supposing β and α respectively are the fixed unknown norms for the converging stochastic coefficients β_i and α_i, then the stochastically convergent coefficients assumption can be written as

(2.22) $$\beta_i=\lambda\beta_{i-1}+(1-\lambda)\beta+\eta_i,$$

$$\alpha_i=\lambda\alpha_{i-1}+(1-\lambda)\alpha+\varepsilon_i,$$

where $0 < \lambda < 1$ is an autoregressive parameter and η_i and ε_i are the stochastic error terms as before. The term $(1-\lambda)$ is referred to as a drift factor to the sequentially varying coefficients. Alternatively, after repeated substitutions and simplification, we may write (2.22) as

(2.23) $$\beta_i=\lambda^i\beta_0+(1-\lambda^i)\beta+\sum_{s=0}^{i-1}\lambda^s\eta_{i-s},$$

$$\alpha_i=\lambda^i\alpha_0+(1-\lambda^i)\alpha+\sum_{s=0}^{i-1}\lambda^s\varepsilon_{i-s}.$$

It is easily seen that for $\lambda=1$ and $\lambda=0$ the stochastic convergent coefficient specification reduces to the adaptive coefficient (2.19) and the purely random coefficient (2.12) specifications, respectively.

We note that the stochastically convergent coefficient specification (2.23) also decomposes the variation in coefficients into a (fixed) deterministic part and a stochastic part. But the errors are serially correlated because they follow a moving average process. For estimation of β_0, β, α_0 and α we can first substitute (2.23) in (2.1) and write

$$y_i= z_{1i}\beta_0+z_{2i}\beta+z_{3i}\alpha_0+z_{4i}\alpha+e_i^{**},$$

where

$$e_i^{**} = u_i+(\sum_{s=0}^{i-1}\lambda^s\eta_{i-s})x_i+\sum_{s=0}^{i-1}\lambda^s\varepsilon_{i-s},$$

and

$$z_{1i} = \lambda^i x_i; \; z_{2i} = (1-\lambda^i)x_i;$$

$$z_{3i} = \lambda^i; \; z_{4i} = (1-\lambda^i).$$

Now, as in the earlier case of the adaptive coefficients model, the nature of e_i^{**} is complex. It is both serially correlated and heteroscedastic. However, an iterative estimation technique, ignoring this nature of e_i^{**}, can be carried out. We can do OLS estimation for different values of λ in the range $0<\lambda<1$, say at a step of 0.1, and stop where the residual sum of squares is minimum. Obviously, the OLS estimates will be inefficient even though unbiased and consistent.

2.4 REVIEW

In Section 2.1 we began with the model

$$y_i = \beta_i x_i + \alpha_i + u_i$$

and emphasized the point that unless we have some prior information about β_i and α_i this model cannot be estimated on the basis of sample information alone. We therefore looked into various possible priors in Sections 2.2 and 2.3. These priors were broadly classified into (A) fixed and systematically varying coefficients; and (B) randomly varying coefficients. In case A the varying coefficients have only a deterministic part whereas in case B, both deterministic and stochastic parts. Alternative specifications under A and B can be summarized in the following way:

A. Systematically Varying Coefficients

(i) Fixed coefficients; $\beta_i=\beta$ and $\alpha_i=\alpha$.

(ii) Functional coefficients; $\beta_i=f(z_i)$, $\alpha_i=g(z_i)$ where z_i is an economic variable.

(iii) Switching coefficients; $\beta_i=f(D_i)$, $\alpha_i=g(D_i)$ where D_i is a binary variable.

B. Randomly Varying Coefficients

(i) Purely random coefficients (Rao, and Hildreth and Houck); these are generally obtained by adding stochastic component in A(i) and A(ii), e.g. $\beta_i=\beta+\eta_i$ or $\beta_i=f(z_i)+\eta_i$.

(ii) Sequentially varying coefficients (Kalman filter type); the two popular ones in this case are:

(a) adaptive coefficients (Cooley and Prescott);

(b) stochastically convergent coefficients (Rosenberg).

Regarding estimation, it was shown that in case A of systematically varying coefficients one can use OLS which is BLUE. On the other hand, in the case of B it was observed that the error structure of the model (2.1) gets complicated, that is, becomes both serially correlated and heteroscedastic. Thus though one could still obtain OLS estimates - which will be consistent and unbiased - they will not be efficient. In the following chapter, therefore, we consider the efficient estimation of the model (2.1) under the randomly varying coefficients specification only.

2.5 A MODEL FOR DISCRIMINATING AMONG ALTERNATIVE VARYING COEFFICIENTS SPECIFICATIONS: AN EXAMPLE

Consider the problem of modelling the evolution of the systematic risk of a stock (or its beta coefficients) over time, that is,

$$y_i=\beta_i x_i+u_i \qquad i=1,2,\ldots,n, \tag{2.24}$$

where y and x represent the excess return, respectively, on the stock and the market portfolio; β is the evolving beta coefficient over time and u is a stochastic error term with zero mean, constant variance σ_u^2, and it is serially uncorrelated. The above single-parameter characterisation of systematic risk is obtained by transforming the usual two-parameter market model through the capital asset pricing model.

Now consider two observations of excess return on the stock, y_i and y_{i+j}, corresponding to two points in time j periods apart. The observation of return y_i is given in (2.24) while the observation of return y_{i+j} is

$$y_{i+j}=\beta_{i+j}x_{i+j}+u_{i+j}. \tag{2.25}$$

Multiplying (2.24) by x_{i+j} and (2.25) by x_i, and subtracting we obtain

$$\begin{aligned} y^*_{i,j}&=y_{i+j}x_i-y_i x_{i+j} \\ &=x_i x_{i+j}(\beta_{i+j}-\beta_i)+x_i u_{i+j}-x_{i+j}u_i. \end{aligned} \tag{2.26}$$

Assuming u_i is independent of $(\beta_{i+j}-\beta_i)$, we can write the mathematical expectation of $y^{*2}_{i,j}$ as

$$(2.27) \qquad E(y^{*2}_{i,j}) = x_i^2 x_{i+j}^2 E(\beta_{i+j}-\beta_i)^2 + (x_i^2+x_{i+j}^2)Eu_i^2,$$

or

$$y^{*2}_{i,j} = x_i^2 x_{i+j}^2 \sigma_\beta^2 + (x_i^2+x_{i+j}^2)\sigma_u^2 + \text{error},$$

where expected value of error is zero. Thus, we can use this regression of $y^{*2}_{i,j}$ on the variables $(x_i^2 x_{i+j}^2)$ and $(x_i^2+x_{i+j}^2)$ to obtain OLS estimates of σ_β^2 and σ_u^2. The estimators are unbiased, that is, $E\hat{\sigma}_\beta^2 = \sigma_\beta^2$ and $E\hat{\sigma}_u^2 = \sigma_u^2$.

Now we observe the nature of $\sigma_\beta^2 = E(\beta_{i+j}-\beta_i)^2$ under alternative specifications on β_i. For example, in the case of fixed betas, $\beta_i=\beta$ and $\sigma_\beta^2 = 0$. In the case of purely random betas $\beta_i=\beta+\varepsilon_i$, where ε_i is distributed with zero mean, variance σ_ε^2 and is serially uncorrelated. Thus

$$\sigma_\beta^2 = E(\beta_{i+j}-\beta_i)^2 = E(\varepsilon_{i+j}-\varepsilon_i)^2 = 2\sigma_\varepsilon^2 .$$

In the case of the adaptive betas $\beta_i=\beta_{i-1}+\eta_i$ where the disturbance term η_i has zero mean, constant variance σ_η^2 and is serially uncorrelated, we get $(\beta_{i+j}-\beta_i) = \sum_{s=1}^{j} \eta_{i+s}$. Thus the variance of betas $\sigma_\beta^2=E(\beta_{i+j}-\beta_i)^2 = j\sigma_\eta^2$ which increases linearly over time. Finally, for the convergent varying betas $\beta_i = \lambda\beta_{i-1}+(1-\lambda)\beta+\mu_i$ and $0<\lambda<1$, we can write

$$\beta_{i+j}-\beta_i = (1-\lambda^j)(\beta-\beta_i)+\sum_{i=1}^{j}\lambda^{j-s}\,\mu_{i+s},$$

where the error term μ_i has zero mean, constant variance σ_μ^2 and is serially uncorrelated. Therefore $E(\beta_{i+j}-\beta_i)^2 = \sigma_\beta^2 = (1-\lambda^j)^2 E(\beta-\beta_i)^2 + \frac{1-\lambda^{2j}}{1-\lambda^2}\sigma_\mu^2$ which increases over time and for $j\to\infty$ converges to the value, $\lim_{j\to\infty} E(\beta_{i+j}-\beta_i)^2 = E(\beta-\beta_i)^2 + \frac{\sigma_\mu{}^2}{1-\lambda^2}$. We note that $\beta_i-\beta = \lambda^i(\beta-\beta_0)+\sum_{s=0}^{i-1}\lambda^s\mu_{s-i}$ [see (2.23)] and thus $E(\beta-\beta_i)^2 = \lambda^{2i}(\beta_0-\beta)^2+\frac{1-\lambda^{2i}}{1-\lambda^2}\,\sigma_\mu^2$. The characteristics of the alternative processes generating betas are summarized in Table 2.1.

A graphical plot of $E(\beta_{i+j}-\beta_i)^2 = \sigma_\beta^2$ against j for alternative models is instructive and is given in Figure 2.1

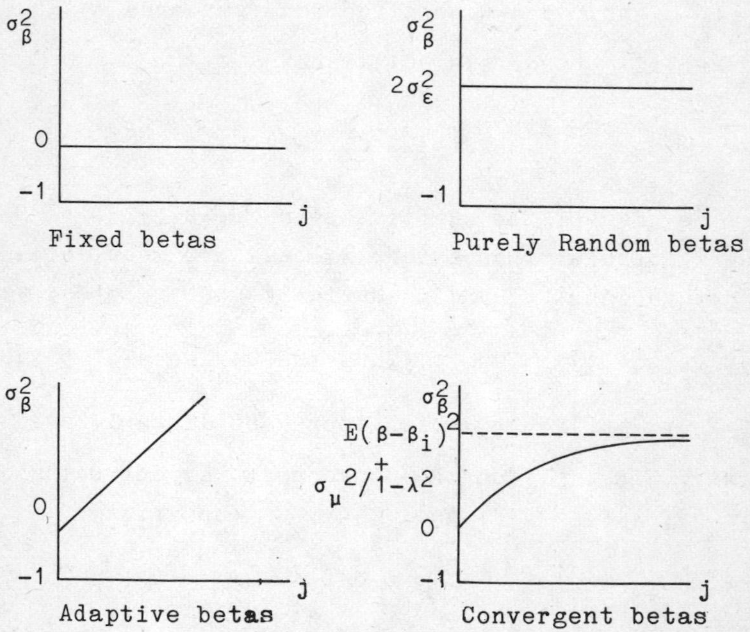

FIGURE 2.1

Table 2.1: Summary of Properties of Alternative Models for Betas

Models	Assumption	$\beta_{i+j}-\beta_i$	$E(\beta_{i+j}-\beta_i)^2$	$\lim_{j\to\infty} E(\beta_{i+j}-\beta_i)^2$
Fixed Coefficient	$\beta_i = \beta$	0	0	0
Purely Random Coefficient	$\beta_i = \beta + \varepsilon_i$	$\varepsilon_{i+j} - \varepsilon_i$	$2\sigma_\varepsilon^2$	$2\sigma_\varepsilon^2$
Adaptive Coefficient	$\beta_i = \beta_{i-1} + \eta_i$	$\sum_{s=1}^{j} \eta_{i+s}$	$j\sigma_\eta^2$	∞
Convergent Coefficient	$\beta_i = \lambda\beta_{i-1}$ $+ (1-\lambda)\beta + \mu_i$	$(1-\lambda^j)(\beta-\beta_i)$ $+ \sum_{s=1}^{j} \lambda^{j-s}\mu_{i+s}$	$(1-\lambda^j)^2 E(\beta-\beta_i)^2$ $+ \frac{(1-\lambda^{2j})}{1-\lambda^2}\sigma_\mu^2$	$E(\beta-\beta_i)^2$ $+ \frac{\sigma_\mu^2}{1-\lambda^2}$

Source: Schaefer et al. (1975).

On the basis of the above characteristics of betas it is important to note that if the fixed coefficient assumption holds then $E\hat{\sigma}_\beta{}^2=\sigma_\beta^2=0$. But, when any of the other three varying coefficient specifications is considered $E\hat{\sigma}_\beta{}^2=\sigma_\beta{}^2 > 0$. Thus, though the test for the null hypothesis $H_o:\sigma_\beta{}^2=0$ against the alternative hypothesis $H_1:\sigma_\beta{}^2>0$ will not discriminate among alternative models it will discriminate between fixed and randomly varying models. However, if the cross-section of time series data are available and one could divide time into convenient subperiods, then one could discriminate among alternative specifications by examining the behaviour of cross-section averaged estimates of $\sigma_\beta{}^2$ for various values of j.

Schaefer et al.(1975) proposed and employed the above methodology to study the variances of excess return on US stocks traded on the New York Stock Exchange over the period 1926 to 1971.

In order to discriminate among alternative beta models the estimates of $\sigma_\beta{}^2$ and $\sigma_u{}^2$ were computed from the equation (2.27) for various values of j between 1 and 50. The results, averaged across stocks and over groups of sequential values of j are given in Table 2.2.

We note that while strong statements about the nature of the process regarding $\hat{\sigma}_\beta^2$ are difficult to make in view of large estimation errors inherent in the methodology, we may make the following weaker statements regarding the problem of discriminating among alternative varying coefficient models.[4] In the periods 1926-1935 and 1936-1945 the value of σ_β^2 tends to increase with j, which suggests that the period 1926-1945 conforms to an adaptive coefficients rather than a random

Table 2.2: Estimate of $E(\beta_{i+j}-\beta_i)^2$ averaged over stocks and over sequential values of j

Range of j	Feb.1926-Dec.1935	Jan.1936-Dec.1945	Jan.1946-Dec.1955	Jan.1956-Dec.1965	Jan.1966-Dec.1971	Feb.1926-Dec.1971
1- 5	0.4760	0.4059	0.1420	-0.0489	-0.0016	0.4244
6-10	0.3790	0.4337	-0.0264	0.1201	0.4753	0.4765
11-15	1.4980	0.4098	0.1434	0.9829	-0.0700	0.6981
16-20	0.9648	0.2628	0.2986	0.1484	0.0261	0.6280
21-25	0.9994	0.5137	0.4882	-0.5609	0.3915	0.5751
26-30	0.6895	0.4514	0.7398	-0.3271	0.4668	0.5189
31-35	1.4628	0.6379	0.4921	-0.2654	-0.1619	0.6068
36-40	1.1876	0.5354	-0.0436	0.3581	-0.9268	0.5264
41-45	1.4370	0.6815	0.4560	0.9329	0.0394	0.5359
46-50	1.7115	0.8626	0.2703	0.3656	-0.8479	0.6118

Source: Schaefer et al. (1975)

coefficients model. The pattern of σ^2_β is weaker in the period 1946-1955 and this period doesn't appear to conform to any of the four models discussed above. Finally, the pattern of σ^2_β in the period 1956-1971 appears to conform to the random coefficients model.

NOTES

1. The switching regression model can be extended in several directions: i) To permit more than two regimes; ii) To permit continuous switching back and forth; and iii) To permit random switching. See Goldfeld and Quandt (1973a, 1973b) and Goldfeld and Quandt (1976), Chapter 1. Also see Poirier (1976) and Suits et al. (1978) for a Spline theoretical approach to the switching regression model.

2. Swamy (1968) independently developed a similar model.

3. See Kalman and Bucy (1961), Sage and Melsa (1971) and Cooper (1973).

4. In addition the problem of negative estimates can arise due to estimation error. The problem of negative variances of randomly varying coefficients is discussed in Chapters 3 and 4.

3. Estimation of Means and Variances of Random Coefficients in a Simple Regression Model

3.1 INTRODUCTION

In Chapter 2 we noted that though the efficient estimation of the model with systematically varying coefficients is straightforward, it is not so in the case of randomly varying coefficients. In this chapter we shall discuss the estimation of the means and variances of purely random coefficient and sequentially varying (adaptive coefficients and stochastically convergent) coefficient models. The estimation of coefficients themselves is considered in the next chapter.

3.2 ESTIMATION OF THE PURELY RANDOM COEFFICIENT MODELS

Consider a simple linear regression model with randomly varying coefficients,

$$(3.1) \qquad y_i = \beta_i x_i + \alpha_i + u_i \qquad i = 1, 2, \ldots, n,$$

where y and x are, respectively, the dependent and explanatory variables and u is the usual error term. We shall assume that u's have zero mean, constant variance σ^2 and are serially uncorrelated. Also, u's are uncorrelated with the x's. The randomly varying regression coefficients are assumed to have decompositions,

(3.2) $\beta_i = \beta + \eta_i$

$\alpha_i = \alpha + \varepsilon_i$

where β and α are fixed systematic parts and ε_i and η_i are random parts. We assume that

(3.3a) $E\,\varepsilon_i = E\eta_i = 0$ for all i;

(3.3b) $V(\varepsilon_i) = E\varepsilon_i^2 = \sigma_\eta^2 = \sigma_\beta^2$,

$V(\eta_i) = E\eta_i^2 = \sigma_\varepsilon^2 = \sigma_\alpha^2$ for all i;

(3.3c) $Cov(\varepsilon_i, \varepsilon_{i'}) = Cov(\eta_i, \eta_{i'}) = 0$ if $i \neq i'$,

$Cov(\varepsilon_i, \eta_i) = 0$ for all i.

Assumptions (3.3) imply that the stochastic parts ε_i and η_i have zero means, constant variances and are serially uncorrelated. Also u_i, ε_i and η_i are contemporaneously uncorrelated. Under these assumptions β and α are the means while σ_β^2 and σ_α^2 are the variances of randomly varying coefficients. The estimation problem in the simple linear regression model (3.1) to (3.3) requires that we obtain efficient estimators of the mean coefficients (β, α), the variances $(\sigma_\beta^2, \sigma_\alpha^2, \sigma^2)$ and the actual coefficients (β_i and α_i). The problem of estimation of the mean coefficients and the variances will be taken up in this chapter. The problem of estimation of the actual coefficients will be discussed in Chapter 4.

3.2.1 The Generalised Least Squares Estimators of the Mean Coefficients

Substituting (3.2) into (3.1), we write

$$y_i=\beta x_i+\alpha+e_i, \tag{3.4}$$

where $e_i=u_i+\varepsilon_i+\eta_i x_i$. Under the assumptions (3.3a) to (3.3c) and also that

$$E(\eta_i x_i)=E(\varepsilon_i x_i)=E(u_i x_i)=0, \tag{3.5}$$

$$E(\varepsilon_i u_i)=E(u_i \eta_i)=0, \tag{3.6}$$

we can obtain the means, variances and covariances of e_i's as

(3.7a) $\quad Ee_i=E(u_i+\varepsilon_i+\eta_i x_i)=0 \quad$ for all i,

(3.7b) $\quad V(e_i)= Ee_i^2= E(u_i+\varepsilon_i+\eta_i x_i)^2$

$$= \sigma^2+\sigma_\alpha^2+ x_i^2\sigma_\beta^2,$$

(3.7c) $\quad Cov(e_i,e_{i'})= E(e_i e_{i'})$

$$= E(u_i+\varepsilon_i+\eta_i x_i)$$

$$(u_{i'}+ \varepsilon_{i'}+ \eta_{i'}x_{i'}) =0,$$

if $i\neq i'$, i, $i'=1,\ldots,n$.

Thus the composite errors e_i's are heteroscedastic but serially uncorrelated even under the simplest assumptions about stochastic terms in the model. It can be easily verified that the composite errors in model (3.4) will be both heteroscedastic and serially correlated when the stochastic terms in

(3.2) or (3.1) are serially correlated. An appropriate method for estimating and in the integrated model is the Generalised Least Squares (GLS) which yields the best linear unbiased estimators (BLUE) when the variances are known. In the GLS method we choose the values of β and α, say $\beta = \hat{\beta}$ and $\alpha = \hat{\alpha}$, that minimise the weighted residual sum of squares,

$$S = \sum_{i=1}^{n} w_i (y_i - \hat{\beta} x_i - \hat{\alpha})^2,$$

where $w_i = 1/[(\sigma^2 + \sigma_\alpha^2) + x_i^2 \sigma_\beta^2] = 1/V(e_i)$ are the weights. To find the values of β and α that minimise S, we have to differentiate S with respect to β and α and equate these derivatives to zero. This gives

$$\frac{\partial S}{\partial \hat{\beta}} = \sum_{i=1}^{n} \frac{\partial w_i (y_i - \hat{\beta} x_i - \hat{\alpha})^2}{\partial \hat{\beta}}$$

$$= -2 \sum_{i=1}^{n} w_i x_i (y_i - \hat{\beta} x_i - \hat{\alpha}) = 0$$

and

$$\frac{\partial S}{\partial \hat{\alpha}} = \sum_{i=1}^{n} \frac{\partial w_i (y_i - \hat{\beta} x_i - \hat{\alpha})^2}{\partial \hat{\alpha}}$$

$$= -2 \sum_{i=1}^{n} w_i (y_i - \hat{\beta} x_i - \hat{\alpha}) = 0.$$

Thus, the GLS estimators $\hat{\beta}$ and $\hat{\alpha}$ of the mean coefficients β and α satisfy the following normal equations:

$$\sum w_i x_i (y_i - \hat{\beta} x_i - \hat{\alpha}) = 0,$$

and

$$\sum w_i (y_i - \hat{\beta} x_i - \hat{\alpha}) = 0.$$

The solution to these equations yields

$$\hat{\beta} = \frac{\Sigma\, w_i \Sigma\, w_i y_i x_i - \Sigma\, w_i x_i \Sigma w_i y_i}{\Sigma\, w_i \Sigma\, w_i x_i^2 - (\Sigma\, w_i x_i)^2}, \tag{3.8}$$

$$\hat{\alpha} = \frac{\Sigma\, w_i x_i^2 \,\Sigma\, w_i y_i - \Sigma\, w_i x_i \Sigma\, w_i y_i x_i}{\Sigma\, w_i \Sigma\, w_i x_i^2 - (\Sigma\, w_i x_i)^2}.$$

The GLS estimators $\hat{\beta}$ and $\hat{\alpha}$ are non operational because the variances of random coefficients and hence w_i are unknown. The estimated or operational GLS estimators of β and α may be obtained by replacing the unknown variances in w_i by their estimators. The question then is how do we get these estimators for the variances? A popular method of deriving them is as follows. Let $\hat{e}$'s be the ordinary least squares (OLS) residuals such that $\hat{e}_i=y_i-bx_i-a$, where $b= \Sigma\,(y_i-\bar{y})(x_i-\bar{x})/\Sigma\,(x_i-\bar{x})^2$ and $a=\bar{y}-b\bar{x}$ are the OLS estimators of β and α respectively in model (3.4). After substituting the OLS estimates of β and α in $\hat{e}_i$'s and rearranging the terms involving x_i's, we can write

$$\hat{e}_i = \sum_{j=1}^{n} m_{ij} y_j = \sum_{j=1}^{n} m_{ij} e_j,$$

where $m_{ij} = -\Sigma x_i^2 + x_i \Sigma\, x_i + x_j \Sigma\, x_i - n x_i x_j + \delta_{ij}$, for $i,j=1,2,\ldots,n$; $\delta_{ij}=1$ when $j=i$ and it is zero when $j\neq i$. Now we obtain the variances of the OLS least squares residuals, viz.,

$$V(\hat{e}_i) = E(\hat{e}_i - E\hat{e}_i)^2 = E\hat{e}_i^2 = E[\sum_{j=1}^{n} m_{ij} e_j]^2, \tag{3.9}$$

$$= \sum_{j=1}^{n} m_{ij}^2 E e_j^2 = \sum_{j=1}^{n} m_{ij}^2 [(\sigma^2+\sigma_\alpha^2)+x_j^2\sigma_\beta^2].$$

In deriving (3.9), we have used the results in (3.7c) and $Ee_i = \Sigma m_{ij} Ee_j = 0$.

Further, defining $\hat{e}_i^2 - E\hat{e}_i^2 = f_i$, we may write equation (3.9) as

$$(3.10) \qquad \hat{e}_i^2 = (\sigma^2+\sigma_\alpha^2)g_{1i}+\sigma_\beta^2 g_{2i}+f_i,$$

where $g_{1i} = \sum_{j=1}^{n} m_{ij}^2$, $g_{2i} = \sum_{j=1}^{n} m_{ij}^2 x_j^2$ and $Ef_i = 0$. The formulation (3.10) can then be considered as a regression of squared OLS residuals, $\hat{e}_i^2$, on g_{1i} and g_{2i} with f_i as the error in regression can. We can therefore estimate $(\sigma^2+\sigma_\alpha^2)$ and σ_β^2 by the least squares method. These OLS estimators of $(\sigma^2+\sigma_\alpha^2)$ and σ_β^2 will be consistent and unbiased since f_i's, as defined above, are uncorrelated with regressor x_i. Substituting these estimators in (3.8) one gets operational GLS estimators of α and β.

To find out whether the OLS estimators of $(\sigma^2+\sigma_\alpha^2)$ and σ_β^2 will be BLUE, we need the variances and covariances of f_i's. Under a simplifying assumption that ε_i, η_i, and u_i are normally distributed, we can easily obtain the variances and covariances of f_i's. The variances of f_i are:

$$(3.11) \qquad V(f_i) = Ef_i^2 = E(\hat{e}_i^2 - E\hat{e}_i^2)^2$$

$$= E\hat{e}_i^4 - (E\hat{e}_i^2)^2 = 2(E\hat{e}_i^2)^2$$

$$= 2[\sum_{j=1}^{n} m_{ij}^2 \{(\sigma^2+\sigma_\alpha^2)+x_j^2\sigma_\beta^2\}]^2,$$

for $i=1,2,\ldots,n$,

where the fourth equality is obtained by using a property of the normal variate f_i that the fourth moment about the mean is equal to three times the square of the variance. Thus the variances of f_i are equal to twice the square of the variances of the respective $\hat{e}_i$'s. The covariance of f_i's, $Ef_i f_{i'}$ for $i \neq i'$, can similarly be shown to be equal to twice the square of the covariance of $\hat{e}_i$'s. Thus

$$(3.12) \qquad Cov(f_i, f_{i'}) = Ef_i f_{i'} = 2[cov(\hat{e}_i, \hat{e}_{i'})]^2$$

$$= 2[\sum_{j=1}^{n} m_{ij} m_{ji'} \{(\sigma^2 + \sigma_\alpha^2) + x_j^2 \sigma_\beta^2\}]^2.$$

It is clear from (3.11) and (3.12) that errors f_i's in (3.10) are both heteroscedastic and serially correlated. Therefore, the OLS estimators of $(\sigma^2+\sigma_\alpha^2)$ and σ_β^2 in (3.10) will not have minimum variance in the class of linear (in $\hat{e}_i^2$) and unbiased estimators. An efficient estimator will therefore be the GLS estimator. However, the expression for the GLS estimator will itself depend on $(\sigma^2+\sigma_\alpha^2)$ and σ_β^2. A way out is to obtain the OLS estimator in the first stage and use this in the GLS estimator to make it operational. The operational GLS estimators of $(\sigma^2+\sigma_\alpha^2)$ and σ_β^2 will be asymptotically more efficient than their OLS estimators. However, the operational GLS estimators obtained for β (and similarly for α) by substituting the GLS or the OLS estimates of $(\sigma^2+\sigma_\alpha^2)$ and σ_β^2 would be asymptotically equivalent. In small samples there may be some possible gains if we use GLS estimates of $(\sigma^2 + \sigma_\alpha^2)$ and σ_β^2.

The use of the estimated w_i in place of the the unknown w_i disturbs the optimal properties of the GLS estimators of β and α in (3.8). It will be shown in Chapter 5 that the finite sample variances of the operational GLS estimators of β and α may be larger than the corresponding variances of the GLS estimators (for known w_i), which are:

$$V(\hat{\beta}) = \frac{\Sigma w_i}{(\Sigma w_i)(\Sigma w_i x_i^2) - (\Sigma w_i x_i)^2},$$

and

$$V(\hat{\alpha}) = \frac{\Sigma w_i x_i^2}{(\Sigma w_i)(\Sigma w_i x_i^2) - (\Sigma w_i x_i)^2}.$$

The derivation of these variances is given for a general case in Chapter 5.

A point to be noted is that the variances σ^2 and σ_α^2 in (3.10) are not identifiable, and we can only obtain an estimate of their sum. Thus the distinction between random disturbances u_i's and the randomly varying intercept (or its stochastic part) becomes purely arbitrary. It is customary, therefore, to subsume the disturbance term into the randomly varying intercept term of the model. We do this in the following chapters, although one could retain it if the model does have an intercept.

A disadvantage of the OLS or GLS estimators of variances $(\sigma^2+\sigma_\alpha^2)$ and σ_β^2 is that they may sometimes give negative estimates. The reason for negative estimates is that the systematic part of regression (3.10) accounts for only one third of the variation in the dependent variable $\hat{e}_i^2$. To prove this we square both sides of $\hat{e}_i^2 = E\hat{e}_i^2+f_i$, take its mathematical expectation and average the results over the n observations. Thus, we obtain

$$\frac{1}{n}\sum_{i=1}^{n} E\hat{e}_i^4 = \frac{1}{n}\sum_{i=1}^{n} (E\hat{e}_i^2)^2 + \frac{1}{n}\sum_{i=1}^{n} Ef_i^2.$$

It follows from (3.11) that the second component is twice as large as the first component under normality. Thus the systematic part $E\hat{e}_i^2$ in the regression relation (3.10) accounts for only one third of the behaviour of the dependent variable $\hat{e}_i^2$. To estimate $(\sigma^2+\sigma_\alpha^2)$ and σ_β^2 with reasonable precision requires a considerable number of observations. The negative estimates of $(\sigma^2+\sigma_\alpha^2)$ and σ_β^2 are not only meaningless, they pose additional problems: (a) The resultant estimator of w_i in (3.8) may become negative and, therefore, the small sample moments of the estimated GLS estimator of β and α may not exist; and (b) Even when the small sample moments exist, the estimated OLS or GLS estimators of β and α may have large mean square errors.

There are two possible solutions to the problem of negative estimates of variances. A simple solution is to replace the negative estimates by zero. The estimators of β and α so obtained may be termed as the truncated GLS estimators. However, this solution is not completely satisfactory because, apart from the fact that it is arbitrary, it implies that the corresponding coefficients are fixed. Another solution is to obtain the constrained nonnegative estimates of the variances. The estimators of β and α so obtained may be termed as constrained (or restricted) GLS estimators. This solution avoids arbitrariness but involves extra computational burden. It is intuitively clear that the restricted GLS and truncated GLS would have smaller mean squared error compared to the unrestricted GLS based on negative estimates (see further discussion in Chapter 5).

3.2.2. Maximum Likelihood (ML)

To estimate $y_i = \beta x_i + \alpha + e_i$ by ML we now assume that e_i's are normally distributed such that [according to (3.7a) to (3.7c)],

$$Ee_i = 0,$$

$$Ee_i^2 = (\sigma^2 + \sigma_\alpha^2) + x_i^2 \sigma_\beta^2 = \omega_i^2,$$

$$Ee_i e_{i'} = 0 \quad \text{for } i \neq i'.$$

Then y_i's are independent normal variates with mean $\beta x_i + \alpha$ and variance ω_i^2. Thus the likelihood and log likelihood functions are:

$$(3.13) \qquad L(\beta, \alpha, \sigma^2 + \sigma_\alpha^2, \sigma_\beta^2 / y_1, \ldots, y_n) = \prod_1^n f(y_i) dy_i$$

$$= \frac{1}{(2\pi)^{n/2} (\prod_1^n \omega_i)} \exp \left[-\frac{1}{2} \sum_1^n \frac{(y_i - \beta x_i - \alpha)^2}{\omega_i^2} \right]$$

and

$$(3.14) \qquad \log L = -\frac{n}{2} \log 2\pi - \frac{n}{2} \sum_1^n \log \omega_i^2$$

$$- \frac{1}{2} \sum_1^n \frac{(y_i - \beta x_i - \alpha)^2}{\omega_i^2}.$$

The ML estimator of β, α, $\sigma^2 + \sigma_\alpha^2$ and σ_β^2 can then be obtained by seeking those values of the parameters for which log L is maximum. In terms of calculus this is achieved by taking the first derivatives of log L (provided it is well behaved and convex) with respect to these parameters and equating them to zero. That is, we obtain:

$$\frac{\partial \log L}{\partial \sigma_\beta^2}=0, \quad \frac{\partial \log L}{\partial \alpha}=0, \quad \frac{\partial \log L}{\partial(\sigma^2+\sigma_\alpha^2)}=0, \quad \frac{\partial \log L}{\partial \sigma_\beta^2}=0.$$

When $(\sigma^2+\sigma_\alpha^2)$ and σ_β^2 are known it can easily be seen that $\frac{\partial \log L}{\partial \beta}=0$ and $\frac{\partial \log L}{\partial \alpha}=0$ would provide the normal equations identical to the GLS case as given earlier, and so the ML estimators of β and α will be the GLS estimators given in (3.8). Note that $w_i=1/\omega_i^2$. The reason for the GLS estimators and ML estimators of β and α to be identical is that the maximisation of log L is the same as the minimisation of $S=\sum_1^n w_i(y_i-\beta x_i-\alpha_i)^2$.

When $(\sigma^2+\sigma_\alpha^2)$ and σ_β^2 are unknown we consider the derivative of log L with respect to $(\sigma^2+\sigma_\alpha^2)$ and σ_β^2. These are

$$\frac{\partial \log L}{\partial(\sigma^2+\sigma_\alpha^2)}=-n\sum_1^n \frac{1}{\omega_i^2}+\sum_1^n \frac{(y_i-\beta x_i-\alpha)^2}{\omega_i^4}=0,$$

$$\frac{\partial \log L}{\partial \sigma_\beta^2}=-n\sum_1^n \frac{x_i^2}{\omega_i^2}+\sum_1^n \frac{x_i^2}{\omega_i^4}(y_i-\beta x_i-\alpha)^2=0,$$

where we use the results

$$\frac{\partial \omega_i^2}{\partial(\sigma^2+\sigma_\alpha^2)}=1 \text{ and } \frac{\partial \omega_i^2}{\partial \sigma_\beta^2}=x_i^2.$$

As is clear, the above normal equations are highly nonlinear in $(\sigma^2+\sigma_\alpha^2)$ and σ_β^2, specially when

$\beta = \hat{\beta}$ and $\alpha = \hat{\alpha}$ are substituted. Therefore, the unique solution for $\sigma^2+\sigma_\alpha^2$ and σ_β^2 cannot be explicitly written. An alternative is to use an iterative nonlinear search procedure to obtain the ML estimator.[1] The resulting ML estimators of $\sigma^2+\sigma_\alpha^2$ and σ_β^2 would, in general, be different from the estimators suggested in the earlier section. This also implies that the operational GLS estimators of β and α would, in general, be different from those of operational ML estimators of β and α, even though they are identical when $\sigma^2+\sigma_\alpha^2$ and σ_β^2 are known. We note that the ML estimates of $\sigma^2+\sigma_\alpha^2$ and σ_β^2 can also sometimes be negative. Again, one can either make the negative estimates to be zero or avoid the negative estimates by applying constrained maximisation of log likelihood.[2] Below we consider a simple model where the ML estimation is not subject to the above problems.

Let us consider a special case of the model (3.1) as $y_i=\beta_i x_i$. For this model the ML estimators of β and σ_β^2 can easily be verified from the equations $\partial \log L/\partial\beta = 0$ and $\partial \log L/\partial\sigma_\beta^2 = 0$, respectively, as

(3.15) $$\hat{\beta} = \frac{1}{n} \sum_1^n \frac{y_i}{x_i}$$

and

(3.16) $$\hat{\sigma}_\beta^2 = \frac{1}{n} \sum_1^n (y_i - \hat{\beta}x_i)^2.$$

Thus, in this special case, we have an explicit solution for $\hat{\sigma}_\beta^2$. Also the ML estimator of β is operational and identical with the GLS estimator of β. This is because the heteroscedasticity in the model $y_i=\beta_i x_i=\beta x_i+\eta_i x_i$ is simply $\sigma_\beta^2 x_i^2$.

3.2.3 Bayesian Estimation

The Bayesian estimator of any parameter is the mean or mode of its posterior density function.[3] If there is more than one parameter involved in a model (as in $y_i = \beta x_i + \alpha_i + e_i$) then one can make inferences about a parameter by considering either its conditional posterior density or marginal posterior density. The mean of the conditional posterior density can then be called the conditional Bayes's estimator and that of the marginal posterior density simply as Bayes's estimator.

To obtain Bayes's estimators of α, β, $(\sigma^2 + \sigma_\alpha^2)$ and σ_β^2 we require their marginal posterior densities. To derive any one of them we first write the joint posterior of all parameters by combining their likelihood (sample information) and joint prior probability density (prior information), and then integrate over the parameters which are of no interest (nuisance parameters). More explicitly, write the likelihood function (given data) from (3.13) as

$$(3.17) \qquad L(\beta, \alpha, \sigma_o^2, \lambda_1) \propto \frac{1}{(\sigma_o^2)^{n/2} \left[\prod_1^n (1+\lambda_1 x_t^2)\right]^{1/2}} \exp\left[-\frac{1}{2\sigma_o^2} \sum_1^n \frac{(y_i - \beta x_i - \alpha)^2}{(1+\lambda_1 x_i^2)}\right],$$

where

$$(3.18) \qquad \sigma_o^2 = \sigma^2 + \sigma_\alpha^2, \quad \lambda_1 = \sigma_\beta^2 / \sigma_o^2.$$

Alternatively, this can be written after some manipulation and simplification as[4]

$$(3.19)\qquad L(\beta,\alpha,\sigma_o^2,\lambda_1) \propto \sigma_o^{-n}\,[\delta(\lambda_1)]^{-1/2}$$

$$\exp[\,-\frac{1}{2\sigma_o^2}\,(\nu s^2+q)],$$

where

$$(3.20)\qquad \delta(\lambda_1) = \sum_1^n \delta_i;\;\; \delta_i = 1+\lambda_1 x_i^2,$$

$$s^2 = \frac{1}{\nu}\sum_1^n [(y_i-\hat{\beta}x_i-\hat{\alpha})^2/\delta_i];\;\; \nu=T-2,$$

$$q=(\beta-\hat{\beta})^2\sum_1^n \frac{x_i^2}{\delta_i}+(\alpha-\hat{\alpha})^2\sum_1^n \frac{1}{\delta_i}$$

$$+\;2(\beta-\hat{\beta})(\alpha-\hat{\alpha})\sum_1^n \frac{x_i}{\delta_i};$$

$\hat{\beta}$ and $\hat{\alpha}$ are the GLS estimators as given in (3.8).

As noted by Griffiths **et al.** (1979), the usual noninformative diffuse prior specification for the parameters is not satisfactory. This is because it produces, along with the likelihood function given above, the posterior density which is improper, that is its integral equals infinity. Thus they use Jeffreys's (1961) rule and formulate the joint prior as

$$(3.21)\qquad p(\beta,\alpha,\sigma_o^2,\sigma_\beta^2) \propto [\,\sum_1^n \left(\frac{1}{\sigma_o^2+x_i^2\sigma_\beta^2}\right)^2 \sum_1^n \left(\frac{x_i^2}{\sigma_o^2+x_i^2\sigma_\beta^2}\right)^2$$

$$-\{\sum_1 \left(\frac{x_i}{\sigma_o^2+x_i^2\sigma_\beta^2}\right)^2\}^2]^{1/2}.$$

The above prior is in fact obtained as

$$p(\beta,\alpha,\sigma_o^2,\sigma_\beta^2) \propto p(\beta,\alpha)p(\sigma_o^2,\sigma_\beta^2)$$

where $p(\beta,\alpha)$, the joint prior for β and α, is diffuse while $p(\sigma_o^2,\sigma_\beta^2)$, the joint informative prior for σ_o^2 and σ_β^2, is

$$(3.22) \quad p(\sigma_o^2,\sigma_\beta^2) \propto [E(-\frac{\partial^2 \log L}{\partial^2 \sigma_o^2})\, E(-\frac{\partial^2 \log L}{\partial^2 \sigma_\beta^2}) - E(-\frac{\partial^2 \log L}{\partial \sigma_o^2 \partial \sigma_\beta^2})^2]^{1/2}.$$

The first and second terms on the right of (3.22) are known as the information with respect to σ_o^2 and σ_β^2, respectively, and the third term is the joint information with respect to σ_o^2 and σ_β^2. These are obtained, using (3.13) as

$$E(-\frac{\partial^2 \log L}{\partial^2 \sigma_o^2}) = \frac{1}{2} \sum_1^n \frac{1}{(\sigma_o^2+\sigma_\beta^2 x_i^2)^2},$$

$$E(-\frac{\partial^2 \log L}{\partial^2 \sigma_\beta^2}) = \frac{1}{2} \sum_1^n \frac{x_i^4}{(\sigma_o^2+\sigma_\beta^2 x_i^2)^2},$$

and

$$E(-\frac{\partial^2 \log L}{\partial \sigma_\beta^2 \partial \sigma_o^2}) = \frac{1}{2} \sum_1^n \frac{x_i^2}{(\sigma_o^2+\sigma_\beta^2 x_i^2)^2}.$$

In terms of variance ratio $\lambda_1 = \sigma_\beta^2/\sigma_o^2$,

$$(3.23) \quad p(\beta,\alpha,\sigma_o^2,\lambda_1) = \sigma_o^2\; p(\beta,\alpha,\sigma_o^2,\sigma_\beta^2) \propto \frac{1}{\sigma_o^2}\, d\ ,$$

where

$$(3.24) \qquad d= [\sum_1^n (\frac{1}{\delta_i^2}) \sum_1^n (\frac{x_i^4}{\delta_i^2}) - \{\sum_1^n (\frac{x_i^2}{\delta_i^2})\}^2]^{1/2} ,$$

and $\delta_i = 1 + \lambda_1 x_i^2$ as in (3.20).

From (3.23) we can write $p(\beta, \alpha, \sigma_o^2, \lambda_1) \propto p(\sigma_o^2, \lambda_1) = p(\sigma_o^2) p(\lambda_1)$. Thus σ_o^2 and λ_1 are a priori independent. Also $p(\sigma_o^2) \propto 1/\sigma_o^2$ is the improper density [considered a noninformative prior] while $p(\lambda_1)$ is a proper density, that is it integrates to one. Thus, $p(\sigma_o^2, \lambda_1)$ can be considered as a kind of noninformative prior. In a special case when $\sigma_\beta^2 = 0$, it is obvious that (3.23) will reduce to the noninformative prior of the fixed coefficients model.

Using Bayes's thereom we can now write the joint posterior density of $\beta, \alpha, \sigma_o^2$ and λ_1 after multiplying the likelihood function by the joint prior. This is

$$(3.25) \qquad p(\beta, \alpha, \sigma_o^2, \lambda_1/y) \propto \sigma_o^{-(n+2)} [\delta(\lambda_1)]^{-1/2} d \; \exp[-\frac{1}{2\sigma_o^2}(\nu s^2 + q)].$$

Using this posterior we can always analyse any parameter either by studying its conditional density or marginal density. The latter is more useful in practice. For example, integrating (3.25) with respect to σ_o^2 provides

$$(3.26) \qquad p(\beta, \alpha, \lambda_1/y) \propto [\delta(\lambda_1)]^{-1/2} d \; [\nu s^2 + q]^{-n/2}.$$

This indicates that the conditional posterior for β and α given λ_1,

$$(3.27) \qquad p(\beta,\alpha/\lambda_i,y) \propto \frac{p(\beta,\alpha,\lambda_1/y)}{p(\lambda_1/y)}$$

$$\propto [\nu s^2 + q]^{-n/2}$$

is a bivariate t-distribution. The mean of this distribution is $(\hat{\beta},\hat{\alpha})$, which is the conditional Bayes's estimator. We note that this is the same as the GLS estimator given in (3.8). If we are only interested in the conditional posterior of β given λ_1 then one can integrate (3.27) over α. This will turn out to be the univariate t-distribution.

To obtain the marginal posterior of say β, requires integration of (3.26) over α and λ_1, that is,

$$p(\beta) = \int_{\alpha} \int_{\lambda_1} p(\beta,\alpha,\lambda_1/y)\,d\beta\,d\alpha\,d\lambda_1.$$

This can be analysed by using a standard bivariate numerical integration technique.[5] The mean of this marginal posterior will be called Bayes's estimator of β.

Following the same principle in the case of σ_o^2, the marginal posterior is obtained as

$$p(\sigma_o^2) = \int_{\beta} \int_{\alpha} \int_{\lambda_1} p(\beta,\alpha,\sigma_o^2,\lambda_1/y)\,d\beta\,d\alpha\,d\lambda_1 \propto \int_{\lambda_1} p(\sigma_o^2,\lambda_1/y)\,d\lambda_1,$$

which requires integration over λ_1. Similarly, one could obtain the posterior density for σ_β^2. The means of these posterior densities of σ_o^2 and σ_β^2 will give the Bayes's estimators of σ_o^2 and σ_β^2. These estimators, in contrast to the estimators

discussed in sections 3.2.1 and 3.2.2, will always be positive

3.2.4 Remarks

Earlier, we considered two methods of estimating the means and variances of the purely random coefficients model, viz.,

1. Classical (Sampling) Method
   (a) GLS estimator
   (b) ML estimator
2. Bayesian Method.

In the classical approach the prior assumption regarding the decomposition of varying coefficients between systematic and stochastic parts is integrated into the model. This integration produces a fixed coefficients linear regression model with a composite error term which is heteroscedastic. Accordingly, the estimates of the fixed coefficients can be obtained by the GLS method. The GLS estimators of the fixed coefficients, which depend on the variances (and more generally on the second moment of randomly varying coefficients), is operational if the variances are replaced by their estimates. The estimation of the variances of the randomly varying coefficients are obtained from the regression relationship between the squares of least squares residuals and the nonlinear transforms of the regressors in the integrated model. Thus, the approach for estimating the means and variances of random coefficients is a two stage procedure. In the first stage the estimates of variances are obtained from the least squares residuals and in the second stage the estimates of the means are obtained through the operational GLS estimators.

Alternatively, the estimation of the means and variances can be obtained simultaneously by the maximum likelihood method. The maximum likelihood and GLS methods produce asymptotically (in the large samples) efficient estimators of the means and variances though the former may be more efficient than the latter in small samples. The normal equations for the estimation of the means in these two methods are the same when variances are known but differ for the estimation of variances. In the former method the iterative solutions of nonlinear equations require a search over the entire range of the values of variances; thus the computational burden can be enormous when the linear regression has more than two regressors. Furthermore, the latter approach can be distribution free while the former approach is not.

In the Bayesian approach the prior assumption regarding the varying coefficients is in the form of a subjective probability distribution. This prior is then combined with the likelihood function using Bayes's Theorem to yield the joint posterior probability distribution of the unknown parameters. The marginal distribution of each parameter is obtained by integrating the joint posterior probability over the remaining parameters. The Bayesian inference entails (though not always) an analysis of the mean (and mode if the posterior distribution is asymmetric) and variance of the posterior marginal distributions. The functional form of the joint posterior distribution of the parameters depends on the form of the prior probability density function which can be taken as normal, gamma, beta, etc. It is often convenient to select the priors such that the functional form of the posterior is the same as that of the prior so that the task of integration to obtain marginal distributions is easilty performed.

A class of such priors for the Bayesian approach in the simple regression model is called the 'conjugate priors'. The advantage of these priors is that every time new sample information is observed the revision of the opinion about the parameter of interest and its posterior distribution can easily be obtained from the previous stage since the posterior distribution has the same functional form as the prior. The disadvantage of these priors is that we may not have such prior knowledge about the parameters, in which case a 'noninformative' or 'diffuse' prior can be used. Such priors recommended by Jeffreys (1961) are also known as 'improper' priors because their probabilities do not add to one. The improper prior about a parameter, which can take any value from $-\infty$ to ∞, is represented by the uniform probability density function. The advantage of noninformative priors is that the posterior distribution is just proportional to the likelihood function. Hence the mode (mean) of the posterior marginal distribution of a regression coefficient is also the Maximum Likelihood (ML) estimator if the likelihood function is asymmetric (symmetric). The interpretation of the Bayesian and classical estimates are of course different even though the noninformative priors yield Bayesian estimates which are similar to the classical estimates.

In the randomly varying coefficients model the Bayesian estimation of the parameters with noninformative priors falls in the class of a multiple parameter problem because the variances cannot be assumed to be a priori independent. The marginal posterior distributions of alternative parameters in the randomly coefficients model are generally intractable analytically and require solutions by numerical integration methods.

The Bayesian approach often involves more algebra and computation than the classical approach. An advantage of this approach, however, is that it incorporates the information about the positiveness of the variances with the result that their estimates are positive. Another advantage of this approach is that the posterior densities of the variances convey more information about the variances than their point estimates obtained from using the classical approach.

3.3 ESTIMATION OF SEQUENTIALLY VARYING COEFFICIENT MODELS

Here we shall consider the estimation of the randomly varying coefficient models under two alternative specifications, that is (a) Adaptive Coefficient; and (b) Stochastically Convergent Coefficient. Under both (a) and (b) we shall first consider the case where only the intercept is changing. Then in Section 3.3.2 we consider the situation where both the intercept and the coefficient of x are changing.

3.3.1 Estimation when Intercept is Random

Consider the adaptive coefficient model:

$$y_i = \alpha_i + \beta x_i + u_i, \tag{3.28}$$

where α_i follows a random walk,

$$\alpha_i = \alpha_{i-1} + \varepsilon_i = \alpha_o + \sum_{s=1}^{i} \varepsilon_s; \tag{3.29}$$

$\sum_{s=1}^{i} \varepsilon_s$ can also be written as $\sum_{s=0}^{i-1} \varepsilon_{i-s}$. The term α_o is the starting value. Alternatively, we can write this model as

$$(3.30) \qquad y_i = \alpha^*_i + \beta x_i,$$

where

$$(3.31) \qquad \alpha^*_i = \alpha_i + u_i, \qquad \alpha_i = \alpha_{i-1} + \varepsilon_i.$$

In this framework the intercept term α_i in (3.28) can be treated as the permanent random component and u_i as the transitory component in the random intercept α^*_i in (3.30).

We assume that:

$$(3.32) \qquad E\varepsilon_i = Eu_i = 0,$$

$$E\varepsilon_i^2 = \sigma_\varepsilon^2, \; Eu_i^2 = \sigma^2,$$

$$E\varepsilon_i u_i = 0,$$

$$E\varepsilon_i \varepsilon_{i'} = Eu_i u_{i'} = 0 \quad \text{for } i \neq i'.$$

Thus the unknown parameters in the adaptive model are the intercept α_o, the regression coefficient β and the variances σ_ε^2 and σ^2. Normally, one would also be interested in estimating or predicting the path of the permanent component α_i over i. This will be discussed in Chapter 4.

To estimate the unknown parameters we substitute (3.29) in (3.28) and write

$$(3.33) \qquad y_i = \alpha_o + \beta x_i + w_i,$$

where $w_i = u_i + \sum_{s=1}^{i} \varepsilon_s$ is the composite error term. We can easily see that

(3.34) $Ew_i = 0;$

and for i,i'=1,...,n,

(3.35) $$Ew_i w_{i'} = \omega_{ii'}$$

$$= i_o \sigma_\varepsilon^2 \quad \text{if } i' \neq i, i_o = \min(i,i')$$

$$= \sigma^2 + i\sigma_\varepsilon^2 \quad \text{if } i' = i.$$

Alternatively, we can write $\omega_{ii'} = \sigma^2 \omega^*_{ii'}$ where $\lambda = \sigma_\varepsilon^2/\sigma^2 > 0$ and

(3.35a) $$\omega^*_{ii'} = (1+i\lambda) \qquad i' = i$$

$$= i_o\lambda, \qquad i' \neq i.$$

Thus the composite disturbance terms w_i's are both heteroscedastic and serially correlated. We can therefore obtain GLS estimators of β and α_0 by minimising

(3.36) $$S = \sum_{i=1}^{n} \sum_{i'=1}^{n} \omega^{*ii'}(y_i - \alpha_0 - \beta x_i)(y_{i'} - \alpha_0 - \beta x_{i'})$$

with respect to α_0 and β; $\omega^{*ii'}$ is the i-i'th element of the inverse of the matrix formed by $\omega^*_{ii'}$. The resulting GLS estimators of α_0 and β will depend only upon unknown variance ratio λ. So unless λ is known the GLS estimator cannot be calculated. An alternative is to consider the search procedure on λ, that is apply an iterative GLS estimator.

One can also obtain the ML estimator by assuming ε's and u's to be normally distributed. The likelihood function is

(3.37) $$L = \frac{1}{(2\pi\sigma^2)^{n/2}[D(\lambda)]^{1/2}} \exp\left[-\frac{1}{2\sigma^2}S\right]$$

$$= L(\alpha_0, \beta, \sigma^2, \lambda/y),$$

where S is as given in (3.36) and $D(\lambda)$ represents the determinant value of the matrix formed by the elements $\omega^*_{ii'}$. The log of the likelihood function is

$$(3.38)\ \log L = -\frac{n}{2}\log(2\pi) - \frac{n}{2}\log\sigma^2 - \frac{1}{2}\log D(\lambda) - \frac{1}{2\sigma^2}S.$$

For known λ, the maximisation of log L with respect to α_o and β is the same as minimisation of S. Thus, in this case, the ML estimators of α_o and β will be identical with their GLS estimators. Let these be $\hat{\alpha}_o(\lambda)$ and $\hat{\beta}(\lambda)$. Further, the ML estimator of σ^2, for given λ, can be obtained by partially differentiating log L with respect to σ^2 and equating it to zero. This gives

$$\hat{\sigma}^2 = \hat{\sigma}^2(\lambda) = \frac{1}{n}S(\lambda),$$

where $S(\lambda)$ is the value of S in (3.36) with $\alpha_o = \hat{\alpha}_o(\lambda)$ and $\beta = \hat{\beta}(\lambda)$.

Since in practice λ is unknown, we should first estimate the ML estimator of λ by maximising log L with respect to λ. An easier way of doing this maximisation is to substitute $\hat{\alpha}_o(\lambda)$, $\hat{\beta}(\lambda)$ and $\hat{\sigma}^2(\lambda)$ in (3.38) and write the log L as

$$(3.38a)\quad \log L_c = \log L_c(\lambda) = -\frac{n}{2}\left(\log\frac{2\pi}{n} + 1\right) - \frac{n}{2}\log S(\lambda) - \frac{1}{2}\log D(\lambda),$$

where $L_c(\lambda)$ is known as the concentrated likelihood function. The maximisation of log L is the same as the maximisation of log L_c. Now we can use an iterative scheme over λ which maximises log L_c. This would give ML estimator of λ. In the process we also obtain the iterative ML estimators

$\hat{\alpha}_0(\lambda)$, $\hat{\beta}(\lambda)$ and $\hat{\sigma}^2(\lambda)$. We note that these iterative ML estimators of α_0 and β, in the case of unknown λ, will not be identical with those of iterative GLS estimators. This is because log L_c contains the term log $D(\lambda)$ in addition to S.

Consider now the stochastically convergent coefficients model

$$(3.39) \qquad y_i = \alpha_i + \beta x_i + u_i,$$

where

$$(3.40) \qquad \alpha_i = (1-\theta)\alpha + \theta\alpha_{i-1} + \varepsilon_i,$$

$$= \theta^i \alpha_0 + (1-\theta^i)\alpha + \sum_{s=1}^{i} \theta^s \varepsilon_s$$

and $0<\theta<1$. To estimate this model one can start again by substituting (3.40) in (3.39). The composite disturbance term, in this case, would again be heteroscedastic and serially correlated, and one can do GLS or ML estimation.

Alternatively, we can write

$$(3.41) \qquad \theta y_{i-1} = \theta\alpha_{i-1} + \theta\beta x_{i-1} + \theta u_{i-1}$$

and then take the difference from (3.39). This gives

$$(3.42) \qquad y_i = \alpha(1-\theta) + \theta y_{i-1} + \beta(x_i - \theta x_{i-1}) + w_i,$$

where

$$w_i = u_i - \theta u_{i-1} + \varepsilon_i$$

is the composite disturbance term such that $Ew_i=0$, and $Ew_i w_{i'} = \omega_{ii'} = \sigma^2 \, {}^*_{ii'}$, where

$$(3.43) \qquad \omega^*_{ii'} = \lambda + (1+\theta^2) \qquad \text{if } i'=i$$

$$= -\theta \qquad \text{if } i' \neq i \text{ and } |i'-i|=1$$

$$= 0 \qquad \text{otherwise,}$$

for all $i,i'=1,\ldots,n$. The (3.43) indicates that w_i's are homoscedastic but serially correlated, and that $\omega^*_{ii'}$ depends on two unknowns: λ and θ. Again, as in the case of the adpative coefficients model, for known θ and λ we can obtain the GLS estimators of α^* and β by minimising

$$S = \sum_{1}^{n} \sum_{1}^{n} \omega^{*ii'}(y^*_i-\alpha^*-\beta x^*_i)(y^*_{i'}-\alpha^*-\beta x^*_{i'}),$$

where $y^*_i=y_i-\theta y_{i-1}$, $x^*_i=x_i-\theta x_{i-1}$, $\alpha^*=\alpha(1-\theta)$, and $\omega^{*ii'}$ is the i-i'^{th} element of the inverse of the matrix based on $\omega^*_{ii'}$ in (3.43). These GLS estimators will be identical with the ML estimators under the assumption of normality of u's and ε's.

When θ and λ are not known we can obtain the GLS estimator by iterating over θ and λ. The ML estimator can also be obtained by writing the log of concentrated likelihood function, corresponding to (3.38a) of the adaptive coefficients case. This is

$$\log L_c(\lambda,\theta) = -\frac{n}{2}(\log\frac{2\pi}{n}+1) - \frac{n}{2}\log S(\lambda,\theta) - \frac{1}{2}\log D(\lambda,\theta),$$

where $S(\lambda,\theta)$ is the value of S after substituting $\alpha^*=\hat{\alpha}^*(\lambda,\theta)$ and $\beta=\hat{\beta}(\lambda,\theta)$, the ML estimators of α^* and β, and $D(\lambda,\theta)$ represents the determinant value of the matrix formed by $\omega^*_{ii'}$ in (3.43). Now we can use an iterative procedure over θ and λ to obtain the estimators of θ and λ for which the log L_c is maximum. This would give us the iterative ML estimators of α^* and β also.

3.3.2 Estimation When Both Intercept and Slope are Random

Now consider the model

(3.44) $$y_i = \beta^*_i x_i + \alpha^*_i,$$

where both the intercept and the coefficient of x_i are sequentially varying as

(3.45) $$\alpha^*_i = \alpha_i + u_i;\ \alpha_i = \alpha_{i-1} + \varepsilon_i = \alpha_0 + \sum_{s=1}^{i} \varepsilon_s,$$

$$\beta^*_i = \beta_i + \nu_i;\ \beta_i = \beta_{i-1} + \eta_i = \beta_0 + \sum_{s=1}^{1} \eta_s.$$

The α_i and β_i are the permanent and u_i and ν_i the transitory components of α^*_i and β^*_i, respectively.[6] We assume that ε's, η's, ν's and u's have zero means, constant variances and are serially uncorrelated. Also ν's, u's, ε's and η's are mutually uncorrelated.

Substituting (3.45) in (3.44) we write

(3.46) $$y_i = \beta_0 x_i + \alpha_0 + w_i,$$

where $w_i = u_i + \sum_{s=1}^{i} \varepsilon_s + x\,(\nu_i + \sum_{s=1}^{i} \eta_s)$ is the composite error term. It is such that $Ew_i = 0$ and $Ew_i w_{i'} = \omega_{ii'}$ where

$$\omega_{ii'} = \sigma^2_u + x^2_i \sigma^2_\nu + i(\sigma^2_\varepsilon + x^2_i \sigma^2_\eta) \qquad \text{if } i=i'$$

$$= i_o(\sigma^2_\varepsilon + x_i x_{i'} \sigma^2_\eta) \qquad \text{if } i \neq i'$$

where i_o = minimum of i and i'. Alternatively, we can write $\omega_{ii'} = \sigma^2_u \omega^*_{ii'}$ where

(3.47) $$\omega^*_{ii'} = (1 + x^2_i \lambda_2) + i\lambda_1(1 + x_i \lambda_3) \qquad \text{if } i=i'$$

$$= i_o \lambda_1 (1 + x_i x_{i'} \lambda_3) \qquad \text{if } i \neq i';$$

$$\lambda_1 = \sigma^2_\varepsilon/\sigma^2_u;\ \lambda_2 = \sigma^2_\nu/\sigma^2_u;\ \lambda_3 = \sigma^2_\eta/\sigma^2_\varepsilon.$$

The λ_1 defines the partitioning in permanent and transitory variance components in the adaptive intercept term and the ratios λ_2 and λ_3 represent the degree of instability in the transitory and permanent components of the adaptive regression coefficients. The ratios λ_2 and λ_3 cannot be independently identifiable; thus these are generally assumed to be known (see a further discussion on this point in Chapter 4). The unknown parameters to be estimated are α_0, β_0, σ_u^2 and λ_1. The ML estimator can be obtained in the same way as in section 3.3.1, except that the concentrated log likelihood function will now be

$$\text{Log } L_c(\lambda_1) = -\frac{n}{2}(\log \frac{2\pi}{n} + 1) - \frac{n}{2} \log S(\lambda_1) - \frac{1}{2} \log D(\lambda_1),$$

$$\text{where } S(\lambda_1) = \sum_{i=1}^{n} \sum_{i'=1}^{n} \omega^{*ii'}(y_i - \hat{\beta}_0 x_i - \hat{\alpha}_0)(y_{i'} - \hat{\beta}_0 x_{i'} - \hat{\alpha}_0)$$

and $D(\lambda_1)$ is the determinant value of the matrix based on $\omega^*_{ii'}$ in (3.47). Furthermore, $\omega^{*ii'}$ is the i-i'th element of the inverse of the matrix formed by $\omega^*_{ii'}$. Finally, $\hat{\beta}_0$ and $\hat{\alpha}_0$ are the GLS estimators of β_0 and α_0, which depend on λ_1. The estimator of σ_u^2 is given by $\hat{\sigma}_u(\lambda_1) = \frac{1}{n} S(\lambda_1)$.

An alternative method of estimating uses scaling by $\sigma^2 = \sigma_u^2 + \sigma_\varepsilon^2 = (1-\gamma)\sigma^2 + \gamma\sigma^2$ where $0 < \gamma < 1$ is the instability parameter representing the decomposition of the total variance (σ^2) into permanent (σ_u^2) and transitory (σ_ε^2) variance components. In this case $\lambda_1 = \gamma\sigma^2$ and $\sigma_u^2 = (1-\gamma)\sigma^2$ and the concentrated likelihood function log $L_c(\lambda_1)$ becomes log $L_c(\gamma)$. Then the test for $\gamma = 0$, based on the ML estimate of γ, provides the test for stability of the coefficients in the model. Further details are given in Chapter 4.

When both coefficients follow a stochastically convergent variation the ML estimation technique can be similarly formulated.

NOTES

1. Three commonly unconstrained methods of optimisation are: (i) The method of Scoring which utilises the first partial derivatives (vector of scores) and the second partial derivatives (Hessian Matrix) to aid in curvature determination (see Rao, 1973, p. 366) (ii) The method of Gradients which utilises the first partial derivatives (gradients). The Davidson-Fletcher-Powell algorithm for this method is discussed in Himmelblau (1972, ch. 5) (iii) The PRAXIS method, which requires no information on derivatives, was developed by Brent (1973, ch. 7). Dent and Hildreth (1977) found that the PRAXIS method is most accurate in identifying the highest local maxima.

2. The procedure is discussed in Chapter 4.

3. These concepts are briefly reviewed in Appendix A.

4. That is, we rewrite $(y_i-\beta x_i-\alpha)$ as $y_i -(\beta-\hat{\beta})x_i-\alpha_i-\hat{\alpha})-\hat{\beta}x_i-\hat{\alpha}=(y_i-\hat{\beta}x_i-\hat{\alpha})-[(\beta-\hat{\beta})x_i+(\alpha_i-\hat{\alpha}_i)$.

5. The numerical integration techniques are discussed in Zellner (1971).

6. This specification is more general than the one considered in Chapter 2. A further generalization of the above specification would be that u's and ν's are correlated.

4. Multiple Regression with Randomly Varying Coefficients

4.1 INTRODUCTION

In this chapter we study the relationship between the dependent variable and a set of explanatory variables when the regression coefficients are purely random, and when they vary sequentially. The results of Chapter 3, with respect to the estimation of means and variances of regression coefficients, are extended to the multiple regression linear model with the help of simple matrix algebra. In addition we discuss the estimation of actual response coefficients. The chapter concludes with the discussion on a study of the Phillips curve with the purely random coefficients.

4.2 PURELY RANDOM COEFFICIENTS SPECIFICATION AND ESTIMATION

Assuming that a linear relationship exists between a dependent variable and K-1 explanatory variables, we may write the multiple linear regression model with varying coefficients as

$$(4.1) \qquad y_i = \beta_{1i} + \sum_{k=2}^{K} \beta_{ki} x_{ki} + \varepsilon_{oi}, \qquad i=1,2,\ldots n,$$

where y is the dependent variable, the x's are explanatory variables and ε_o is the usual disturbance term. We assume that ε_o is independently distributed with zero mean and constant variance σ_0^2 and that the varying regression coefficients β's are random variables such that

$$(4.2) \qquad \beta_{ki} = \beta_k + \varepsilon_{ki}, \qquad k=1,2,\ldots,K,$$

where β_k and ε_{ki} are respectively the deterministic and random parts. The estimation of β_k and also of β_{ki} in model (4.1) to (4.2) under simplifying assumptions regarding the random part will be discussed in this chapter. Some of these assumptions will be modified in a following chapter. Accordingly, we assume that the random coefficients β_{ki}'s are independently and identically distributed with fixed means β_k and variances σ_k^2, that is,

$$(4.3) \qquad E\beta_{ki} = \beta_k, \qquad \text{for all } i,$$

$$V(\beta_{ki}) = E(\beta_{ki} - \beta_k)^2 = \sigma_k^2, \qquad \text{for all } i,$$

$$\text{cov}(\beta_{ki}, \beta_{k'i'}) = E(\beta_{ki} - \beta_k)(\beta_{k'i'} - \beta_{k'})$$

$$= 0, \qquad \text{for } i \neq i' \text{ and } k \neq k',$$

where $i'=1,\ldots,n$ and $k'=1,\ldots,K$. Alternatively, assumptions (4.3) can be stated as

$$(4.4) \qquad E\varepsilon_{ki} = 0, \qquad \text{for all } i \text{ and } k,$$

$$V(\varepsilon_{ki}) = E\varepsilon_{ki}^2 = \sigma_k^2, \qquad \text{for all } i,$$

$$\text{cov}(\varepsilon_{ki}, \varepsilon_{k'i'}) = 0, \qquad \text{for } i \neq i' \text{ and } k \neq k'.$$

Further, we assume that the x's are linearly independent fixed numbers.

The multiple regression model with randomly varying coefficients under these assumptions may be written as

$$(4.5) \qquad y_i = \beta_1 + \sum_{k=2}^{K} \beta_k x_{ki} + u_i,$$

where

$$(4.6) \qquad u_i = \varepsilon_{1i}^{*} + \sum_{k=2}^{K} x_{ki}\varepsilon_{ki} \text{ with } \varepsilon_{1i}^{*} = \varepsilon_{oi} + \varepsilon_{1i},$$

which has been obtained by substituting (4.2) into (4.1). Note that the usual disturbance term has been added to random part ε_{1i} of the randomly varying intercept term β_{1i}. The means, variances and covariances of u_i's under assumptions(4.4) are easily obtained and are given below:

$$(4.7) \qquad Eu_i = E(\varepsilon_{oi} + \varepsilon_{1i}) + \sum_{k=2}^{K} x_{ki} E\varepsilon_{ki} = 0 \qquad \text{for all } i$$

$$V(u_i) = Eu_i^2 = E(\varepsilon_{oi} + \varepsilon_{1i} + \sum_{k=2}^{K} x_{ki}\varepsilon_{ki})^2$$

$$= (\sigma_o^2 + \sigma_1^2) + \sum_{k=2}^{K} \sigma_k^2 x_{ki}^2 = d_{ii},$$

$$\text{cov}(u_i, u_{i'}) = E(\varepsilon_{1i}^{*} + \sum_{k=2}^{K} x_{ki}\varepsilon_{ki})$$

$$(\varepsilon_{1i'}^{*} + \sum_{k=2}^{K} x_{ki'}\varepsilon_{ki'}) = 0.$$

It was noted in Chapter 3 that σ_o^2 and σ_1^2 can not be identified separately while the sum $(\sigma_o^2 + \sigma_1^2)$ is identified. To simplify the notation we will henceforth drop σ_o^2 from $V(u_i)$ in Section (4.2) without any loss of generalities.

The n observations for (4.5) can be compactly written as

$$(4.8) \qquad y = X\beta + u,$$

where

$$y = \begin{bmatrix} y_1 \\ y_2 \\ \vdots \\ y_n \end{bmatrix}, \qquad X = \begin{bmatrix} 1 & x_{21} & \cdots & x_{K1} \\ 1 & x_{22} & \cdots & x_{K2} \\ \vdots & \vdots & & \vdots \\ 1 & x_{2n} & \cdots & x_{Kn} \end{bmatrix},$$

$$\beta = \begin{bmatrix} \beta_1 \\ \beta_2 \\ \vdots \\ \beta_K \end{bmatrix} \quad \text{and } u = \begin{bmatrix} u_1 \\ u_2 \\ \vdots \\ u_n \end{bmatrix}.$$

Also assumptions (4.7) can be compactly written as

(4.9) $Eu = E(u_1, u_2, \ldots, u_n)' = 0,$

$$Euu' = \begin{bmatrix} Eu_1^2 & Eu_1u_2 & \cdots & Eu_1u_n \\ Eu_2u_1 & Eu_2^2 & \cdots & Eu_2u_n \\ \vdots & \vdots & & \vdots \\ Eu_nu_1 & Eu_nu_2 & \cdots & Eu_n^2 \end{bmatrix}$$

$$= \text{diag.}(d_{11}, d_{22}, \ldots, d_{nn}) = D.$$

We note that the multiple regression model with random coefficients reduces to the model (4.5) or (4.8) with fixed coefficients and heteroscedastic variances. A typical diagonal element in the variance-covariance matrix D, viz., $d_{ii} = \sigma_1^2 + \sum_{k=2}^{K} \sigma_k^2 x_{ki}^2$, is the sum of the product of K variances of the stochastic coefficients and the square of the ith observation corresponding to the intercept and K-1 other explanatory variables. This heteroscedasticity will be present even if $\sigma_k^2 = \sigma^2$ for k=1,2,...,K so long as the square of the explanatory variables are present. No doubt, the problem of estimation in the varying coefficients model is considerably simpler when $\sigma_k^2=\sigma^2$ for all k.

4.2.1 The Generalised Least Squares Estimator of the Vector of Means of the Randomly Varying Coefficients

If we assume that σ_k^2's are known, then the GLS estimators of β's are obtained by minimising the criterion function

$$(4.10) \qquad \sum_{i=1}^{n} d^{ii}u_i^2,$$

where $d^{ii}= 1/(\sigma_1^2+\sum_{k=2}^{K}\sigma_k^2x_{ki}^2)$ is the ith diagonal element of D^{-1}. This criterion function weights the square of the disturbances by the reciprocals of their variances. These weights differentiate explicitly the information contents among all observations with smaller and larger variances, and assigns them larger and smaller weights, respectively.

Substituting $u_i=y_i-\beta_1-\beta_2x_{2i}-\cdots-\beta_Kx_{Ki}$, the criterion function (4.10) becomes

$$(4.11) \qquad S = \sum_{1}^{n} d^{ii}(y_i-\beta_1-\beta_2x_{2i}-\cdots-\beta_Kx_{Ki})^2,$$

or in matrix notation

$$(4.12) \qquad S= (y-X\beta)'D^{-1}(y-X\beta).$$

To choose β such that S is minimum we differentiate (4.12) with respect to β and then equate this derivative to zero. This gives, for $\beta = \hat{\beta}$, the normal equations as

$$(4.13) \qquad (X'D^{-1}X)\hat{\beta} = X'D^{-1}y,$$

where $\hat{\beta} = (\hat{\beta}_1, \hat{\beta}_2, \ldots, \hat{\beta}_K)'$ is a Kx1 column vector. Premultiplying (4.13) by $(X'D^{-1}X)^{-1}$, we obtain the estimator of β, called a GLS estimator, as

$$(4.14) \qquad \hat{\beta} = (X'D^{-1}X)^{-1}X'D^{-1}y.$$

In writing (4.14) we have used the assumptions that the explanatory variables are linearly independent or the rank of the matrix X is K and the variance-covariance matrix D is positive definite; thus the inverse of $X'D^{-1}X$ exists.

It is easily verified that the estimation problem in the model (4.8) to (4.9) can be equivalently handled by premultiplying the model (4.8) by $D^{-1/2} = \text{diag.}(\sqrt{d}^{11}, \sqrt{d}^{22}, \ldots, \sqrt{d}^{nn})$ to yield the transformed model

$$(4.15) \qquad y_a = X_a\beta + u_a,$$

where

$$(4.16) \qquad y_a = D^{-1/2}y, \; X_a = D^{-1/2}X \text{ and } u_a = D^{-1/2}u.$$

Now the transformed model (4.15) satisfies all the assumptions of the standard linear regression model with fixed coefficients. In particular,

$$Eu_a u_a' = D^{-1/2}E(uu')D^{-1/2} = D^{-1/2}DD^{-1/2} = I_n.$$

The ordinary least squares estimator of β in (4.15) is given by

$$(4.17) \qquad \hat{\beta} = (X_a'X_a)^{-1}X_a'y_a = (X'D^{-1}X)^{-1}X'D^{-1}y,$$

where the second equality is obtained by using

(4.16). Thus, the estimator $\hat{\beta}$ is a best (minimum variance) linear estimator of β, with variance-covariance matrix

$$(4.18) \qquad V(\hat{\beta})= E(\hat{\beta}-\beta)(\hat{\beta}-\beta)'= (X_a'X_a)^{-1}= (X'D^{-1}X)^{-1}.$$

The multiple correlation coefficient is defined as

$$R^2= 1- \frac{\hat{u}_a'\hat{u}_a}{y_a'Ay_a},$$

where $A= I- \frac{1}{n} \iota\iota'$ and ι is a column vector of ones.

The least squares estimator of β in the general linear model (4.8) would be

$$(4.19) \qquad b= (X'X)^{-1}X'y,$$

which would be linear in y's, consistent and unbiased, but would not have minimum variance in the class of linear and unbiased estimators. This is because the variance-covariance matrix of b is

$$(4.20) \qquad V(b)=E(b-\beta)(b-\beta)'=E[(X'X)^{-1}X'uu'X(X'X)^{-1}]$$

$$= (X'X)^{-1}X'DX(X'X)^{-1},$$

so that (using $D^{-1}= D^{-1/2}D^{-1/2}$),

$$(4.21) \qquad [V(b)]^{-1}-[V(\hat{\beta})]^{-1}= -X'[D^{-1}-X(X'DX)^{-1}X']X$$

$$= -X'D^{-1/2}[I-D^{1/2}X(X'DX)^{-1}X'D^{1/2}]D^{-1/2}X.$$

Since $I-D^{1/2}X(X'DX)^{-1}X'D^{1/2}$ is an indempotent matrix the right hand side of (4.21) is a negative definite matrix. Thus $[V(b)]^{-1}-[V(\hat{\beta})]^{-1} \leqslant 0$, or

$$(4.22) \qquad V(b)-V(\hat{\beta}) \geqslant 0.$$

This result implies that if one proceeds with regression analysis under a false belief that the coefficients are fixed when they are in fact randomly varying, then one might get inefficient estimates of the coefficients. Also the confidence intervals will be different from the true ones.

4.2.2 The Estimation of the Variances of the Random Coefficients

For the estimation of the variances of the random coefficients, viz., $\sigma_1^2,\ldots,\sigma_K^2$, we consider the following property of the least squares residuals in the multiple regression model (4.8). Let $e=(e_1,e_2,..,e_n)'$ be the least squares residual column vector given as

$$(4.23) \qquad e= y-Xb,$$

with b as the least squares estimator of β in the model (4.8). Substituting the value of b from (4.19) and y from (4.8), we can write (4.23) as

$$(4.24) \qquad e= My= Mu,$$

where $M= I-X(X'X)^{-1}X'$ is a symmetric idempotent matrix[1] of order (nxn), which is orthogonal to matrix of regressors X; thus $M=M'$, $M^2=M$ and $MX=0$. The ith element of e is $e_i= \sum_{j=1}^{n} m_{ij}u_j$, where m_{ij} is the i,j^{th} element of M. Thus, using (4.7) we can obtain

$$(4.25a) \qquad Ee_i= E(\sum_{j=1}^{n} m_{ij}u_j)= 0,$$

(4.25b) $$Ee_i^2 = V(e_i) = E(\sum_{j=1}^{n} m_{ij}u_j)^2$$

$$= \sum_{j=1}^{n} \sum_{j'=1}^{n} m_{ij}m_{ij'}(Eu_j u_{j'})$$

$$= \sum_{j=1}^{n} m_{ij}^2(\sigma_1^2 + \sum_{k=2}^{K} x_{kj}^2 \sigma_k^2)$$

$$= \sum_{j=1}^{n} m_{ij}^2 d_{jj}.$$

We may write n observations in (4.25a) and (4.25b) compactly as

(4.26) $$E\dot{e} = \dot{M}\dot{X}\dot{\sigma},$$

where

$$\dot{e} = e*e = \begin{bmatrix} e_1 \\ e_2 \\ \vdots \\ e_n \end{bmatrix} * \begin{bmatrix} e_1 \\ e_2 \\ \vdots \\ e_n \end{bmatrix} = \begin{bmatrix} e_1^2 \\ e_2^2 \\ \vdots \\ e_n^2 \end{bmatrix},$$

$$\dot{M} = M*M = \begin{bmatrix} m_{11} & m_{12} & \cdots & m_{1n} \\ m_{21} & m_{22} & \cdots & m_{2n} \\ \vdots & \vdots & & \vdots \\ m_{n1} & m_{n2} & \cdots & m_{nn} \end{bmatrix} * \begin{bmatrix} m_{11} & m_{12} & \cdots & m_{1n} \\ m_{21} & m_{22} & \cdots & m_{2n} \\ \vdots & \vdots & & \vdots \\ m_{n1} & m_{n2} & \cdots & m_{nn} \end{bmatrix}$$

$$= \begin{bmatrix} m_{11}^2 & m_{12}^2 & \cdots & m_{1n}^2 \\ m_{21}^2 & m_{22}^2 & \cdots & m_{2n}^2 \\ \vdots & \vdots & & \vdots \\ m_{n1}^2 & m_{n2}^2 & \cdots & m_{nn}^2 \end{bmatrix}$$

$$\dot{X}=X*X=\begin{bmatrix} 1 & x_{21} & .. & x_{K1} \\ 1 & x_{22} & .. & x_{K2} \\ \vdots & \vdots & & \vdots \\ 1 & x_{2n} & .. & x_{Kn} \end{bmatrix} * \begin{bmatrix} 1 & x_{21} & .. & x_{K1} \\ 1 & x_{22} & .. & x_{K2} \\ \vdots & \vdots & & \vdots \\ 1 & x_{2n} & .. & x_{Kn} \end{bmatrix}$$

$$= \begin{bmatrix} 1 & x_{21}^2 & .. & x_{K1}^2 \\ 1 & x_{22}^2 & .. & x_{K2}^2 \\ \vdots & \vdots & & \vdots \\ 1 & x_{2n}^2 & .. & x_{Kn}^2 \end{bmatrix},$$

$$\dot{\sigma} = \begin{bmatrix} \sigma_1^2 \\ \sigma_2^2 \\ \vdots \\ \sigma_K^2 \end{bmatrix}$$

and * represents the Hadamard matrix product.[2] The regression relation conditional on the explanatory variables implied by (4.26) can be written as

(4.27) $\dot{e}= G\dot{\sigma}+w,$

where $G=\dot{M}\dot{X}$ and w is an nx1 disturbance vector such that

(4.28) $Ew= 0.$

The variance-covariance matrix of the disturbance vector w is easily derived under the assumption that the random coefficients β's are normally distributed. It is shown below that the disturbances w's are both heteroscedastic and serially correlated. The variance-covariance matrix of w is

$$(4.29) \qquad Eww' = E(\dot{e} - G\dot{\sigma})(\dot{e} - G\dot{\sigma})' = E(\dot{e} - E\dot{e})(\dot{e} - E\dot{e})'$$

$$= E\dot{e}\dot{e}' - (E\dot{e})(E\dot{e})',$$

where

$$\dot{e} = \begin{bmatrix} e_1^2 \\ \\ e_2^2 \\ \vdots \\ e_n^2 \end{bmatrix} = \begin{bmatrix} (\sum_{j=1}^{n} m_{1j}u_j)^2 \\ \\ (\sum_{j=1}^{n} m_{2j}u_j)^2 \\ \vdots \\ (\sum_{j=1}^{n} m_{nj}u_j)^2 \end{bmatrix} = \begin{bmatrix} \sum_{j=1}^{n} \sum_{j'=1}^{n} m_{1j}m_{1j'}u_ju_{j'} \\ \\ \sum_{j=1}^{n} \sum_{j'=1}^{n} m_{2j}m_{2j'}u_ju_{j'} \\ \vdots \\ \sum_{j=1}^{n} \sum_{j'=1}^{n} m_{nj}m_{nj'}u_ju_{j'} \end{bmatrix}$$

and e_i is the ith element of the column vector e in (4.24). The $(i,i')^{th}$ element in the moment matrix of $E\dot{e}\dot{e}'$ is

$$(4.30) \quad Ee_i^2e_{i'}^2 = E(\sum_{j=1}^{n} \sum_{j'=1}^{n} m_{ij}m_{ij'}u_ju_{j'})$$

$$(\sum_{j''=1}^{n} \sum_{j'''=1}^{n} m_{i'j''}m_{i'j'''}u_{j''}u_{j'''}),$$

$$= \sum_{j=1}^{n} \sum_{j'=1}^{n} \sum_{j''=1}^{n} \sum_{j'''=1}^{n} m_{ij}m_{ij'}m_{i'j''}m_{i'j'''}$$

$$E(u_ju_{j'}u_{j''}u_{j'''}).$$

The mathematical expectation of the term $u_ju_{j'}u_{j''}u_{j'''}$ is nonzero when either j, j', j", j‴ are pairwise equal or when they are all equal. In the former case the value of the expression on the right hand side of (4.30) is equal to

$$\sum_{j=1}^{n} \sum_{j''=1}^{n} m_{ij}^2 m_{i'j''}^2 d_{jj} d_{j''j''} - \sum_{j''=1}^{n} m_{ij''}^2 m_{i'j''}^2 d_{j''j''}^2,$$

where $V(u_j) = E(u_j^2) = d_{jj}$. In the latter case the value of the expression is equal to

$$3 \sum_{j=1}^{n} m_{ij}^2 m_{i'j}^2 d_{jj}^2,$$

which is obtained by using the fact that the fourth moment about the mean of a normal variable is equal to three times the square of its variance. Thus, the $(i,i')^{th}$ element of the moment matrix of $\dot{e}$ about zero is

$$(4.31) \qquad Ee_i^2 e_{i'}^2 = [\sum_{j=1}^{n} m_{ij}^2 d_{jj}][\sum_{j'=1}^{n} m_{i'j'}^2 d_{j'j'}] + 2[\sum_{j=1}^{n} m_{ij} m_{i'j} d_{jj}]^2.$$

The nxn elements in (4.31) for i,i'=1,2,...,n, can be compactly written as

$$(4.32) \qquad E\dot{e}\dot{e}' = E(\dot{e})E(\dot{e})' + 2\Psi * \Psi,$$

where $\Psi = Eee' = EMuu'M = MDM$ is the variance-covariance of e and * represents the Hadamard matrix product. Substituting (4.31) into (4.29), we obtain the variance-covariance matrix of w as

$$(4.33) \qquad Eww' = 2\dot{\Psi}$$

where $\dot{\Psi} = \Psi * \Psi$.

The generalised least squares estimator of $\dot{\sigma}$ in the multiple regression model (4.27), assuming σ_j^2's are known, can be obtained by minimising the criterion function

$$(4.34) \qquad S = w'(2\dot{\Psi})^{-1}w = (\dot{e} - G\dot{\sigma})'(2\dot{\Psi})^{-1}(\dot{e} - G\dot{\sigma}).$$

Differentiating (4.34) with respect to $\dot{\sigma}$ and equating this derivative to zero, we can write the K normal equations compactly as

$$(4.35) \qquad (G'\dot{\Psi}^{-1}G)\dot{\sigma} = (G'\dot{\Psi}^{-1}\dot{e}).$$

Thus, the generalised least squares estimator of $\dot{\sigma}$ can be written as

$$(4.36) \qquad \hat{\dot{\sigma}} = (G'\dot{\Psi}^{-1}G)^{-1}G'\dot{\Psi}^{-1}\dot{e}.$$

The solution (4.36) has been obtained from (4.35) under the assumption that the columns of the matrix of regressors G are linearly independent and the variance-covariance matrix D (and hence $\dot{\Psi}$) is positive definite.

The variance-covariance matrix of $\hat{\dot{\sigma}}$ is

$$(4.37) \qquad V(\hat{\dot{\sigma}}) = E(\hat{\dot{\sigma}} - E\hat{\dot{\sigma}})(\hat{\dot{\sigma}} - E\hat{\dot{\sigma}})' = E(\hat{\dot{\sigma}} - \dot{\sigma})(\hat{\dot{\sigma}} - \dot{\sigma})'$$

$$= E[(G'(2\dot{\Psi})^{-1}G)^{-1}G'(2\dot{\Psi})^{-1}ww'(2\dot{\Psi})^{-1}$$

$$G(G'(2\dot{\Psi})^{-1}G)^{-1}]$$

$$= (G'(2\dot{\Psi})^{-1}G)^{-1}G'(2\dot{\Psi})^{-1}(Eww')(2\dot{\Psi})^{-1}$$

$$G(G'(2\dot{\Psi})^{-1}G) = (G'(2\dot{\Psi})^{-1}G)^{-1}.$$

4.2.3 The Operational Generalised Least Squares Estimators of the Vector of Means and Variances of the Stochastic Coefficients

The estimators (4.14) and (4.36) of β and $\dot{\sigma}$ respectively are nonoperational because the variance-covariance matrices D and $2\dot{\Psi}$ of disturbance vectors u and w are functions of unknown variances of the stochastic coefficients. However, the operational generalised least squares (OGLS) estimators of β and $\dot{\sigma}$ may be obtained by using the estimators of $\hat{D}$ and $2\hat{\dot{\Psi}}$ in (4.14) and (4.36) respectively in place of the unknown D and $2\dot{\Psi}$.

An estimator of the vector of variances of the random coefficients $\dot{\sigma}$ may be obtained by applying the least squares principle to the multiple regression model (4.27); it is given by

$$(4.38) \qquad \dot{s}_1 = (G'G)^{-1}G'\dot{e} = (\dot{X}'\dot{M}^2\dot{X})^{-1}\dot{X}'\dot{M}^2\dot{e}.$$

Another consistent estimator of $\dot{\sigma}$ based on a procedure introduced by Rao is called a minimum norm quadratic unbiased estimator[3] (MINQUE), given by

$$(4.39) \qquad \dot{s}_2 = (\dot{X}'\dot{M}\dot{X})^{-1}\dot{X}'\dot{M}\dot{e}.$$

In fact a class of consistent estimators, which are linear functions of e_i^2, is given by

$$(4.40) \qquad \dot{s}_3 = (\dot{X}'\dot{M}^{g+1}\dot{X})^{-1}\dot{X}'\dot{M}^{g+1}\dot{e},$$

where g is a characterising scalar. It should be noted that estimators $\dot{s}_1$ and $\dot{s}_2$ are special cases of the estimator $\dot{s}_3$ for g=1 and g=0 respectively.

Alternative sets of operational generalised least squares estimators of β and $\dot{\sigma}$ can be obtained by using (4.40) for the unknowns in D and $\dot{\Psi}$ respectively. Accordingly, we may write a set of operational generalised least squares estimators of β and $\dot{\sigma}$ respectively as

(4.41) $$\tilde{\beta} = (X'\hat{D}^{-1}X)^{-1}X'\hat{D}^{-1}y$$

and

(4.42) $$\tilde{\dot{\sigma}} = (G'\hat{\dot{\Psi}}^{-1}G)^{-1}G'\hat{\dot{\Psi}}^{-1}\dot{e},$$

where $\hat{D} = \text{diag.}(\hat{d}_{11},\ldots,\hat{d}_{nn})$ with $\hat{d}_{ii} = \hat{\sigma}_1^2 + \sum_{k=2}^{K} \hat{\sigma}_k^2 x_{ki}^2$ and $\hat{\dot{\Psi}} = \hat{\Psi} * \hat{\Psi}$, with $\hat{\Psi} = M\hat{D}M$ are consistent estimators of D and $\dot{\Psi}$ respectively, which are obtained by replacing the unknown σ_k^2's by their consistent least squares estimators from (4.40).

4.2.4 Properties of the Estimators

It can easily be shown that the operational GLS estimators of β, where D is replaced by a consistent estimator, are all equivalent to the GLS estimator (4.14) with known D, in the sense that $\sqrt{n}(\tilde{\beta}-\hat{\beta})$ converges in probability to zero as $n\to\infty$. This is because both estimators $\tilde{\beta}$ and $\hat{\beta}$ are asymptotically normally distributed with mean vector β and covariance matrix $(X'D^{-1}X)^{-1}$. Similarly, the operational GLS estimators of $\dot{\sigma}$, where $\dot{\Psi}$ is replaced by a consistent estimator, are all asymptotically equivalent to the GLS estimator $\hat{\dot{\sigma}}$, in the sense that $\sqrt{n}(\tilde{\dot{\sigma}}-\hat{\dot{\sigma}})$ converges in probability to zero as $n\to\infty$. Both the estimators $\tilde{\dot{\sigma}}$ and $\hat{\dot{\sigma}}$ being asymptotically normally distributed with mean $\dot{\sigma}$ and variance-covariance matrix

$$(G'(2\mathring{\Psi})^{-1}G')^{-1} \approx (G'(2\dot{D})^{-1}G')^{-1}.$$

These limiting properties of the operational generalised estimators are proved in Chapter 6.

Despite the fact that the alternative operational estimators of β and $\dot{\sigma}$ are asymptotically (large sample) equally efficient, this may not be so in the finite samples. In Chapter 5 we shall discuss the evaluation of relative efficiency of various estimation procedures when the sample is small. We note there that if the sample is small the variances of the $\tilde{\beta}$ obtained from the asymptotic variance-covariance matrix formula underestimate the value obtained by true variances. The true variance refers to the finite sample variance of $\tilde{\beta}$.

4.2.5 Maximum Likelihood Estimation

Assuming, in addition to (4.4), that the disturbance ε_{ki} in the random coefficients β_{ki} are normally distributed, we can use the maximum likelihood (ML) estimation procedure for the estimation of β_k and σ_k^2. Since, under normality, the distribution of y is a multivariate normal with mean $X\beta$ and variance-covariance matrix D we can write the likelihood function as

$$(4.43) \qquad L=L(\beta,\sigma_1^2,..,\sigma_K^2/y,X)= (2\pi)^{-n/2}\,|D|^{-1/2}$$
$$\exp\,[-1/2\,(y-X\beta)'D^{-1}(y-X\beta)],$$

where the matrix D contains $\sigma_1^2,...,\sigma_K^2$ and is as given in (4.9). Thus the log likelihood is

$$(4.44) \qquad \log L= -\,\frac{n}{2}\log(2\pi)-\,\frac{1}{2}\log|D|$$
$$-\,\frac{1}{2}\,(y-X\beta)'\,D^{-1}(y-X\beta).$$

Since the maximisation of log L for given D, is the same as minimisation of $S=(y-X\beta)'D^{-1}(y-X\beta)$, the ML estimator of β is identical with the GLS estimator $\hat{\beta}=(X'D^{-1}X)^{-1}X'D^{-1}y$. One can obtain this by solving $\partial \log L/\partial\beta=0$.

To obtain the ML estimator of $\sigma_1^2,\ldots,\sigma_K^2$ we first substitute $\hat{\beta}$ in the log likelihood and write it as[4]

$$\begin{aligned}(4.45)\qquad \log L_c &= \log L_c(\sigma_1^2,\ldots,\sigma_K^2/y,X)\\ &= \text{const.}-\frac{1}{2}\log|D|-\frac{1}{2}\hat{u}'D^{-1}\hat{u}\\ &= \text{const.}-\frac{1}{2}\sum_{i=1}^{n}\log\left(\sum_{k=1}^{K}x_{ki}^2\sigma_k^2\right)\\ &\quad -\frac{1}{2}\sum_{i=1}^{n}\left(\hat{u}_i^2/\sum_{k=1}^{K}x_{ki}^2\sigma_k^2\right),\end{aligned}$$

where $\hat{u}=y-X\hat{\beta}$ and $\hat{u}_i$ is its ith element. The $\log L_c$ in (4.45) is a concentrated log likelihood function of σ_k^2, $k=1,\ldots,K$. Unfortunately, this is highly nonlinear in σ_k^2's and hence $\partial\log L/\partial\sigma_k^2=0$ does not provide an explicit ML solution for σ_k^2 (except for K=1 and in this case the resulting ML estimator of σ_1^2 is as given in Chapter 3). In general the ML estimators of $\sigma_1^2,\ldots,\sigma_K^2$ are obtained by using available nonlinear maximisation programmes which solve $\log L_c(\sigma_i^2,\ldots,\sigma_K^2)$ by an iterative method. The converging solution of this iterative process will be the ML estimators for σ_k^2's, and substituting this into $(X'D^{-1}X)^{-1}X'D^{-1}y$ provides the operational ML estimator of β. This operational ML estimator will be different from the operational GLS estimator considered in (4.41).

Since the domain of the parameters σ_k^2's is nonnegative, it is appropriate to maximise the function (4.45) subject to the restrictions that $\sigma_k^2 \geq 0$ if the negative solutions for σ_k^2's from (4.45) are to be avoided. The above constrained maximisation problem can be cast in terms of the unconstrained maximisation problem by using a square root transformation.[5] Accordingly, we may set $\sigma_j=\theta_j^2$ in (4.45) and apply one of the several available search procedures to obtain the maxima of the log of the concentrated likelihood function. However, it is important to note two points: first, the function (4.45) may have regions of different concavity and more than one maximum. It is therefore important to use an efficient search procedure so that it is sufficiently discriminating among alternative local maxima. Second, we need a starting guess for the search procedure. A reasonable and efficient starting point can be obtained by applying restricted generalised least squares estimator of the vector $\dot{\sigma}=(\sigma_1^2,\ldots,\sigma_K^2)'$ which minimises the criterion function

$$(4.46) \qquad (\dot{\hat{u}}-G\dot{\sigma})'(2\dot{\Psi})^{-1}(\dot{\hat{u}}-G\dot{\sigma}),$$

subject to restrictions $\dot{\sigma} \geq 0$. A reasonably inexpensive and almost as efficient starting point can be obtained by letting $2\dot{\Psi}=I$ in (4.46) and obtaining the restricted least squares estimator of the vector $\dot{\sigma}$.[6] The maximum likelihood estimation is computationally more expensive but can be more efficient than the operational generalised least squares estimators in small samples (see the Monte Carlo evidence reported in Chapter 5).

4.2.6. Testing for the Randomly Varying Coefficients

We have seen that the effect of introducing stochastic variation in coefficients is that the errors in the reduced model become heteroscedastic. Thus, testing for varying parameters implies testing for the heteroscedasticity. One way to do this is to apply the likelihood ratio test, which is derived from an important principle due to Neyman and Pearson for testing the plausibility of one set of the parameters against another. Specifically, the likelihood ratio is the ratio of the maximum values of the likelihood function under the null and alternative hypotheses about the parameters of the model. The test statistic is then minus two times the log likelihood, and it is asymptotically distributed as χ^2 with the degrees of freedom equal to the number of restrictions.

An alternative approach is to apply the Lagrange-multiplier (LM) test which is also known as Rao's efficient score test.[7] The statistic for this test, which is due to Aitchison and Silvey (1960), is obtained from the LM corresponding to the maximisation of the likelihood function subject to the parameter restrictions implied by the null hypothesis. The LM test has the same asymptotic properties as the likelihood ratio (LR) test. It is computationally a simple test since it is based on least squares residuals. We discuss this method below.

Let us consider model (4.5), viz.,

$$(4.47) \qquad y_i = \beta_1 + \sum_{k=2}^{K} x_{ki}\beta_k + u_i,$$

where $u_i = \varepsilon^*_{1i} + \sum_{k=2}^{K} x_{ki}\varepsilon_{ki}$ such that $Eu_i = 0$ and

$$Eu_i^2 = \sigma_1^2 + \sum_{k=2}^{K} x_{ki}^2 \sigma_k^2 = \dot{x}_i \dot{\sigma};$$

$\dot{x}_i = (1, x_{1i}^2, \ldots, x_{Ki}^2)'$ is the ith row of $\dot{X}$ in (4.26) and $\dot{\sigma} = (\sigma_1^2, \ldots, \sigma_K^2)'$ as given before. Thus in this model the test for the hypothesis

$$H_0 : \sigma_2^2 = \ldots = \sigma_K^2 = 0$$

implies the test for zero variation of the type $\beta_{ki} = \beta + \varepsilon_{ki}$ for k=2,...,K in model (4.1).

The LM test statistic for testing the above hypothesis is

$$\text{(4.48)} \qquad LM = \hat{d}'\hat{I}^{-1}\hat{d},$$

which is asymptotically distributed as χ^2 with K-1 degrees of freedom when H_0 is true. The $\hat{d}$ and $\hat{I}$ are given respectively as

$$\text{(4.49)} \qquad \hat{d} = \left[\frac{\partial \log L}{\partial \dot{\sigma}}\right]_{\dot{\sigma} = \hat{\dot{\sigma}}};$$

$$\text{(4.50)} \qquad \hat{I} = E\left[-\frac{\partial^2 \log L}{\partial \dot{\sigma}\partial \dot{\sigma}'}\right]_{\dot{\sigma} = \hat{\dot{\sigma}}},$$

where log L represents the log likelihood function given in (4.44), and $\hat{\dot{\sigma}}$ is the ML estimate of $\dot{\sigma}$ under the restriction imposed by H_0.

To see the values of $\hat{d}$ and $\hat{I}$ more explicitly, it would be convenient to use concentrated log likelihood in (4.45) and write it as

$$(4.51)\quad \log L_c(\dot{\sigma}) = \text{const.} - \frac{1}{2}\sum_{i=1}^{n}\log d_{ii} - \frac{1}{2}\sum_{i=1}^{n}\frac{\hat{u}_i^2}{d_{ii}},$$

where $d_{ii} = \dot{x}_i\dot{\sigma}$ and $\hat{u}_i$ is the ith element of restricted LS residual vector $\hat{u} = y - X\hat{\beta}$. Note that $\hat{\beta} = (X'X)^{-1}X'y$ is the ML estimator under the restrictions $\sigma_2^2 = \ldots = \sigma_K^2 = 0$. Now

$$(4.52)\quad \frac{\partial \log L_c}{\partial \dot{\sigma}} = -\frac{1}{2}\sum_{i=1}^{n}\frac{\dot{x}_i'}{d_{ii}} + \frac{1}{2}\sum_{i=1}^{n}\frac{\hat{u}_i^2\dot{x}_i'}{d_{ii}^2}$$

$$= \frac{1}{2}\sum_{i=1}^{n}\frac{\dot{x}_i'}{d_{ii}}\left(\frac{\hat{u}_i^2}{d_{ii}} - 1\right).$$

But when $\sigma_2^2 = \ldots = \sigma_K^2 = 0$, $d_{ii} = \sigma_1^2$ and its ML estimator is $\hat{\sigma}_1^2 = (\sum_1^n \hat{u}_i^2)/n$; thus the restricted ML estimator of $\dot{\sigma} = (\sigma_1^2, \ldots, 0)'$ is $\hat{\dot{\sigma}} = (\hat{\sigma}_1^2, \ldots, 0)'$. Hence

$$(4.53)\quad \hat{d} = \left[\frac{\partial \log L_c}{\partial \dot{\sigma}}\right]_{\dot{\sigma}=\hat{\dot{\sigma}}} = \frac{1}{2\hat{\sigma}_1^2}\left[\sum_{i=1}^{n}\dot{x}_i'(\hat{\sigma}_1^{-2}\hat{u}_i^2 - 1)\right].$$

Similarly,

$$(4.54)\quad \hat{I} = \frac{1}{2\hat{\sigma}_1^4}\sum_{i=1}^{n}\dot{x}_i'\dot{x}_i = \frac{\dot{X}'\dot{X}}{2\hat{\sigma}_1^4},$$

where

$$\dot{X} = \begin{bmatrix} 1 \\ \dot{x}_2 \\ \vdots \\ \dot{x}_n \end{bmatrix}$$

as given in (4.26).

Substituting d and I in (4.48), we can write

$$(4.55) \qquad LM = \frac{1}{2}\dot{g}'\dot{X}(\dot{X}'\dot{X})^{-1}\dot{X}'\dot{g} \sim \chi^2_{K-1},$$

where $\dot{g}$ is nx1 vector whose i^{th} element is $g_i = (\hat{\sigma}_1^{-2}\hat{u}_i^2 - 1)$. This statistic is then simply one half of the explained sum of squares in the regression of $\dot{g}$ on $\dot{X}$. The computation of LM is quite simple because $\dot{g}$ is based on the LS residuals $\hat{u}_i$ from (4.47).[8]

4.3 ESTIMATION OF THE ACTUAL COEFFICIENTS

In the earlier sections we discussed the estimation of the means of random coefficients β_k's in the model (4.1). Here we shall take up the estimation of actual coefficients β_{ki}'s which are useful for efficient prediction of the values of y.[9]

We first rewrite the model (4.1) under (4.2) as

$$(4.56) \qquad y_i = x_i\beta_i + \varepsilon_{oi},$$

$$(4.57) \qquad \beta_i = \beta + \varepsilon_i,$$

where x_i is a 1x(K-1) vector

$$(4.58) \qquad x_i = (x_{2i}, \ldots, x_{Ki}),$$

β is (K-1)x1 vector and

$$(4.59) \qquad \beta_i = (\beta_{2i}, \ldots, \beta_{Ki})'; \; \varepsilon_i = (\varepsilon_{2i}, \ldots, \varepsilon_{Ki})'$$

are (K-1)x1 vectors. We note that the random intercept β_{1i} has been dropped (without any loss of generality) for the sake of simplicity in exposition. The vector x_i can be considered as the ith

row of the matrix X in (4.8) excluding the first term. Further, following (4.4) it can be easily seen that $E\varepsilon_{oi}=0$, $E\varepsilon^2_{oi}=\sigma^2_o$, and also

$$(4.60) \qquad E\varepsilon_i = 0; \; E\varepsilon_i \varepsilon_i' = \Sigma = \text{diag.}(\sigma_2^2, .., \sigma_K^2)$$

The linear model (4.56) with the stochastic prior information on β_i in (4.57), viz., that β_i is a random vector with common unknown mean β and covariance matrix Σ, can be considered as a kind of mixed estimation model of Theil and Goldberger (1961). However, we should take note that since β is not observable we have the case of nonobservable prior. With known β, σ^2_o and Σ, we can obtain the estimator of β_i by incorporating the prior information (4.57) with the sample information in (4.56). For this we write

$$(4.61) \qquad S = S(\beta_i) = \frac{\varepsilon^2_{oi}}{\sigma^2_o} + \varepsilon_i' \, \Sigma^{-1} \varepsilon_i$$

$$= \frac{(y_i - x_i \beta_i)^2}{\sigma^2_o} + (\beta_i - \beta)' \, \Sigma^{-1} (\beta_i - \beta)'$$

and minimise it with respect to β_i. Equating the first order derivative of S with respect to $\beta_i = \hat{\beta}_i$ gives

$$(4.62) \qquad \frac{-x_i'(y_i - x_i \hat{\beta}_i)}{\sigma^2_o} + \Sigma^{-1}(\hat{\beta}_i - \beta) = 0.$$

Further simplifying, we obtain

$$(4.63) \qquad \hat{\beta}_i = \left(\frac{x_i'x_i}{\sigma_o^2} + \Sigma^{-1}\right)^{-1} \left(\frac{x_i'y_i}{\sigma_o^2} + \Sigma^{-1}\beta\right).$$

If the model in (4.56) and (4.57) is true, then $\hat{\beta}_i$ is the best linear unbiased estimator. The unbiased property of $\hat{\beta}_i$ follows from the fact that it is based on complete information. Further, one can easily show that it is the GLS estimator of the combined model (4.56) and (4.57). The mean vector and covariance matrix of $\hat{\beta}_i$ is

$$(4.64) \qquad E\hat{\beta}_i = \beta_i,$$

$$(4.65) \qquad V(\hat{\beta}_i) = E(\hat{\beta}_i - \beta_i)(\hat{\beta}_i - \beta_i)' = \left(\frac{x_i'x_i}{\sigma_o^2} + \Sigma^{-1}\right)^{-1}.$$

Another method of obtaining the estimator of β_i is by ML approach. In this we first assume the normality of ε_{oi} and ε_i in addition to the earlier assumptions. Then since ε_{oi} and ε_i are independent one can specify the likelihood of the combined model (4.56) and (4.57) as

$$(4.66) \qquad L(\beta_i) = L(\beta_i/y_i, x_i, \sigma_o^2)\, L(\beta_i/\beta, \Sigma),$$

where the first term can be called 'sample likelihood', such that[10]

$$(4.67) \qquad L(\beta_i/y_i, x_i) = \frac{1}{\sqrt{(2\pi)}(\sigma_o)} \exp\left[-\frac{1}{2}\, \frac{(y_i - x_i\beta_i)^2}{\sigma_o^2}\right];$$

while the second term may be called 'prior likelihood', such that

$$(4.68) \quad L(\beta_i/\beta,\Sigma) = \frac{1}{(2\pi)^{\frac{K-1}{2}} |\Sigma|^{1/2}} \exp[-\tfrac{1}{2}(\beta_i-\beta)'\Sigma^{-1}(\beta_i-\beta)].$$

Using these sample and prior likelihood expressions in (4.66) and taking log it becomes clear that the maximisation of log $L(\beta_i)$ is the same as the minimisation of $S(\beta_i)$ in (4.66) with respect to β_i. Thus, under normality, $\hat{\beta}_i$ in (4.63) is also the ML estimator.

In the Bayesian framework the 'prior likelihood' is termed as prior probability distribution and we obtain the posterior of β_i as

$$(4.69) \quad p(\beta_i/y_i,\beta,\sigma_o^2,\ \Sigma) \propto L(\beta_i/y_i,x_i,\sigma_o^2)p(\beta_i/\beta,\ \Sigma),$$

where L( ) is as before and p( ) is a prior. If prior of β_i is normal with mean β and covariance matrix Σ, then the posterior of β_i is

$$(4.70) \quad p(\beta_i/y_i,\beta,\sigma_o^2,\ \Sigma) \propto [\exp -\tfrac{1}{2}\, q],$$

where

$$q = \frac{(y_i - x_i\beta_i)^2}{\sigma_o^2} + (\beta_i-\beta)'\ \Sigma^{-1}(\beta_i-\beta)$$

$$= \frac{\beta_i'x_i'x_i\beta_i}{\sigma_o^2} + \beta_i'\ \Sigma^{-1}\beta_i - \frac{2\beta_i'x_i'y_i}{\sigma_o^2}$$

$$- 2\beta_i'\ \Sigma^{-1}\beta + \frac{y_i^2}{\sigma_o^2} + \beta'\ \Sigma^{-1}\beta.$$

Adding and subtracting $\beta_i^{*\prime}\left(\frac{x_i'x_i}{\sigma_o^2} + \Sigma^{-1}\right)\beta_i^*$ in q, and making a perfect square in terms of β_i, we can write

$$(4.71)\qquad q=(\beta_i-\beta_i^*)'A(\beta_i-\beta_i^*)+\frac{y_i^2}{\sigma_o^2}-\beta_i^{*}{}'A\beta_i^*+\beta'\Sigma^{-1}\beta,$$

where

$$(4.72)\qquad \beta_i^*=\left(\frac{x_i'x_i}{\sigma_o^2}+\Sigma^{-1}\right)^{-1}\left(\frac{x_i'y_i}{\sigma_o^2}+\Sigma^{-1}\beta\right)$$

and

$$(4.73)\qquad A=\left(\frac{x_i'x_i}{\sigma_o^2}+\Sigma^{-1}\right).$$

Thus the posterior density of β_i is

$$(4.74)\qquad p(\beta_i/y_i,\beta,\sigma_o^2,\Sigma)\propto \exp[-\tfrac{1}{2}(\beta_i-\beta_i^*)'A(\beta_i-\beta_i^*)],$$

which is a multivariate normal with mean vector β_i^* and covariance matrix A^{-1}. The conditional Bayes estimator is therefore β_i^*, the posterior mean, and is identical with the estimator in (4.63). Further, variance of the posterior density is in fact identical with the variance of the estimator $\beta_i^*=\hat{\beta}_i$ as given in (4.65). We should note that the unconditional Bayes estimator obtained under assumptions of the prior density of σ_o and Σ may not be the same as $\hat{\beta}_i$.

4.3.1 Operation Version of $\hat{\beta}_i$

The mixed ML and Bayes estimator $\hat{\beta}_i$ in (4.63) cannot be used in practice in their current form. This is because they depend on unknown σ_o, Σ and β. A way out is to replace them by their estimates obtained in an earlier section. For example, estimators for σ_o and Σ can be obtained from $\tilde{\sigma}$ given in (4.42) and that of β from $\tilde{\beta}$ in (4.41). Then an operational version of β_i can be written as

$$(4.75) \qquad \tilde{\beta}_i = \left(\frac{x_i'x_i}{\tilde{\sigma}_o^2} + \tilde{\Sigma}^{-1}\right)^{-1} \left(\frac{x_i'y_i}{\tilde{\sigma}_o^2} + \tilde{\Sigma}^{-1}\hat{\beta}\right).$$

This estimator will be asymptotically BLUE and has the same distribution as $\hat{\beta}_i$.

With this estimator $\tilde{\beta}_i$ one can get the best linear unbiased predictor (asymptotically) of y_i as

$$(4.76) \qquad \tilde{y}_i = x_i\tilde{\beta}_i.$$

4.4 SPECIFICATION AND ESTIMATION OF SEQUENTIALLY VARYING COEFFICIENT MODELS (ADAPTIVE COEFFICIENT CASE)

Here we shall consider the estimation problem of a linear regression model first when the intercept in the model is varying sequentially and then when both the intercept and slope coefficients are varying.

4.4.1 Adaptive Intercept Model

Let us consider the case when only the intercept is random in model (4.1), that is

$$(4.77) \qquad y_i = \beta_{1i} + \beta_2 x_{2i} + \cdots + \beta_K x_{Ki} + \varepsilon_{oi}$$
$$= \beta_{1i} + x_i\beta + \varepsilon_{oi},$$

where $x_i=(x_{2i}\dots x_{Ki})$ as defined in (4.59) and β is (K-1)x1 vector. We now use adaptive coefficient specification for β_{1i} which is

(4.78) $$\beta_{1i}= \beta_{1,i-1}+\varepsilon_{1i}.$$

The assumptions about ε_{oi} and ε_{1i} are as stated in Section 4.3. The unknown parameters of the model (4.77) and (4.78) are the regression coefficient vector β and the variances σ_o^2 and σ_1^2. One would also be interested in estimating or predicting the path of the permanent component β_{1i} over i=1,...,n. We shall first, however, consider the estimation of β, σ_o^2 and σ_1^2.

Write the model (4.77) for i=i-1 as

(4.79) $$y_{i-1}= \beta_{1,i-1}+x_{i-1}\beta+\varepsilon_{o,i-1} \qquad i=2,\dots,n.$$

Now we subtract (4.79) from (4.77) and write the model in the first difference form as

(4.80) $$y_i-y_{i-1}= (x_i-x_{i-1})\beta+(\varepsilon_{oi}-\varepsilon_{o,i-1})+\varepsilon_{1i}$$

or simply as

(4.81) $$y_i^*= x_i^*\beta+u_i^*,$$

where $y_i^*= y_i-y_{i-1}$, $x_i^*= x_i-x_{i-1}$ and

(4.82) $$u_i^*= \varepsilon_{oi}-\varepsilon_{o,i-1}+\varepsilon_{1i}.$$

The disturbance term u_i^* is such that $Eu_i^*=0$ and

(4.83) $$Eu_i^* = \sigma_1^2 + 2\sigma_o^2,$$

$$Eu_i^* u_{i-s}^* = -\sigma_o^2, \qquad \text{for } s=1$$

$$= 0, \qquad \text{for } |s| > 1.$$

Given this behaviour of u_i^* one can write u_i^* in terms of a first order moving average (MA[1]) representation, that is

(4.84) $$u_i^* = v_i - \theta v_{i-1}, \qquad 0 \leqslant \theta < 1,$$

for some choice of θ. The disturbances v_i are independent and identically distributed with zero mean and variance σ_v^2. To obtain the value of θ for which (4.82) and (4.84) have identical representations we observe the following relations:

(4.85) $$Eu_i^{*2} = \sigma_v^2(1+\theta^2) = \sigma_1^2 + 2\sigma_o^2,$$

$$Eu_i^* u_{i-1}^* = -\sigma_o^2 = \theta\sigma_v^2,$$

$$\rho_1 = \frac{\text{cov}(u_i^*, u_{i-1}^*)}{\sqrt{V(u_i^*)}\sqrt{V(u_{i-1}^*)}} = \frac{-\theta}{1+\theta^2} = \frac{-\sigma_o^2}{\sigma_1^2 + 2\sigma_o^2}.$$

These relations give

(4.86) $$\sigma_1^2 = \sigma_v^2(1-\theta)^2,$$

$$\theta = \frac{-1+\sqrt{1-4\rho_1^2}}{2\rho_1} = 1 + \frac{1}{2}\frac{\sigma_1^2}{\sigma_o^2} - \frac{\sigma_1}{\sigma_o}\sqrt{1 + \frac{1}{4}\frac{\sigma_1^2}{\sigma_o^2}},$$

$$\sigma_o^2 = -\theta\sigma_v^2.$$

Thus for the value of θ in (4.86) the MA(1) process $u_i^* = v_i - \theta v_{i-1}$ has identical representation with (4.82). The implication of this is that we can estimate the regression model (4.79) under MA(1) process.[11] It would be convenient now to write the model in matrix notation:

$$(4.87) \qquad y^* = X^* \beta + u^*,$$

where y^* is an $(n-1)x1$ vector, X^* is an $(n-1)x(K-1)$ matrix and β is a $(K-1)x1$ vector. Further u^* is an $(n-1)x1$ vector such that $Eu^*=0$ and variance-covariance matrix

$$(4.88) \qquad Eu^*u^{*\prime} = \Omega = \sigma_v^2 \begin{bmatrix} (1+\theta^2) & -\theta & \cdots & 0 \\ -\theta & (1+\theta^2) & & 0 \\ \vdots & & \ddots & -\theta \\ 0 & 0 \cdots & -\theta & (1+\theta^2) \end{bmatrix}$$

is of order $(n-1)x(n-1)$. The i, i'th element of Ω^{-1} is $\frac{1}{\sigma_v^2}\omega^{ii}$ where

$$(4.89) \qquad \omega^{ii'} = \frac{(-\theta)^{i-i'}}{1-\theta^2} \frac{[1-\theta^{2i}][1-\theta^{2(n-i'+1)}]}{(1-\theta^{2n+2})}$$

$$= \frac{(-\theta)^{i-i'}}{1-\theta^2} \qquad \text{if } |\theta|<1$$

An alternative way to invert Ω is[12]

$$(4.90) \qquad \Omega^{-1} = \frac{1}{\sigma_v^2} H' \Lambda^{-1} H,$$

where the ith element of Λ is given by

$$(4.91) \qquad \lambda_i = \theta^2 + 2\theta \cos\left(\frac{i\lambda}{n+1}\right) + 1, \qquad i=1,2,\ldots,n.$$

Further,

(4.92) $$H=\left(\frac{2}{n+1}\right)^{1/2}(h_i,h_2,\ldots,h_n)',$$

where

$$h_i=\left(\sin\left[\frac{i\lambda}{n+1}\right],\sin\left[\frac{2i\lambda}{n+1}\right],\ldots,\sin\left[\frac{ni\lambda}{n+1}\right]\right)'.$$

Thus, for given θ the GLS estimator of β is

(4.93) $$\hat{\beta}=(X^{*\prime}\Omega^{-1}X^{*})^{-1}X^{*\prime}\Omega^{-1}y^{*}.$$

When θ is not known an iterative GLS estimator of β can be obtained by using a search routine for θ in $0\leqslant\theta<1$.

An approximate GLS estimator, which is computationally easier, can be obtained by replacing the first diagonal element $(1+\theta^2)$ of Ω by 1. In this case

(4.94) $$\Omega_a=\sigma_v^2\begin{bmatrix} 1 & -\theta & \cdots & 0 \\ -\theta & 1+\theta^2 & \cdot & 0 \\ \cdot & & \cdot & -\theta \\ 0 & \cdot & -\theta & 1+\theta^2 \end{bmatrix}=\sigma_v^2QQ',$$

where

(4.95) $$Q=\begin{bmatrix} 1 & 0 & \cdots & 0 \\ 1-\theta & 1 & \cdot & \cdot \\ \cdot & & \cdot & 0 \\ 0 & 0 & 1-\theta & 1 \end{bmatrix}.$$

and the approximate GLS estimator is

(4.96) $$\hat{\beta}_a=(X^{*\prime}Q'^{-1}Q^{-1}X^{*})^{-1}X^{*\prime}Q'^{-1}Q^{-1}y^{*}.$$

For given θ, the calculation of $\hat{\beta}_a$ then involves simple least squares on the regression of $Q^{-1}X^*$ on $Q^{-1}y^*$. Note that Q is a special case of the triangular matrix.

To obtain the simultaneous ML estimation of β, θ and σ_v^2 we first assume the normality of ε_{oi} and ε_{1i} and write the likelihood function as

$$(4.97) \qquad L = L(\beta, \theta, \sigma_v^2/y) = (2\pi\sigma_v^2)^{-n/2}|\Omega|^{-1/2}$$

$$\exp\left[-\frac{1}{2\sigma_v^2}(y^*-X^*\beta)'\Omega^{-1}(y^*-X^*\beta)\right].$$

Partially differentiating log L with respect to σ_v^2 and β and equating to zero, we obtain the ML estimators of σ_v^2 and β, for known θ, as

$$(4.98) \qquad \hat{\beta} = (X^{*\prime}\Omega^{-1}X^*)^{-1}X^{*\prime}\Omega^{-1}y^*$$

and

$$(4.99) \qquad \hat{\sigma}_v^2 = \frac{1}{n}(y^*-X^*\hat{\beta})'\Omega^{-1}(y^*-X^*\hat{\beta}).$$

Note that for known θ the ML estimator of β is the same as the GLS estimator.

When θ is unknown we may substitute $\hat{\sigma}_v^2$ and $\hat{\beta}$ in log L and write the concentrated log likelihood function as

$$(4.100) \qquad \log L_c = -\frac{n}{2}(\log\frac{2\pi}{n}+1) - \frac{1}{2}\log|\Omega|$$

$$-\frac{n}{2}\log(y^*-X^*\hat{\beta})'\Omega^{-1}(y^*-X^*\hat{\beta})$$

$$= \log L_c(\theta/y).$$

The ML estimators of β and θ can now be obtained by using a search routine for $0<\theta<1$. Substitution of this in (4.98) then provides the iterative ML estimators of β and σ_v^2. If we use Ω_a for Ω we will get the approximate ML estimators of θ, β and σ_v^2. Note that the ML and approximate ML estimators will in general be different from the GLS estimator. This is because of the term log $|\Omega|$ in log L which makes maximisation of log L different from the minimisation of only $(y^*-X^*\beta)'\Omega^{-1}(y^*-X^*\beta)$ in the GLS case. After the ML estimators of θ, β and σ_v^2 have been obtained one can get the estimators of σ_o^2 and σ_1^2 from the relations in (4.85) and (4.86).

An alternative ML(GLS) method of estimating the model (4.77) was discussed in Chapter 3 for the case where K=1. Following this we first write

$\beta_{1i}=\beta_{1i-1}+\varepsilon_{1i}$ as

(4.101) $$\beta_{1i}=\beta_{1o}+\sum_{s=1}^{i}\varepsilon_{1s}$$

and then substitute this in (4.77) to write it as

(4.102) $$y_i=\beta_{1o}+x_i\beta+w_i,$$

where $w_i=\varepsilon_{oi}+\sum_{s=1}^{i}\varepsilon_{1s}$. In matrix notation

(4.103) $$y=Z\beta_o+w,$$

where $\beta_o=(\beta_{1o}\beta)'$ is a Kx1 and $Z=[\iota X]$; ι is an nx1 vector of unity; and w is an nx1 vector such that Ew=0 and

$$(4.104) \quad Eww' = \sigma_o^2 \begin{bmatrix} (1+\lambda) & \lambda & \cdots & \lambda \\ \lambda & (1+2\lambda) & & 2\lambda \\ \lambda & 2\lambda & \ddots & 2\lambda \\ \vdots & \vdots & & \vdots \\ \lambda & 2\lambda & \cdots & (1+n\lambda) \end{bmatrix} = \Omega_0,$$

where $\lambda = \sigma_1^2/\sigma_o^2$. (See [3.35a] in Chapter 3). The matrix Ω_0 can also be written as

$$(4.104a) \quad \Omega_0 = \sigma_o^2[I+\lambda Q_o] = [\sigma_o^2 I + \sigma_i^2 Q_o],$$

where Q_o is an nxn matrix such that

$$q_{ii'} = i_o = \min(i,i'), \qquad \text{if } i \neq i'.$$

Now the GLS estimator of β_0 for known λ is

$$(4.105) \quad \hat{\beta}_0 = (Z'\Omega_0^{-1}Z)^{-1}Z'\Omega_0^{-1}y.$$

Since in practice λ is not known, a search procedure on λ can be carried out to obtain an iterative GLS estimator of β_0.

If we further assume ε_{oi} and ε_{1i} to be normally distributed the iterative ML estimator of β can be obtained. The likelihood function in this case is

$$(4.106) \quad L = L(\beta_0/\sigma_o^2, \lambda, y) = \frac{(\sigma_o^2)^{-n/2}}{(2\pi)^{n/2}|\Omega_0|^{1/2}}$$

$$\exp[-\frac{1}{2\sigma_o^2}(y-Z\beta_0)'\Omega_0^{-1}(y-Z\beta_0)].$$

To obtain the ML estimators of β and σ^2 we take the partial derivatives of log L with respect to β and σ_o^2 and equate them to zero. This gives

$\hat{\beta}_o = (Z'\Omega_o^{-1}Z)^{-1}Z'\Omega_o^{-1}y$, as in (4.105), and

$$\hat{\sigma}_o^2 = \frac{1}{n}(y-Z\hat{\beta}_o)'\Omega_o^{-1}(y-Z\hat{\beta}_o). \tag{4.107}$$

These estimators depend upon λ and therefore are not useful. An alternative, as discussed before, is first to obtain the ML estimator of λ. For this we substitute $\hat{\beta}_o$ and $\hat{\sigma}_o^2$ in L and write the concentrated log likelihood function of λ as

$$\log L_c(\lambda) = -\frac{n}{2}(\log\frac{2\pi}{n}+1) - \frac{1}{2}\log|\Omega_o| - \frac{n}{2}\log(y-Z\hat{\beta}_o)'\Omega_o^{-1}(y-Z\hat{\beta}_o). \tag{4.108}$$

The iteration is then carried over λ and the converging value is taken as the ML estimator of λ. Using this value the ML estimators of β_o and σ_o are calculated.

It is useful to compare the apparently different estimators $\hat{\beta}$ in (4.93) and $\hat{\beta}$ obtained from $\hat{\beta}_o$ given in (4.105). We will show below that they are identical. Using the inversion rule for a partitioned matrix, we write $\hat{\beta}$ and $\hat{\beta}_{1o}$ from $\hat{\beta}_o$ as

$$\hat{\beta} = [X'(\Omega_o^{-1}-\Omega_o^{-1}\iota(\iota'\Omega_o^{-1}\iota)^{-1}\iota'\Omega_o^{-1})X]^{-1} X'(\Omega_o^{-1}-\Omega_o^{-1}\iota(\iota'\Omega_o^{-1}\iota)^{-1}\iota'\Omega_o^{-1})y \tag{4.109}$$

and

$$\hat{\beta}_{1o} = (\iota'\Omega_o^{-1}\iota)^{-1}\iota'\Omega_o^{-1}(y-X\hat{\beta}). \tag{4.110}$$

Now introduce the (n-1)xn matrix B as

$$B=\begin{bmatrix} -1 & 1 & 0 & \dots & 0 \\ 0 & -1 & 1 & \dots & 0 \\ \vdots \\ 0 & 0 & \cdots & -1 & 1 \end{bmatrix},$$

which is such that $y^*=By$, $u^*=Bu$ and $X^*=BX$ in (4.87). Also if we write the matrix Ω in (4.88) as

$$\Omega=\sigma_u^2[(1+\theta^2)I-\theta P],$$

where

$$P=\begin{bmatrix} 0 & 1 & 0 & \dots & 0 \\ 1 & 0 & 1 & & 0 \\ 0 & 1 & \ddots & & \vdots \\ \vdots & & \ddots & 0 & 1 \\ 0 & 0 & 0 & 1 & 0 \end{bmatrix},$$

then

$$\Omega=\sigma_v^2[(1+\theta^2)I-\theta P]=(\sigma_u^2+2\sigma_o^2)I-\sigma_o^2P$$

$$=B\Omega_0B'=\sigma_o^2BB'+\sigma_v^2I$$

because $BB'=2I-P$ and $B\Omega_0B'=I$. Finally, noting that B is rank of n-1 and $B\iota=0$ we can verify that

$$(\Omega_0^{-1}-\Omega_0^{-1}\iota(\iota'\Omega_0^{-1}\iota)^{-1}\Omega_0^{-1})X=B(B\Omega_0B')^{-1}BX.$$

Thus it follows that $\hat{\beta}$ in (4.109) is identical to that of $\hat{\beta}$ in (4.93).

Now to obtain the estimator of the permanent path of β_{1i} we write the model for given β and β_{1o} as

$$y_i - x_i\beta = \beta_{1i} + \varepsilon_{oi},$$

$$\beta_{1i} = \beta_{1o} + \varepsilon_{1i}.$$

If we minimise $\varepsilon_{oi}^2/\sigma_o^2 + \varepsilon_{1i}^2/\sigma_1^2$ with respect to β_{1i} for given β and β_{1o} we get the mixed estimator of β_{1i} as

$$\hat{\beta}_{1i} = \left(\frac{1}{\sigma_o^2} + \frac{1}{\sigma_1^2}\right)^{-1}\left(\frac{(y_i - x_i\beta)}{\sigma_o^2} + \frac{\beta_{1o}}{\sigma_1^2}\right)$$

$$= (1+\lambda)^{-1}[(y_i - x_i\beta) + \lambda\beta_{1o}].$$

This is the BLUE predictor of β_{1i}. In practice, an operational variant of $\hat{\beta}_{1i}$ will be

$$\hat{\hat{\beta}}_{1i} = (1+\hat{\lambda})^{-1}[(y_i - x_i\hat{\beta}) + \hat{\lambda}\hat{\beta}_{1o}],$$

where $\hat{\lambda}$, $\hat{\beta}_{1o}$ and $\hat{\beta}$ are the ML estimates as discussed before. The $\hat{\hat{\beta}}_{1i}$ is asymptotically unbiased and efficient.

4.4.2 Estimation When all the Coefficients are Adaptive

Let us write model (4.1) in this case as

$$(4.111)\qquad y_i = Z_i\beta_i^*,$$

where $Z_i = (1, x_{2i}, \ldots, x_{Ki})$ is a 1xK vector and $\beta_i^* = (\beta_{1i}^*, \ldots, \beta_{Ki}^*)'$ is a Kx1 random vector such that

$$(4.112)\qquad \beta_i^* = \beta_i + u_i.$$

The Kx1 vectors $\beta_i = (\beta_{1i}, \ldots, \beta_{Ki})'$ and $u_i = (u_{1i}, \ldots, u_{Ki})'$

are the permanent and transitory components respectively of β_i^*. We specify an adaptive scheme for β_i as

$$(4.113) \quad \beta_i = \beta_{i-1} + \varepsilon_1,$$

where $\varepsilon_i = (\varepsilon_{1i}, \ldots, \varepsilon_{Ki})'$ is a Kx1 vector of random errors in β_i. In the model of Section 4.4.1, we had $u_i = (u_{1i}, 0, \ldots, 0)'$ and $\varepsilon_i = (\varepsilon_{1i}, 0, \ldots, 0)'$. Further, in the special case where K=2, the model (4.111) is analysed in Chapter 3.

The above specification implies that the permanent component of β_i^* will drift systematically over i=1,...,n away from its initial value without returning towards a mean value. The nature of this specification is therefore different than that considered in the purely random coefficient case.

The u_i and ε_i are independently and identically distributed as normal variates with mean vectors zero and diagonal covariance matrices $Eu_iu_i' = \Sigma_u^*$ and $E\varepsilon_i\varepsilon_i' = \Sigma_\varepsilon^*$ respectively. The diagonality of Σ_u^* and Σ_ε^* imply that the elements in both u_i and ε_i are mutually independent. The results below can, however, be used even when this assumption is not made. We also assume that

$$Eu_iu_{i'}' = 0 = E\varepsilon_i\varepsilon_{i'}' \quad \text{for } i \neq i' = 1, \ldots, n;$$

and

$$Eu_i\varepsilon_i' = 0 \qquad \text{for all } i.$$

The problem with regard to the estimation of model (4.111) under (4.112) is that the matrices Σ_u^* and Σ_ε^* cannot be determined independently from the available information. One therefore uses the following reparameterisation, viz.:

$$(4.113a) \quad \Sigma_u^* = (1-\gamma)\sigma^2\, \Sigma_u;\ \Sigma_\varepsilon^* = \gamma\sigma^2\, \Sigma_\varepsilon,$$

where σ^2 is the scaling parameter to be estimated and $0 \leq \gamma \leq 1$ represents the partition of the total variance of the adaptive coefficient between permanent and transitory components. Further, Σ_u and Σ_ε are known matrices up to a scalar factor. This means that the degree of instability in each coefficient relative to the other has to be prespecified. The reparameterisation can be explained by considering a special case of K=2. Let Σ_u^* and Σ_ε^* be

$$\Sigma_u^* = \begin{bmatrix} \sigma_{11} & 0 \\ 0 & \sigma_{22} \end{bmatrix}, \quad \Sigma_\varepsilon^* = \begin{bmatrix} \omega_{11} & 0 \\ 0 & \omega_{22} \end{bmatrix},$$

where σ_{11} is the transitory variance and ω_{11} is the permanent variance of the intercept. Similarly, σ_{22} and ω_{22} are the transitory and permanent variances for the slope efficient. Now we can write

$$\Sigma_u^* = \sigma_{11} \begin{bmatrix} 1 & 0 \\ 0 & \lambda_1 \end{bmatrix}, \quad \Sigma_\varepsilon^* = \omega_{11} \begin{bmatrix} 1 & 0 \\ 0 & \lambda_2 \end{bmatrix},$$

where $\lambda_1 = \sigma_{22}/\sigma_{11}$ and $\lambda_2 = \omega_{22}/\omega_{11}$ are the ratios of variance of the slope coefficient to the intercept variance for the transitory and permanent components respectively. These ratios (degree of instability) are assumed to be known. Now if we denote the total variation in the intercept as $\sigma^2 = \sigma_{11} + \omega_{11}$ and define γ for the partitioning of σ^2 in transitory and permanent components, we can write $\sigma^2 = (1-\gamma)\sigma^2 + \gamma\sigma^2$. This implies that if we take $\sigma_{11} = (1-\gamma)\sigma^2$ then $\omega_{11} = \gamma\sigma^2$. Alternatively, $\sigma_{11}/\omega_{11} = (1-\gamma)/\gamma$. In view of this we can write

$$\Sigma_u^* = (1-\gamma)\sigma^2 \begin{bmatrix} 1 & 0 \\ 0 & \lambda_1 \end{bmatrix} = (1-\gamma)\sigma^2 \Sigma_u, \text{ for } 0 \leq \gamma \leq 1,$$

and

$$\Sigma_\varepsilon^* = \gamma\sigma^2 \begin{bmatrix} 1 & 0 \\ 0 & \lambda_2 \end{bmatrix} = \gamma\sigma^2 \Sigma_\varepsilon;$$

the parameter γ thus specifies the relative variance of the permanent and transitory components in the β_i^*. The greater the value of γ, the more important is permanent relative to transitory change. The objective of any estimation procedure would be to estimate σ^2, γ and the permanent component in β_i^*.

The coefficient levels in the adaptive process are nonstationary; therefore likelihood functions for them cannot be specified. But a likelihood function conditional on some specific realisation at some point in time can be defined and the value of the coefficient at that point can be estimated. Considering this point to be i=0 we can write

$$\beta_i = \beta_0 + \sum_{s=1}^{i} \varepsilon_s,$$

and

$$\beta_i^* = \beta_0 + \sum_{s=1}^{i} \varepsilon_s + u_i.$$

The model can be rewritten as

(4.114) $\quad y_i = Z_i \beta_0 + w_i,$

where

$$(4.115)\quad w_i = Z_i\left(\sum_{s=1}^{i} \varepsilon_s + u_i\right)$$

is the combined disturbance vector such that $Ew_i=0$ and

$$(4.116)\quad Ew_i w_{i'}' = \sigma^2 \gamma i_o Z_i \Sigma_\varepsilon Z_{i'}' \qquad \text{if } i \neq i',$$

$$= (1-\gamma)\sigma^2 Z_i \Sigma_u Z_i'$$

$$+ \sigma^2 \gamma i_o Z_i \Sigma_\varepsilon Z_i' \qquad \text{if } i = i'.$$

In a more compact matrix form the model can be written as

$$(4.117)\quad y = Z\beta_o + w,$$

where y is an nx1 vector, Z is an nxK matrix and β_o is a Kx1 vector. Further, w is an nx1 vector such that, using (4.115) and (4.116), Ew=0 and

$$Eww' = \sigma^2[(1-\gamma)R + \gamma Q] = \sigma^2 \Omega(\gamma),$$

where R is an nxn diagonal matrix whose i^{th} diagonal element is

$$r_{ii} = Z_i \Sigma_u Z_i'$$

and Q is an nxn matrix whose $(i, i)^{th}$ element is

$$q_{ii'} = i_o Z_i \Sigma_\varepsilon Z_{i'}'.$$

A special case of Eww' appeared in (4.104a). From (4.116) it follows that y is distributed normally with mean $Z\beta_0$ and covariance matrix $\sigma^2\Omega(\gamma)$.

When γ is known, the estimate of β_0 can be obtained by applying GLS because $\Omega(\gamma)$ is a function of Z and γ alone. This is

$$(4.118) \quad \hat{\beta}_0 = (Z'\Omega^{-1}(\gamma)Z)^{-1}Z'\Omega^{-1}(\gamma)y.$$

However, the parameter γ which indicates how fast the β's are adapting to structural change is rarely known. Thus $\hat{\beta}_0$ is not operational. One can therefore use the maximum likelihood method of estimation.

We can write the likelihood function as

$$(4.119) \quad L(\beta_0, \sigma^2, \gamma/y, Z) = \frac{1}{(2\pi\sigma^2)^{n/2}\,|\Omega(\gamma)|^{1/2}}$$

$$\exp[-\frac{1}{2\sigma^2}(y-Z\beta_0)'\Omega^{-1}(\gamma)(y-Z\beta_0)].$$

Taking log on both sides and then equating the partial derivatives with respect to β_0 and σ^2 to zero gives the estimators of β_0 and σ^2, for given γ, as

$$(4.120) \quad \hat{\beta}_0(\gamma) = (Z'\Omega^{-1}(\gamma)Z)^{-1}Z'\Omega^{-1}(\gamma)y,$$

$$\hat{\sigma}^2(\gamma) = \frac{1}{n}(y-Z\hat{\beta}_0)'\Omega^{-1}(\gamma)(y-Z\hat{\beta}_0).$$

These can be substituted into the likelihood to obtain the concentrated log likelihood function of γ as

$$(4.121) \quad \log L_c(\gamma) = -\frac{n}{2}(\log\frac{2\pi}{n}+1) - \frac{1}{2}\log|\Omega(\gamma)|$$

$$-\frac{n}{2}\log(y-Z\hat{\beta}_0)'\Omega^{-1}(\gamma)(y-Z\hat{\beta}_0).$$

Now one can use an iterative scheme over $0 \leq \gamma \leq 1$ and choose a γ for which $\log L_c(\gamma)$ is maximum. Using this ML estimator of γ one can then obtain the ML estimators $\hat{\beta}_0$ and $\hat{\sigma}^2(\gamma)$. For ease in computations one could use transformations which will reduce $\Omega(\gamma)$ into a diagonal matrix $D(\gamma)$. The transformation is

$$P'R^{-1/2}y = P'R^{-1/2}Z\beta_0 + P'R^{-1/2}w,$$

such that

$$\begin{aligned} E(P'R^{-1/2}ww'R^{-1/2}P) &= \sigma^2 P'(R^{-1/2}\Omega(\gamma)R^{-1/2})P \\ &= \sigma^2 P'[(1-\gamma)I + \gamma Q^*]P \\ &= \sigma^2[(1-\gamma) + \gamma P'Q^*P] \\ &= \sigma^2[(1-\gamma) + \gamma D] = \sigma^2 D(\gamma); \end{aligned}$$

where $Q^* = R^{-1/2}QR^{-1/2}$, P is the matrix of the orthonormal eigenvectors of the matrix Q^* and D is the diagonal matrix of eigenvalues of Q^*. The matrix P is such that $P'P = I$ and $P'Q^*P = D$.

The ML estimators of β_0, σ^2 and γ are consistent and asymptotically efficient. Further, while the asymptotic distribution of $\sqrt{n}(\hat{\beta}_0 - \beta) \sim N[0, \sigma^2 (Z'\Omega^{-1}(\gamma)Z)^{-1}]$, the asymptotic distribution of $\delta = (\gamma, \sigma^2)$ is[13] $\sqrt{n}(\hat{\delta} - \delta) \sim N[0, I(\delta)^{-1}]$, where

$$I(\delta) = -\frac{1}{\sqrt{n}} E\left(\frac{\partial^2 L}{\partial \delta \partial \delta'}\right)$$

$$= \frac{1}{2n} \begin{bmatrix} \sum_1^n \frac{(d_i - 1)^2}{d_i(\gamma)} & -\sigma^2 \sum_1^n \frac{(d_i - 1)}{d_i(\gamma)} \\ -\sigma^2 \sum_1^n \frac{(d_i - 1)}{d_i(\gamma)} & n\,\sigma^4 \end{bmatrix},$$

$d_i(\gamma) = (1-\gamma)+\gamma d_i$ and d_i represent the ith diagonal element of the matrix D. Inverting $I(\delta)$, the asymptotic variance of $\hat{\gamma}$ can be written as

$$(4.122)\quad V[\sqrt{n}(\hat{\gamma}-\gamma)] = 2/[\frac{1}{n}\sum_1^n \frac{(d_i-1)^2}{d_i(\gamma)^2} - (\frac{1}{n}\sum_1^n \frac{(d_i-1)^2}{d_i(\gamma)})]^2 .$$

This can be used to construct the test statistic, $\hat{\gamma}/\sqrt{V(\hat{\gamma})} \sim N[0,1]$, for testing the significance of permanent change in the coefficient vector β_i^*.

An alternative estimation can be carried out by using Bayesian methods. Assume that the prior information about the parameters β_0, σ and γ can be represented by the following locally uniform, independent distributions:

$$p(\gamma) = d\gamma, \qquad 0 \leq \gamma \leq 1$$

$$p(\beta_0) \propto \text{constant},$$

$$p(\sigma) \propto \frac{1}{\sigma} d\sigma.$$

Then, using Bayes's theorem, the joint density of β, γ, σ^2 is obtained by multiplying its prior density with the likelihood function given in (4.119). This is

$$(4.123)\quad p(\ ) \propto D(\gamma) \exp[-\frac{1}{2\sigma^2}(y-Z\beta_i)'\Omega^{-1}(\gamma)(y-Z\beta_0)]$$

$$\propto D(\gamma) \exp[-\frac{1}{2\sigma^2}(\beta_0-\hat{\beta}_0)'(Z'\Omega^{-1}(\gamma)Z)(\beta_0-\hat{\beta}_0)+ S],$$

where $p(\ ) = p(\beta_0,\sigma^2,\gamma/y)$, $D(\gamma) = (\sigma\ )^{-(n+1)}|\Omega(\gamma)|^{-1/2}$, and $S=(y-Z\hat{\beta}_0)'\Omega^{-1}(\gamma)(y-Z\hat{\beta}_0)$ is the residual sum of squares. The final expression on the right of (4.123) has been obtained by writing

$$y-Z\beta_0 = y-Z(\beta_0-\hat{\beta}_0) - Z\hat{\beta}_0.$$

It is obvious that the posterior density of β_0, conditional on σ^2 and γ, is normal with mean $\hat{\beta}_0$ (the GLS estimator) and variance $\sigma^2(Z'\Omega^{-1}(\gamma)Z)^{-1}$. Further the marginal posterior density for γ is

$$p(\gamma) = \iint_{\beta\sigma} p(\beta\ ,\sigma,\gamma/y)\,d\beta d\sigma$$

$$\propto |\Omega(\gamma)|^{-\frac{1}{2}}|(Z'\Omega^{-1}(\gamma)Z)^{-1}|^{\frac{1}{2}}\ S^{-(n-K)/2}.$$

The expected value (Bayesian estimator) of this posterior density of γ can be obtained by numerical integration.

An advantage of the Bayesian estimation is that one can incorporate the prior information about γ. Though the above posterior for γ is based on the diffuse prior of γ, in principle the analysis can be done with some other available priors. Another advantage is that the Bayesian analysis could be utilised to calculate the posterior odds, especially when one needs to discriminate between alternative models.

4.5 AN APPLICATION: THE SHIFTING PHILLIPS CURVE

Gordon and Hynes (1970) have identified a number of factors generating instability in the short run Phillips curve relationship. Among these factors are improper characterisation of labour markets, learning lags, erratic macroeconomic policy shocks, and adjustment costs. A simple way to characterise the instability of the Phillips curve is to adopt a varying coefficients specification; that is the individual coefficients are allowed to vary from observation to observation in purely random manner. Accordingly, we may consider a simple model of money wage disequilibrium

$$w = f(u, m, p),$$

where w is the percentage rate of change of money wages, u is the employment rate, m is the percentage rate of change of the money stock and p is the percentage rate of change of labour productivity. We further assume that coefficients of this simple model are randomly varying. Allowing the coefficients in the above relationship to be stochastically varying can provide a means for incorporating short run deviations from a long run average Phillips curve. Furthermore, a bad predictive performance of the wage inflation relationship with stochastic coefficients can serve as an indirect test for the shifting Phillips curve -- that is worsening tradeoff relationship between wage inflation and unemployment. A systematic or permanent shift in the Phillips curve over the long run would imply that the coefficients shifted significantly from the estimation period to the prediction period, resulting in steadily worsening of predictive performance of the equation (see Rappoport and Kniesner, 1974).

The following wage equation, with purely random coefficients specification of Section 4.2, is estimated using the annual data from 1930-1966; that is

$$(4.124) \qquad w_i = \beta_{1i} + \beta_{2i} u_i + \beta_{3i} m_i + \beta_{4i} p_i, \qquad i = 1, \ldots, n,$$

where a typical variable representing the percentage rate of change of the variable (say S_i) is defined as $S_i = (S_i - S_{i-1})/S_{i-1}$. The effect of u on w is expected to be negative while the effect of m and p is expected to be positive. Each stochastically varying coefficient is assumed to be the sum of a fixed systematic part and a stochastic part; that is $\beta_{ki} = \beta_k + \varepsilon_{ki}$; $k=1,\ldots,4$. The stochastic parts are assumed to be distributed with zero mean, constant variances and zero correlations. When they estimated the wage inflation equation obtained by using the inefficient least square estimator $b = (X'X)^{-1}X'y$ of vector $\beta = (\beta_1, \beta_2, \beta_3, \beta_4)'$, they obtained

$$(4.125)\quad \hat{w}_i = \underset{(.0135)}{.04033} - \underset{(.00111)}{.00201}\, u_i + \underset{(.11033)}{.3533}\, m_i + \underset{(.06335)}{.1284}\, p_i,$$

$$\bar{R}^2 = .70,\ DW = 1.84,\ n = 37,$$

where the numbers in parentheses are standard errors. Then they estimated the wage equation using the asymptotic efficient estimator

$$\hat{\beta} = (X'\hat{D}^{-1}X)^{-1}X'\hat{D}^{-1}y$$

of β and obtained the following estimated equation:

$$(4.126)\quad \hat{w}_i = \underset{(.0134)}{.0537} - \underset{(.00119)}{.00264}\, u_i + \underset{(.06031)}{.2522}\, m_i + \underset{(.0468)}{.1689}\, p_i,$$

where $\hat{D}$ is a consistent estimator of the dispersion matrix D of the error vector, and is obtained by using the least squares estimator of the vector of variances $\dot{\sigma} = (\sigma_1^2, \sigma_2^2, \sigma_3^2, \sigma_4^2)'$. The estimated vector of variances is

$$\hat{\dot{\sigma}} = (8.4\text{x}10^{-3},\ .14\text{x}10^{-3},\ 700\text{x}10^{-3},\ 520\text{x}10^{-3})'.$$

We note that the estimates of the constant term β_1 and the coefficient of unemployment β_2 are larger for the stochastic coefficients version of the Phillips curve than those of the fixed coefficients version; this suggests that the fixed coefficient in formulating the wage inflation equation is too rigid. Furthermore, the notion of long run Phillips curve relation once the influence of some important variables is accounted for appears not too unwarranted in view of the correct sign of the coefficient of β_1.

The point predictions obtained via estimated wage equations (4.125) and (4.126) are given below:

	1967	1968	1969	1970	1971	1972
w	.04044	.06330	.05980	.05329	.05952	.07022
$\hat{w}$	.05219	.06584	.06203	.04090	.05428	.07128
$\tilde{w}$	.04431	.06279	.06034	.04481	.05594	.07150.

It is clear from these point predictions that the wage inflation is better predicted from stochastic varying coefficients specifications than from the fixed coefficients specification. In order to compare the predictive performance under the stochastic coefficients and fixed coefficients specification, we may compare the prediction variances of various $\hat{w}$'s and $\tilde{w}$'s. The prediction variances of $\hat{w}$'s are obtained from $E(\hat{y}_f - y_f)^2 = \sigma^2(1 + x_f'(X'X)^{-1}x_f)$, where x_f' is the row vector of actual values of exogenous variables, y_f is the actual value of the dependent variable and σ^2 is the variance of the disturbance term in the forecast period. The prediction variances of $\tilde{w}$'s are obtained from

$$E(\tilde{y}_f - y_f)^2 = \sigma_*^2 + x_f'\Sigma x_f + x_f'[\Sigma + \sigma_*^2 (X'X)^{-1}]x_f,$$

where $\Sigma = \text{diag.}(\sigma_1^2, \ldots, \sigma_4^2)$ and σ_*^2 is the variance of disturbance term in the forecast period. We note that there are two sources of prediction errors in the fixed coefficients model, viz. the error due to estimating the fixed regression coefficients and the error due to the disturbance term in the forecast period. However, the predictions using random coefficients specification entails three sources of errors. The first error is due to estimating the fixed means of the stochastic coefficients. The second error is due to the deviations of various stochastic coefficients around their sample means. The third error is due to the disturbance term in the forecast period.[14] The variances of forecasts of $\hat{w}$'s and $\tilde{w}$'s are

	1967	1968	1969	1970	1971	1972
$E(\hat{w}_i - w_i)^2$	1.380	.050	.0497	1.54	.275	.001
$E(\tilde{w}_i - w_i)^2$	0.149	.004	.003	0.84	.167	.005.

The prediction variances $\tilde{w}_i$'s are smaller than those of the $\hat{w}_i$'s except for the year 1972. The estimates of σ^2 and σ_*^2 used above are 1.60×10^{-3} and 1.82×10^{-3} respectively.

We can conclude that modelling wage inflation with random coefficients generates more precise forecasts than modelling with fixed coefficients. Furthermore, the wage inflation equation with stochastic coefficients forecast rather well, which suggests that the shift in the Phillips curve for the years following 1966 probably did not take place.

It should be noted that the point predictions reported above are not the best linear unbiased predictions of the percentage rate of change of money wages since they are based on the means of coefficients and not the actual repsonse coefficients. The predictions of w, if obtained from equation (4.76), could be even more accurate than reported above.

NOTES

1. The matrix A of order nxn is said to be idempotent if AA=A. The characteristic roots are either zero or one. Further, if the rank of A is r then Trace of A (tr[A])= (Rank [A])= r. See Dhrymes (1978), p. 484.

2. The Hadamard matrix product of two matrices $A=[a_{ij}]$ and $B= [b_{ij}]$ each of order nxn is defined as $A*B= [a_{ij}\ b_{ij}]$. For its properties see Rao (1973), p. 30.

3. See Rao (1973), p. 303.

4. See Rubin (1950); Swamy (1973); Horn, Horn and Duncan (1975).

5. See Box (1966), p. 72.

6. The FORTRAN algorithm for the restricted least squares is given in Ravindran (1972), among other places.

7. See Rao (1973), p. 417.

8. The negative estimates of σ^2's can be a problem here. Appropriate restriction for positive solution may be a proper answer for this problem. See Breusch and Pagan (1980).

9. See Griffiths (1972), Swamy and Mehta (1975), Lee and Griffiths (1979) and Griffiths, Dryman and Prakash (1979).

10. See Edwards (1969).

11. See Reinsel (1979).

12. See Pesaran (1973).

13. See Cooley and Prescott (1973a and 1973b). Also see Pagan (1980).

14. See Swamy (1971).

5. Properties of the Purely Random Coefficient Models

5.1 INTRODUCTION

In this chapter we will examine the properties of various estimators in a multiple regression model when regression coefficients are purely random. First we will discuss and compare the asymptotic (or large sample) properties of some of the commonly used estimators. Then we will discuss the Monte Carlo results regarding the small sample performance of these and other estimators of the means and variances of purely random coefficients. The motivation for studying the small sample performance is that there are large numbers of estimators of means and variances which yield asymptotically equivalent variance-covariance matrices. Thus, asymptotic properties of estimators do not often provide information on the comparative small sample performance for these estimators. Finally, we will obtain a small sigma approximation to the moment matrix of the asymptotic distribution of an operational generalised least squares estimator of the mean response vector.

The motivation for obtaining this approximation is that the variances of the operational generalised least squares estimates obtained from the conventional asymptotic moment matrix underestimate the corresponding variances obtained from the small sigma approximate moment matrix. Thus, in the applications of the random coefficients model the 'standard errors' of estimates should preferably be obtained from an appropriate approximate finite sample moment matrix rather than from the easily available asymptotic moment matrix. This derivation will be obtained for the operational generalised least squares estimators wherein the least squares estimates of variances are utilised to estimate the true variance-covariance matrix of the error vector.

5.2 ASYMPTOTIC PROPERTIES

The asymptotic properties of some of the more commonly used estimators of the vectors of means and variances of purely random coefficients are derived below.[1] The derivation of the several other estimators discussed in Chapter 4 can be patterned on the lines of proofs given below. The proofs for the asymptotic efficiency of the maximum likelihood estimators of the vectors of means and variances are quite involved and hence not included here; see Swamy (1973).

5.2.1 Asymptotic Properties of the Estimators of Variances of Purely Random Coefficients

In Section 4.2.3 of Chapter 4 several operational estimators of the vector of variances of random coefficients $\dot{\sigma}= (\sigma_1^2, \sigma_2^2,\ldots,\sigma_k^2)'$ were obtained.

One of these estimators is the ordinary least squares estimator (4.38), viz., (omitting the subscript 1)

$$(5.1) \qquad \dot{s}= (G'G)^{-1} G'\dot{e},$$

where $G= \ddot{M}X$; $e= My$ with $M= I-X(X'X)^{-1}X'$ is the vector of least squares residuals in the model

(4.8), that is $y=X\beta+u$; and the dot on a vector or matrix represents the Hadamard vector or matrix product of the vector or matrix with itself. This estimator, among several others, was proposed by Hildreth and Houck (1968); we call it the Hildreth and Houck (HH) estimator. Another estimator of $\dot{\sigma}$ is the operational generalised least squares estimator (OGLS) discussed in (4.42), viz.,

$$(5.2) \qquad \tilde{\dot{\sigma}} = (G'\hat{\dot{\Psi}}^{-1}G)^{-1}G'\hat{\dot{\Psi}}^{-1}\dot{e},$$

where $\hat{\dot{\Psi}}$ is a consistent estimator of $\dot{\Psi}$ obtained by replacing the unknowns σ_k^2's by their consistent estimates from $\dot{s}$ where Ψ = MDM with D= Euu' and $E(\dot{e}-E\dot{e})(\dot{e}-E\dot{e})' = 2\dot{\Psi}$. A varient of the OGLS estimator $\tilde{\dot{\sigma}}$ proposed by Theil and Mennes (TM) (1959) which may be termed the OTM estimator, is given by

$$(5.3) \qquad \tilde{\dot{\sigma}}_* = (G'\hat{\dot{\Psi}}_*^{-1}G)^{-1}\ G'\hat{\dot{\Psi}}_*^{-1}\dot{e},$$

where $\hat{\dot{\Psi}}_*$ is another consistent estimator of $\dot{\Psi}$ obtained by replacing the unknowns σ_k^2's by their consistent estimates from $\dot{s}$. The $\hat{\dot{\Psi}}_*$ differs from $\hat{\dot{\Psi}}$ in that its off diagonal elements are replaced by zeros. The motivation for this is that the new weight matrix $\hat{\dot{\Psi}}_*^{-1}$ in $\tilde{\dot{\sigma}}_*$ is now a diagonal matrix instead of a full weight matrix $\hat{\dot{\Psi}}^{-1}$. Thus a considerable ease in computation is achieved without losing asymptotic efficiency because the off diagonal terms in $2\hat{\dot{\Psi}}$ are of lower order of magnitude than its diagonal terms. We now show that the OGLS and OTM estimators of $\dot{\sigma}$ are asymptotically efficient whereas the HH estimator is asymptotically inefficient. We will prove the following results:

(i) The sampling error of the HH estimator of $\dot{\sigma}$ is of order $n^{-1/2}$ in probability, that is $\dot{s}-\dot{\sigma} = O_p(n^{-1/2})$;

(ii) The sampling error of the OGLS estimator of $\dot{\sigma}$ is of order $n^{-1/2}$ in probability, that is $\tilde{\dot{\sigma}}-\dot{\sigma}= O_p(n^{-1/2})$;

(iii) The sampling error of the OTM estimator of $\dot{\sigma}$ is of order $n^{-1/2}$ in probability, that is $\tilde{\dot{\sigma}}*-\dot{\sigma}= O_p(n^{-1/2})$;

(iv) The OGLS estimator of $\dot{\sigma}$ is more efficient than the corresponding HH estimator since the asymptotic moment matrix of the HH estimator minus the moment matrix of the OGLS estimator is equal to a positive definite matrix, that is $AV(\dot{s})-AV(\tilde{\dot{\sigma}})=C$ (a positive definite matrix), where AV represents a asymptotic variance-covariance or moment matrix.

(v) The OGLS and the OTM estimators of $\dot{\sigma}$ are asymptotically efficient in the sense that they are consistent estimators and their moment matrices are identical to the efficient GLS estimator, that is

$$AV(\tilde{\dot{\sigma}})= AV(\tilde{\dot{\sigma}}*)= AV(\hat{\dot{\sigma}}),$$

where

(5.4) $$\hat{\dot{\sigma}}= (G'\dot{\Psi}^{-1}G)^{-1}G'\dot{\Psi}^{-1}\dot{e}$$

and

(5.5) $$AV(\hat{\dot{\sigma}})= 2(\dot{X}'\dot{D}^{-1}\dot{X})^{-1}.$$

To establish these properties, we assume that x's are weakly nonstochastic and, for fixed n, $\lim n\to\infty\ [n^{-1}(X'X)]$ and $\lim n\to\infty\ [n^{-1}(G'D^{-1}G)]$ are finite positive definite matrices. Note that this assumption implies that the time pattern of the explanatory variables is bounded by some finite limits even though it is not necessary for the time pattern of the variables to repeat itself.

Also note that each of the estimators $\dot{s}$, $\tilde{\dot{\sigma}}$ and $\tilde{\dot{\sigma}}*$ is obtained by applying an appropriate minimisation of the sum of squares of errors criterion from the relation

(5.6) $\dot{e}= G\dot{\sigma}+w,$

where w is the disturbance vector such that Ew=0 and $Eww'=2\dot{\Psi}$. For example, the HH estimator of $\dot{\sigma}$ minimises the errors sum of squares, w'w, whereas the OGLS and OTM estimators minimise the weighted errors sum of squares $w'(2\hat{\dot{\Psi}})^{-1}w$ and $w'(2\hat{\dot{\Psi}}_*)^{-1}w$ respectively.

Now substituting (5.6) into (5.1) we can write

(5.7) $\dot{s}= \dot{\sigma}+(G'G)^{-1}G'w$

and the sampling error of the HH estimator of $\dot{\sigma}$ is

(5.8) $\dot{s}-\dot{\sigma}=(G'G)^{-1}G'w.$

Thus, $E(\dot{s}-\dot{\sigma})= 0$, that is the HH estimator is unbiased and its variance-covariance matrix is

(5.9) $V(\dot{s})= E(\dot{s}-\dot{\sigma})(\dot{s}-\dot{\sigma})'=(G'G)^{-1}G'(2\dot{\Psi})G(G'G)^{-1}.$

Further, since the matrix $X(X'X)^{-1}X'$ (= A say) is of order n^{-1} we can write the matrix $\dot{M}=M*M$, where * represents the Hadamard matrix product and $M= I-X(X'X)^{-1}X'$, neglecting the terms of higher order of smallness, as

(5.10) $\dot{M}= I+O(n^{-1}).$

Thus, to the order of our approximation we can write matrices Ψ and $\dot{\Psi}$, as

(5.11) $\quad \Psi = MDM = D + O(n^{-1})$

and

(5.12) $\quad \dot{\Psi} = \Psi^* \Psi = \dot{D} + O(n^{-1})$.

Combining (5.12) and (5.9) we can write n times the asymptotic variance-covariance matrix of $\dot{s}$ as

$$\lim n\to\infty\ n\ AV(\dot{s}) = \lim n\to\infty\ n(\dot{X}'\dot{X})^{-1}\dot{X}'(2\dot{D})\dot{X}(\dot{X}'\dot{X})^{-1},$$

assuming $\lim n\to\infty[n^{-1}(\dot{X}'\dot{X})^{-1}]$ exists. Finally, using Chebyshev's inequality, we obtain result (i) above, that is $\dot{s}$ is a consistent estimator of $\dot{\sigma}$, or

(5.13) $\quad \dot{s} - \dot{\sigma} = O_p(n^{-1/2})$.

Next, when the HH estimates of σ_k^2's are used to obtain the estimator of D as

$$\hat{D} = \text{diag.}(\hat{d}_{11}, \hat{d}_{22}, \ldots, \hat{d}_{nn}),$$

where

$$\hat{d}_{ii} = \sum_{k=1}^{K} x_{ki}^2 s_k^2, \quad \text{for } i=1,2,..,n$$

we can write $\hat{D} = D + O_p(n^{-1/2})$, and hence

(5.14) $\quad \hat{\dot{D}} = \dot{D} + O_p(n^{-1/2})$,

where the terms of higher order of smallness have been neglected. Further, using (5.12) and (5.14), we obtain

(5.15) $\quad \hat{\dot{\Psi}} = \dot{\Psi} + O_p(n^{-1/2})$, where once again we have neglected the terms of higher order of smallness. Then, writing $\hat{\Psi}^{-1}$ as

$$(5.16)\qquad \hat{\Psi}^{-1} = (\hat{\Psi}-\dot{\Psi}+\dot{\Psi})^{-1}$$

$$= (E+\dot{\Psi})^{-1}$$

$$= \dot{\Psi}^{-1}+\dot{\Psi}^{-1}E\dot{\Psi}^{-1},$$

where $E= \hat{\Psi}-\dot{\Psi}= O_p(n^{-1/2})$ as noted in (5.15) above.

Now the sampling error of the OGLS estimator $\tilde{\dot{\sigma}}$, which is easily obtained by combining (5.6) with (5.2), can be written as

$$(5.17)\qquad \tilde{\sigma}-\dot{\sigma}= (G'\hat{\Psi}^{-1}G)^{-1}G'\hat{\Psi}^{-1}w.$$

Using (5.16) and neglecting the terms of higher order of smallness we can write n^{-1} times the order in probability of the individual terms in (5.16) as

$$(5.18)\qquad n^{-1}(G'\hat{\Psi}^{-1}G)= n^{-1}(G'\dot{\Psi}^{-1}G)+O_p(n^{-1/2})$$

and

$$(5.19)\qquad n^{-1}(G'\hat{\Psi}^{-1}w)= n^{-1}(G'\dot{\Psi}^{-1}w)+O_p(n^{-1/2}).$$

Also note that $G'\dot{\Psi}^{-1}w= O_p(n^{1/2})$ and $G'\dot{\Psi}^{-1}E\dot{\Psi}^{-1}w=O_p(1)$ since $\dot{\Psi}^{-1}E\ \dot{\Psi}^{-1}= O_p(n^{1/2})$ and $G'w= O_p(n^{1/2})$. Further, $(G'\dot{\Psi}^{-1}G)= O(n)$ because $\lim n\to\infty\ [n^{-1}(G'\dot{\Psi}^{-1}G)]$ is assumed to be positive definite matrix.

Thus the sampling error in (5.17), neglecting the terms of higher smallness, can be written as

$$(5.20)\qquad \tilde{\dot{\sigma}}-\dot{\sigma}= \hat{\sigma}-\sigma+O_p(n^{-1}),$$

where

$$(5.21) \qquad \hat{\dot{\sigma}}-\dot{\sigma}= (G'\dot{\Psi}^{-1}G)^{-1}G'\dot{\Psi}^{-1}w$$

is the sampling error of the GLS estimator $\hat{\dot{\sigma}}$ in (5.4). But the GLS estimator is unbiased, i.e. $E(\hat{\dot{\sigma}}-\dot{\sigma})=0$ and its variance-covariance matrix is

$$(5.22) \qquad V(\hat{\dot{\sigma}})= E(\hat{\dot{\sigma}}-\dot{\sigma})(\hat{\dot{\sigma}}-\dot{\sigma})'= 2(G'\dot{\Psi}^{-1}G)^{-1}.$$

Combining (5.22) with the facts that $G'\dot{\Psi}^{-1}w=O_p(n^{1/2})$ and that the $\lim n\to\infty\ n^{-1}(G'\dot{\Psi}^{-1}G)$ is finite, we obtain the asymptotic variance-covariance matrix of $\hat{\dot{\sigma}}$ as

$$(5.23) \qquad \lim n\to\infty\ nAV(\hat{\dot{\sigma}})= \lim n\to\infty\ [n2(\dot{X}'\dot{D}^{-1}\dot{X})^{-1}].$$

Further, using Chebyshev's inequality, we obtain the result that

$$(5.24) \qquad \hat{\dot{\sigma}}-\dot{\sigma}= O_p(n^{-1/2}).$$

Finally, neglecting terms of higher order of smallness and combining (5.24) with (5.20) we obtain the result in (ii) above, viz.:

$$(5.25) \qquad \tilde{\dot{\sigma}}-\dot{\sigma}= O_p(n^{-1/2}).$$

The proof for the result that the OTM estimator $\tilde{\dot{\sigma}}_*$ is of order $n^{-1/2}$ is easily patterned on the lines of proof in (ii) above. Note that in this estimator the matrix $\hat{\dot{\Psi}}_*$ is used in place of the unknown matrix $\dot{\Psi}$ in the GLS estimator because the off diagonal terms of $\dot{\Psi}$ are of order $O(n^{-2})$, which is of lower order than the order of our approximation in (5.25). Thus the asymptotic moment matrix of $\tilde{\dot{\sigma}}_*$ given in (5.23) is the same as the asymptotic variance-covariance of $\hat{\dot{\sigma}}$.

The result in (iv) is easily proved by noting that the asymptotic variance-covariance of $\dot{s}$, which is also the moment matrix because $\dot{s}$ is an unbiased estimator, can be written as

$$(5.26) \qquad AV(\dot{s}) = AV(\tilde{\dot{\sigma}}) + B\dot{D}B' = AV(\tilde{\dot{\sigma}}) + C,$$

where

$$B = (\dot{X}'\dot{X})^{-1}\dot{X}' - (\dot{X}'\dot{D}^{-1}\dot{X})^{-1}\dot{X}'\dot{D}^{-1},$$

such that

$$B\dot{X} = 0.$$

Further, since $C = \dot{B}\dot{D}\dot{B}'$ is at least a positive definite matrix, we can write

$$(5.27) \qquad AV(\dot{s}) \geq AV(\tilde{\dot{\sigma}}),$$

that is the OGLS estimator is asymptotically more efficient than the HH estimator.

The result in (v) follows easily from the result proved in (iii) above that the asymptotic moment matrices of $\tilde{\dot{\sigma}}$ and $\tilde{\dot{\sigma}}_*$ are identical to the moment matrix of the GLS estimator given in (5.5).

5.2.2 Asymptotic Properties of Means of Purely Random Coefficients

The best linear unbiased estimator of the vector of means of random coefficients $\beta = (\beta_1, \beta_2, \ldots, \beta_k)'$ in the model $y = X\beta + u$ [where $Eu = 0$ and $Euu' = D = \text{diag.}$

$(d_{11}, d_{22}, \ldots, d_{nn})$ with $d_{ii} = \dot{X}_i \dot{\sigma}$, and $\dot{X}_i$ is the ith row vector of matrix $\dot{X} = X * X]$ is the GLS estimator given below:

$$(5.28) \qquad \hat{\beta} = (X'D^{-1}X)^{-1}X'D^{-1}y.$$

This estimator $\hat{\beta}$ is asymptotically normally distributed with mean β and variance-covariance matrix $(X'D^{-1}X)^{-1}$, that is

$$(5.29) \qquad \sqrt{n}(\hat{\beta}-\beta) \sim N[0, \lim n \to \infty\, n^{-1}(X'D^{-1}X)^{-1}].$$

When variances of purely random coefficients σ_k^2's are not known, an operational GLS estimator can be obtained by using an estimated variance-covariance matrix in place of the unknown true matrix in the GLS estimator. Accordingly, we can obtain the HH, OGLS and OTM estimators of vector of means by using estimated variance-covariance matrix $\hat{D}$ (say) obtained by the HH, OGLS and OTM estimates of σ_k^2's from (5.1), (5.2) and (5.3) respectively. For example, the OGLS estimator of β may be written as

$$(5.30) \qquad \tilde{\beta} = (X'\hat{D}^{-1}X)^{-1}X'\hat{D}^{-1}y,$$

where $\hat{D}$ is an estimator of D obtained by using the OGLS estimates of σ_k^2's from (5.3).

In the previous section we have shown that the sampling error of the OGLS estimator $\tilde{\dot{\sigma}} - \dot{\sigma} = O_p(n^{-1/2})$, that is the OGLS estimator $\tilde{\dot{\sigma}}$ is a consistent estimator of $\dot{\sigma}$. Now since $\hat{D} = \text{diag.}(\hat{d}_{11}, \hat{d}_{22}, \ldots \hat{d}_{nn})$ where $\hat{d}_{ii} = \dot{X}_i \hat{\dot{\sigma}}$, the sampling error $\hat{D} - D$ of the estimator $\hat{D}$ is also of order $n^{-1/2}$ in probability, that is

(5.31) $\hat{D}-D = O_p(n^{-1/2})$.

Further, introducing $F=\hat{D}-D$ and writing $\hat{D}^{-1}[\hat{D}-D+D]^{-1} = (F+D)^{-1}=D^{-1}-D^{-1}FD^{-1}$ + terms of higher order of smallness, and following steps similar to (5.16) to (5.20), it is easily shown that the sampling error of $\tilde{\beta}$ can be written as

(5.32) $\tilde{\beta}-\beta= \hat{\beta}-\beta+O_p(n^{-1})$.

Also, the sampling error $(\hat{\beta}-\beta)$ of $\hat{\beta}$, which is of order $n^{-1/2}$ in probability, is asymptotically normally distributed with zero mean and variance-covariance matrix $(X'D^{-1}X)^{-1}$. Thus using (5.32) we prove the result that the OGLS AND GLS are asymptotically normally and identically distributed.

It is clear from the above arguments that the HH and OTM estimators, which use estimates of σ_k^2's from consistent estimators $\dot{s}$ and $\tilde{\hat{\sigma}}^*$, will also have identical distributions with the GLS estimator. The proofs for the asymptotic properties of the HH and OTM estimators of β are therefore omitted.

5.3 MONTE CARLO EVIDENCE

The first question Monte Carlo studies have attempted to answer is whether the asymptotic differences between the ordinary least squares estimator of mean response coefficients on the one hand and various operational generalised least squares estimators on the other show up clearly in small samples. The second question Monte Carlo studies have attempted to answer concerns the small sample rankings of various estimators whose asymptotic properties are identical. The third question examined in Monte Carlo studies is whether large sample mean squared error (MSE) differences between various truncated estimators of means and variances on the one hand and the unrestricted estimators on the other continue to show up in small samples. The truncated estimators of variances are obtained when negative elements in an estimator of the vector of variances are replaced by zeros.

It is noted that replacing negative estimates by zero is arbitrary. To avoid negative solutions for the estimates of variances of the randomly varying coefficients one should more appropriately optimise suitable criterion function subject to the restrictions $\sigma_k^2 \geqslant 0$ for all $k=1,2,\ldots,K$. Various estimators of the vector of means and variances so obtained are referred to as the restricted estimators of means and variances.

The fourth question examined in some Monte Carlo studies concerns the small sample performance of various restricted estimators. In particular whether the restricted maximum likelihood estimator performs better than other unrestricted estimators, in the small samples, and whether this estimator is worth the extra cost. Also, whether the use of restricted estimates of variances in computing the estimator of the vector of means is more efficient than the corresponding unrestricted estimator.[2]

The usual criterion for comparison is the mean squared error of the sampling distribution of various estimators. The mean squared error combines additively the variance of an estimator of a parameter about its expected value and square of its bias. The bias of an estimator is the difference between the estimate of expected value of an estimator and its true value.

5.3.1 Small Sample Properties of the Alternative Estimators of Variances

Unrestricted Estimators. Various unrestricted estimators of the vector of variances of the random coefficients studied are: (i) HH, (ii) OTM, and (iii) OGLS. The OTM and OGLS estimators of the vector of variances $\dot{\sigma}$ have the same asymptotic distribution as the GLS estimator with true variance-covariance matrix, and both of them are asymptotically more efficient than the HH estimator as shown in the previous section. The small sample results for alternative estimators are generally in accordance with the corresponding asymptotic rankings discussed above. For example, on the criterion of smaller number of negative variance estimates for sample of size 50, the OTM and OGLS estimators perform equally well while each estimator performs better than the HH estimator. The OGLS estimator is most efficient among the three estimators on the above criterion for a sample of size 20. The frequency of negative estimates decreases as sample size increases.

Truncated Estimators. Since the HH, OTM and OGLS estimators frequently yield negative estimates, one may obtain truncated estimators wherein the negative estimates are replaced by zeros. Let $\hat{\dot{\sigma}}*$ be an unrestricted estimator of $\dot{\sigma}$ with $\hat{\sigma}_k^{*2}$ as its typical element. Then a restricted estimator of σ_k^2 corresponding to the estimator $\hat{\sigma}_k^{*2}$ is given by $\hat{\sigma}_k^{*2}= \max[0,\sigma_k^2]$ for $k=1,2,...,K$. A restricted estimator is biased but has smaller mean squared error than the corresponding unrestricted estimator. Thus, corresponding to the HH, OTM and OGLS estimators, we may obtain the truncated HH (THH), truncated OTM (TOTM) and truncated OGLS (TOGLS) estimators respectively. The Monte Carlo results suggest that a truncated estimator should be preferred in small samples also to an untruncated estimator on the criterion of MSE. Furthermore, the bias of a truncated estimator is small provided the true parameter value does not lie near zero.

Restricted Estimators. Various restricted estimators optimise an appropriate criterion function subject to the restriction $\dot{\sigma} \geq 0$. For example, the restricted HH (RHH) estimator of $\dot{\sigma}$ is obtained by minimising $(\dot{e}-G\dot{\sigma})'(\dot{e}-G\dot{\sigma})$ subject to restriction $\dot{\sigma} \geq 0$. Further, the restricted OTM (ROTM) estimator of $\dot{\sigma}$ is obtained by minimising $(\dot{e}-G\dot{\sigma})'(2\hat{\Psi}_*)^{-1}(\dot{e}-G\dot{\sigma})$ subject to restriction $\dot{\sigma} \geq 0$, where $2\hat{\Psi}_*$ is the diagonal estimate of covariance matrix of w in (5.6). The calculations for these estimators are involved and costly since a quadratic programming method needs to be applied for the optimisation of the quadratic function subject to the inequality constraint. The restricted maximum likelihood estimator (RML) of $\dot{\sigma}$ may be obtained by maximising the concentrated likelihood function for $\hat{\dot{\sigma}}$ given in (4.45). Note that an unrestricted method of optimisation method can be applied for optimisation of (4.45) under a square root transformation as explained in the previous chapter.

The Monte Carlo evidence on various restricted estimators indicates that for sample size of 25 the RML estimators perform best among alternative restricted estimators on the criterion of mean squared error. Thus, the restricted maximum likelihood estimator is worth the extra computationed effort involved. Furthermore, for small samples the RHH estimator is least biased. It is also least efficient on the criterion of MSE among the restricted estimators. However, the restricted estimators are to be preferred over both truncated and untruncated estimators on the criterion of the MSE.

5.3.2 Small Sample Properties of the Alternative Estimators of Means

An operational estimator of the mean response vector is obtained by using an estimated variance-covariance matrix in place of the unknown true matrix in GLS estimator. Furthermore, the estimators of σ^2's and hence D are obtained by one of the methods of estimation outlined in 5.3.1 above. For example, if the estimates from the HH estimator of $\dot{\sigma}$ are used in the GLS estimator of β, we would obtain the HH estimator. Similarly, the OTM and OGLS estimators of β are obtained when estimates from the OTM and OGLS estimators of $\dot{\sigma}$ respectively are used. It is shown in Section 5.1 that the asymptotic distributions of the HH, OTM and OGLS estimators of β are identical to the GLS estimator. The Monte Carlo results on the alternative unrestricted estimators of β indicate that for samples of size 50 the OGLS estimator is most efficient while the HH estimator is least efficient among HH, OTM and OGLS estimators on the criterion of the MSE. Further, the small sample performance of the LS estimator $b=(X'X)^{-1}X'y$, which is an unbiased, consistent but inefficient estimator of β, suggests that it may be preferable to the other asymptotic efficient estimators for sample sizes 10 and 20 for a model with two or three explanatory variables.

With regard to the alternative truncated estimators of β, which are biased but have lower mean squared errors than the unrestricted estimators discussed above, the small sample evidence suggests that a truncated estimator is to be preferred over the corresponding unrestricted estimator even in small samples on the criterion of the MSE. Finally, a restricted estimator of β, which is obtained by using restricted estimates from any one of the RHH, RTM and RGLS estimators of $\dot{\sigma}$, is to be preferred to both truncated and unrestricted estimators. For small samples the RML estimator of β is most efficient, followed by the RGLS estimator among all estimators on the criterion of MSE.

5.4 THE SMALL SIGMA APPROXIMATE MOMENT MATRIX OF AN ESTIMATOR OF THE MEAN RESPONSE VECTOR

In this section we will derive the finite sample approximation of the moment matrix of the limiting distribution of the HH estimator of β. The finite sample approximate moment matrix of the OTM and OGLS estimators of β can be obtained similarly. The derivation of the finite sample approximate moment matrix is based on the small disturbance approach, which is briefly explained below along with the derivation of the finite sample approximate moment matrix.[3]

First we note that the HH estimator of β may be obtained from the regression equation

$$(5.33) \qquad \dot{e} = G\dot{\sigma} + \delta v,$$

where $\delta v = \dot{e} - G\dot{\sigma}$ is the disturbance vector such that δ tends to zero. The regression equation (5.33) differs from the regression equation (5.6) in Section 5.2 in that the disturbance vector w is redefined as a product of a small delta δ and a new disturbance vector v. This technique, first proposed by Kadane (1970,71), is commonly known as small sigma (in our example δ) asymptotic expansion technique. Secondly, we note that the validity of the finite sample approximate expression for the moment matrix depends on the existence of moments of the HH estimator $\hat{\hat{\beta}}$. The sufficient condition for the existence of the mean of $\hat{\hat{\beta}}$ can be shown to be that the elements of the disturbance vector u are symmetrically distributed about zero with finite fourth order moments. Further, the sufficient condition for the existence of the second order moments of the estimator $\hat{\hat{\beta}}$ is that the variable of the reciprocal of the smallest diagonal element of the error vector is finite.

Now, we may write the sampling errors of the estimators $\hat{\hat{\beta}}$ and $\dot{s}$, using $y=X\beta+u$ and $\dot{e}=G\dot{\sigma}+\delta v$ respectively as

$$(5.34) \qquad \hat{\hat{\beta}}-\beta= (X'\hat{D}^{-1}X)^{-1}X'\hat{D}^{-1}u$$

and

$$(5.35) \qquad \dot{s}-\dot{\sigma}= \delta(G'G)^{-1}G'v.$$

Further, let $\hat{d}_{ii}-d_{ii}=\dot{X}_i(\dot{s}-\dot{\sigma})$. Then the sampling error of the estimator of the variance-covariance matrix D may be written as

$$(5.36) \qquad \hat{D}-D= \delta N,$$

where δN is an nxn matrix formed with elements $\dot{X}_i(\dot{s}-\dot{\sigma})(i=1,2,...,n)$. Writing (5.36) as $\hat{D}=D+\delta N$ taking its inverse, we obtain

$$(5.37)\qquad \hat{D}^{-1} = D^{-1} - \delta D^{-1} N D^{-1} + \delta^2 D^{-1} N D^{-1} N D^{-1} - \delta^3 D^{-1} N D^{-1} N D^{-1} N \hat{D}^{-1}$$

by making use of the result: For any two square matrices A and B, the inverse of the sum of matrices A and B, when A and (A+B) are invertable, is

$$(5.38)\qquad (A+B)^{-1} = A^{-1} - A^{-1}BA^{-1} + A^{-1}BA\ BA^{-1} - A^{-1}BA^{-1}BA^{-1}B(A+B)^{-1}.$$

Substituting (5.37) in the sampling error of the estimator $\hat{\hat{\beta}}$ in (5.34), we obtain

$$(5.39)\qquad \hat{\hat{\beta}} - \beta = \gamma + O_p(\delta^3),$$

where

$$\begin{aligned}
\gamma &= \mu_o + \delta\mu_1 + \delta^2\mu_2, \\
\mu_o &= \Omega X' D^{-1} u, \\
\mu_1 &= -\Omega X' D^{-1} NPu, \\
\mu_2 &= \Omega X' D^{-1} NPNPu, \\
P &= D^{-1} - D^{-1} X\Omega X' D^{-1}, \\
\Omega &= (X' D^{-1} X)^{-1}.
\end{aligned}$$

The finite sample approximation to the moment matrix of the asymptotic distribution of the estimator $\hat{\hat{\beta}}$ up to asymptotic order δ^3 can now be obtained by calculating the mathematical expectation of the matrix of sum of squares and cross products of the sampling errors. This finite sample approximate moment matrix up to order δ^3 is given by

$$(5.40)\quad E(\hat{\hat{\beta}}-\beta)(\hat{\hat{\beta}}-\beta)' = E\mu_0\mu_0' + \delta E(\mu_0\mu_1' + \mu_1\mu_0') + \delta^2 E(\mu_0\mu_2' + \mu_1\mu_1' + \mu_2\mu_0') = \Omega + \Omega X'D^{-1}HD^{-1}X\Omega,$$

where

$$H = 2(F\dot{\Psi}F')*P + 4(F*M)\Psi(M*F') + 4Q,$$
$$F = \dot{X}(G'G)^{-1}G',$$
$$\dot{\Psi} = (M\dot{D}M)*(M\dot{D}M) = \Psi*\Psi,$$

while the (j,j') element of matrix Q is given by

$$q_{jj'} = \sum_{i,i'}^{n} f_{ji} m_{j'i} \Psi_{ii'} f_{j'i'},$$

such that f_{ji} is the $(j,i)^{th}$ element of matrix F, $m_{j'i}$ is the $(j',i)^{th}$ element of the matrix $M = I - X(X'X)^{-1}X'$ and $\Psi_{ii'}$ is the $(i,i')^{th}$ element of matrix Ψ. We note that the task of evaluating the mathematical expectations of the individual terms is lengthy but straightforward. Further, comparing the finite sample approximate moment matrix $\hat{\hat{\beta}}$, in (5.40) with the asymptotic moment matrix Ω, we can say that the matrix $\Omega X'D^{-1}HD^{-1}X\Omega$ provides a measure of underestimation/overestimation to the moment matrix Ω of the asymptotic distribution of the estimator $\hat{\hat{\beta}}$ up to order δ^3.

We now present the summary results of the extent of underestimation/overestimation in small samples by examining the relative sizes of the determinant values of the moment matrix of the asymptotic distribution and its finite sample approximation for a few hypothetical models, namely:

Model I $\quad y_i = \beta_{i1} + \beta_{i2}x_{i2},$

Model II $\quad y_i = \beta_{i1} + \beta_{i3}x_{i3} + \beta_{i4}x_{i4}.$

In Table 5.2 the percentage ratio of the determinant values of the asymptotic and its finite sample approximate moment matrices are given for the sample sizes 10, 20 and 40. The values of various x's for the sample 10 were taken from a typical economic series while the values of the alternative explanatory variables were obtained by repeating the observations on them two and four times respectively. The sample means, standard deviations for alternative explanatory variables are given in Table 5.1. The correlation coefficient between x_3 and x_4 was 0.248. The value of σ_1^2 and σ_3^2 used in the numerical experiments was fixed at 0.9 and 0.5 respectively.

TABLE 5.1: Sample Size, Sample Means and Standard Deviations for x's in Models I and II

Sample Size	Variable	Mean	Standard Deviation
10	x_2	3.740	0.664
20	x_2	3.740	0.646
40	x_2	3.740	0.638
10	x_3	0.882	0.621
20	x_3	0.882	0.605
40	x_3	0.882	0.597
10	x_4	1.373	0.948
20	x_4	1.373	0.919
40	x_4	1.373	0.907

The values of both σ_2^2 and σ_4^2 were varied between 0.1 and 0.9 in Model I and Model II.

The summary conclusions are: (i) The determinant value of the moment matrix Ω of the asymptotic distribution underestimates the determinant value of the finite sample approximate moment matrix

TABLE 5.2: Percentage Ratio Measure of Underestimation of the Asymptotic Moment Matrix for Models I and II

Model I

Sample Size	0.1	0.2	0.3	0.4	0.5	0.6	0.7	0.8	0.9
10	120.064	121.914	123.008	123.717	124.211	124.576	124.855	125.075	125.254
20	107.067	107.711	108.093	108.341	108.514	108.642	108.740	108.817	108.880
40	103.012	103.283	103.443	103.548	103.621	103.675	103.716	103.749	103.775

Model II

Sample Size	0.1	0.2	0.3	0.4	0.5	0.6	0.7	0.8	0.9
10	299.317	310.665	324.766	340.934	358.783	378.084	398.693	420.517	443.492
20	148.296	149.810	151.947	154.504	157.367	160.467	163.757	167.208	170.797
40	118.542	118.929	119.558	120.347	121.248	122.224	123.282	124.381	125.526

(5.40) of the estimator $\hat{\hat{\beta}}$ for small samples. Thus, in the applications of the random coefficients model it would be desirable to use the finite sample approximate moment estimator to obtain the standard errors of estimates of the means of the random coefficients rather than obtaining them from the usual asymptotic moment matrix; (ii) The size of underestimation of moment matrix of $\hat{\hat{\beta}}$ varies inversely and directly proportional to the sample size and variance of the random coefficients respectively.

NOTES

1. Also see Swamy and Mehta (1977).

2. See Griffiths (1971b), Froehlich (1973a, 1973b), Raj (1973), Dent and Hildreth (1977).

3. See Raj, Srivastava and Upadhyaya (1976, 1980).

6. Contemporaneous Correlation and Autocorrelation

6.1 INTRODUCTION

Two of the important assumptions of the purely random coefficients linear model in Chapter 4 were that the stochastic components of the varying coefficients are contemporaneously and serially uncorrelated. When the varying coefficients are normally distributed these assumptions imply that all the pairwise random coefficients are both serially and contemporaneously independent. However, there are likely to be circumstances in which the assumption of either the contemporaneous or the serial independents is unacceptable. For example, the assumption of the pairwise contemporaneous dependency is plausible in situations where one may incorrectly specify the form of the systematic part of the varying coefficients. A misspecification will occur if we specify a fixed systematic part when the true specification requires a varying systematic part, say a linear function of a policy variable.

Similarly, a misspecification would occur if we specify the systematic part as a linear function of varying coefficient when the true relationship is nonlinear. The contamination of the stochastic part due either to omitted variables and/or to the incorrect form of the systematic part can violate the assumptions of pairwise contemporaneous and serial independence. The pairwise contemporaneous correlation between the coefficients can occur if all the coefficients were influenced by the same set of omitted policy variables. Similarly, the pairwise serial dependence can occur if the serial correlation in the omitted variable is pervasive.

In this chapter we discuss the problem of estimation in a general linear model with purely random coefficients when the coefficients are (a) contemporaneously correlated; and (b) autocorrelated.

6.2 THE GENERAL LINEAR MODEL WITH CONTEMPORANEOUSLY CORRELATED RANDOM COEFFICIENTS

Consider the model

$$(6.1) \qquad y_i = \beta_{1i} + \sum_{k=2}^{K} \beta_i x_{ki}, \qquad i=1,2,\ldots,n$$

with

$$(6.2) \qquad \beta_{ki} = \beta_k + \varepsilon_{ki} \qquad k=1,2,\ldots,K,$$

where the usual disturbance term in the regression (6.1) has been subsumed into ε_{1i}. The simplifying assumptions of the model are

(6.3) (a) $E\varepsilon_{ki} = 0,$ for all k and i.

(b) $E\varepsilon_{ki}^2 = \sigma_k^2 = \sigma_{kk},$ for all k and i.

(c) $E\varepsilon_{ki}\varepsilon_{ki'} = 0,$ for all $i \neq i'$.

(d) $E\varepsilon_{ki}\varepsilon_{k'i} = \sigma_{kk'}$ for $k \neq k'$ and $k,k' = 1,2,\ldots,K$.

The assumptions (6.3a) and (6.3b) respectively imply that each stochastically varying regression coefficient in (6.2) has a fixed mean and homoscedastic variance (which is assumed to be finite). The assumptions (6.3c) and (6.3d) respectively imply that the stochastically varying coefficients are pairwise serially uncorrelated and pairwise contemporaneously correlated. We will also assume that the ε_{ki} is uncorrelated with x_{ki}.

Substituting (6.2) into (6.1), we obtain

$$(6.4) \qquad y_i = \beta_1 + \sum_{k=2}^{K} \beta_k x_{ki} + u_i,$$

where

$$u_i = \varepsilon_{1i} + \sum_{k=2}^{K} \varepsilon_{ki} x_{ki}$$

such that $Eu_i = 0$, $\mathrm{var}(u_i) = \sum_{k=1}^{K} \sum_{k'=1}^{K} \sigma_{kk'} x_{ki} x_{k'i}$ with $x_{1i}=1$ for all i and $\mathrm{cov}(u_i, u_{i'})=0$ for $i \neq i'$ $(i,i'=1,2,\ldots,n)$. Note that in obtaining the mean, variance and covariance of u_i, we have made use of assumptions (6.3a) to (6.3d) and that x_{ki} is uncorrelated with ε_{ki}.

6.2.1 Estimation of β

The model (6.4) can be compactly written as

$$(6.5) \qquad y = X\beta + u,$$

where y is an nx1 vector of observations on the dependent variable, X is an nxK matrix of observations on the K nonstochastic explanatory variables and of rank K, β is a Kx1 vector of mean response coefficients and u is an nx1 vector of disturbances, such that

$$(6.6) \qquad Eu = 0 \text{ and } Euu' = D_o = \text{diag.}(d^o_{11}, d^o_{22}, \ldots, d^o_{nn}),$$

where

$$d^o_{ii} = \sum_{k=1}^{K} \sum_{k'=1}^{K} \sigma_{kk'} x_{ki} x_{k'i}$$

and

$$x_{1i} = 1 \text{ for all } (i=1,2,\ldots,n).$$

Note that the least squares estimator of β in (6.5) is inefficient because the variance-covariance matrix for u is not a scalar times an identity matrix. Thus the best linear unbiased estimator of β can be obtained by generalised least squares (GLS) procedure when the values of the parameters $\sigma_{kk'}$'s are known. The GLS of β in (6.5) is given by

$$(6.7) \qquad \hat{\beta} = (X' D_o^{-1} X)^{-1} X' D_o^{-1} y$$

and the variance-covariance matrix of $\hat{\beta}$ is

$$(6.8) \qquad V(\hat{\beta}) = (X' D_o^{-1} X)^{-1},$$

where

$$D_o^{-1} = \text{diag.}(1/d^o_{11}, 1/d^o_{22}, \ldots, 1/d^o_{nn}).$$

The estimator (6.7) can be obtained alternatively by applying least squares to the transformed model:

$$(6.9) \qquad y_o = X_o \beta + u_o,$$

where

$$y_o = D_o^{-1/2}y, X_o = D_o^{-1/2}X \text{ and } u_o = D_o^{-1/2}u$$

with

$$D_o^{-1/2} = \text{diag.}(1/\sqrt{d_{11}^o}, 1/\sqrt{d_{22}^o}, \ldots, 1/\sqrt{d_{ii}^o}).$$

Then $\hat{\beta} = (X_o'X_o)^{-1}X_o'y_o$ and its variance-covariance matrix is $V(\hat{\beta}) = (X_o'X_o)^{-1}$, which are equal to (6.7) and (6.8) respectively.

To illustrate this estimation method we consider the following bivariate model:

(6.10) $$y_i = \beta_{1i} + \beta_{2i}x_{2i}, \qquad i = 1,2,\ldots,n,$$

with

(6.11) $$\beta_{1i} = \beta_1 + \varepsilon_{1i},$$
$$\beta_{2i} = \beta_2 + \varepsilon_{2i},$$

where once again we have subsumed the usual disturbance term into ε_{1i}.

The simplifying assumptions are:

(6.12) $E\varepsilon_{ki} = 0,$ for $k=1,2$ and $i=1,2,\ldots,n.$

$E\varepsilon_{ki}^2 = \sigma_{kk},$ for all k and i.

$E(\varepsilon_{ki}\varepsilon_{k'i}) = \sigma_{kk'},$ for $k \neq k'$ and $k,k'=1,2.$

$E(\varepsilon_{ki}\varepsilon_{ki'}) = 0,$ for all k and $i \neq i'$ $(i,i'=1,2,\ldots,n).$

$E\,\varepsilon_{ki}x_{ki} = 0,$ for all k and i.

Substituting (6.11) into (6.10), we can write

$$(6.13)\qquad y_i = \beta_1 + \beta_2 x_i + u_i,$$

where $u_i = \varepsilon_{1i} + \varepsilon_{2i} x_{2i}$ such that $Eu_i = 0$ for all i, $\text{var}(u_i) = \sigma_{11} + \sigma_{22} x_{2i}^2 + 2\sigma_{12} x_{2i} = d_{ii}^o$ for $i = 1,2,\ldots,n$ and $E(u_i u_{i'}) = 0$ for $i \neq i'$ $(i,i' = 1,2,\ldots,n)$. Writing $w_i = 1/\sqrt{d_{ii}^o}$ for all i and multiplying (6.13) by w_i, we obtain

$$(6.14)\qquad w_i y_i = \beta_1 w_i + \beta_2 w_i x_{2i} + w_i u_i$$

or

$$y_i^o = \beta_1 x_{1i}^o + \beta_2 x_{2i}^o + u_i^o.$$

It is easily verified that $Eu_i^o = w_i Eu_i = 0$ and $\text{var}(u_i^o) = \text{var}(w_i u_i) = w_i^2 \text{ var } u_i = 1$ for all i and $E(u_i^o\ u_{i'}^o) = E(w_i u_i w_{i'} u_{i'}) = w_i w_{i'}\ E(u_i u_{i'}) = 0$. Thus, in (6.14) the best linear estimators of β_1 and β_2 when $\sigma_{kk'}$'s are known, can be obtained by the ordinary least squares (OLS). The OLS estimators of β_1 and β_2 may be obtained from

$$\hat{\beta} = \begin{bmatrix} \hat{\beta}_1 \\ \hat{\beta}_2 \end{bmatrix} = \begin{bmatrix} \Sigma x_{1i}^{o^2} & \Sigma x_{1i}^o x_{2i}^o \\ \Sigma x_{2i}^o\ x_{1i}^o & \Sigma x_{2i}^{o2} \end{bmatrix}^{-1} \begin{bmatrix} \Sigma x_{1i}^o y_i^o \\ \Sigma x_{2i}^o y_i^o \end{bmatrix}$$

$$= \frac{1}{A} \begin{bmatrix} \Sigma x_{2i}^{o^2} & -\Sigma\ x_{1i}^o x_{2i}^o \\ -\Sigma x_{2i}^o x_{1i}^o & \Sigma\ x_{1i}^{o2} \end{bmatrix} \begin{bmatrix} \Sigma x_{1i}^o y_i^o \\ \Sigma x_{2i}^o y_i^o \end{bmatrix},$$

where $A = \Sigma x_{1i}^{o^2} \Sigma x_{2i}^{o^2} - (\Sigma x_{1i}^{o} x_{2i}^{o})^2$.

Therefore,

$$(6.16) \qquad \hat{\beta}_1 = \frac{\Sigma x_{2i}^{o^2} \Sigma x_{1i}^{o} y_{1i}^{o} - \Sigma x_{1i}^{o} x_{2i}^{o} \Sigma x_{2i}^{o} y_{i}^{o}}{\Sigma x_{1i}^{o^2} \Sigma x_{2i}^{o^2} - (\Sigma x_{1i}^{o} x_{2i}^{o})^2}$$

and

$$(6.17) \qquad \hat{\beta}_2 = \frac{\Sigma x_{1i}^{o^2} \Sigma x_{2i}^{o} y_{i}^{o} - \Sigma x_{1i}^{o} x_{2i}^{o} \Sigma x_{1i}^{o} y_{i}^{o}}{\Sigma x_{1i}^{o^2} \Sigma x_{2i}^{o^2} - (\Sigma x_{1i}^{o} x_{2i}^{o})^2}.$$

6.2.2 Estimation of $\sigma_{kk'}$

Consider the vector of least squares residuals in (6.5), that is

$$(6.18) \qquad e = Mu,$$

where $M = I - X(X'X)^{-1}X'$ is a symmetric idempotent matrix of order nxn. The mathematical expectation of the Hadamard matrix product of the residual vector e with itself is

$$(6.19) \qquad Ee*e = E\dot{e} = E(e_1^2, e_2^2, \ldots, e_n^2)'$$

$$= E((\sum_{i=1}^{n} m_{1i} u_i)^2, \ldots, (\sum_{i=1}^{n} m_{ni} u_i)^2)' ,$$

In writing the last equality result in (6.19) we have made use of (6.18) so that

$$e_i^2 = \left(\sum_{i'=1}^{n} m_{ii'} u_{i'} \right)^2 \qquad \text{for } i=1,2,\ldots,n.$$

Further, since

$$E\left(\sum_{i'=1}^{n} m_{ii'} u_{i'} \right)^2 = \sum_{i'=1}^{n} \sum_{i''=1}^{n} m_{ii'} m_{ii''} E(u_{i'} u_{i''}),$$

we obtain

$$(6.20) \qquad Ee_i^2 = \sum_{i'=1}^{n} m_{ii'}^2 d_{i'i'}^o, \qquad \text{if } i'=i''$$

$$= 0 \qquad \text{otherwise}$$

where

$$d_{ii}^o = \sum_{k=1}^{K} \sum_{k'=1}^{K} \sigma_{kk'} x_{ki} x_{k'i}$$

and

$$E\dot{e} = \left(\sum_{i=1}^{n} m_{1i}^2 d_{ii}^o, \ldots, \sum_{i=1}^{n} m_{ni}^2 d_{ii}^o \right)'.$$

The mathematical expectation of the Hadamard matrix product of the residual vector e with itself in the linear model with contemporaneously correlated but serially uncorrelated random coefficients can be compactly written as

$$(6.21) \qquad E\dot{e} = \dot{M}\dot{Z}\sigma_o,$$

where $\dot{M}=M*M$, $\dot{Z}=Z*Z$ and the * represents the Hadamard matrix product such that

$$(6.22)\quad \dot{Z}=\begin{bmatrix} 1 & .. & 2x_{K1} & x_{21}x_{21} & .. & 2x_{21}x_{K1} & .. & x_{K1}x_{K1} \\ 1 & .. & 2x_{K2} & x_{21}x_{22} & .. & 2x_{22}x_{K2} & .. & x_{K2}x_{K2} \\ \vdots & & \vdots & \vdots & & & & \\ 1 & .. & 2x_{Kn} & x_{2n}x_{2n} & .. & 2x_{2n}x_{K2} & .. & x_{Kn}x_{Kn} \end{bmatrix}$$

is an nx(K(K+1)/2) matrix having: K columns corresponding to the Hadamard product of each column of the matrix X with itself; K(K-1)/2 columns which are two times the Hadamard product of the K column vectors of the matrix X with each of the remaining columns of X having a higher column index than the column used to obtain the Hadamard matrix product. Finally, the $\dot{\sigma}_o$ is a (K(K+1)/2)x1 column vector of variances and contemporaneous covariances of the stochastically varying coefficients, i.e.

$$(6.23)\quad \dot{\sigma}_o=(\sigma_{11},\sigma_{12},..,\sigma_{1K},..,\sigma_{K-1,1},..,\sigma_{K-1,K},\sigma_{KK})'.$$

The regression relation (6.21) can be written as[1]

$$(6.24)\quad \dot{e}= \dot{M}\dot{Z}\dot{\sigma}_o+w_o= \dot{G}_o\dot{\sigma}_o+w_o,$$

where w_o is a disturbance vector such that $Ew_o= 0$. It can be shown that when the σ_{ki}'s are normally distributed the variance-covariance matrix of w_o is

$$(6.25)\quad Ew_ow_o'= 2\dot{\Psi}_o= (MD_oM)*(MD_oM),$$

where $D_o= \text{diag.}(d^o_{11},d^o_{22},...,d^o_{nn})$ and the * represents the Hadamard matrix product. Note that the proof for (6.25) is similar to the proof for $Eww' = 2\dot{\Psi}$ in Chapter 4.

Since the dispersion matrix of w_o is not a scalar times an identity matrix, the ordinary least squares estimator of $\dot{\sigma}_o$ in (6.24) is inefficient, and best linear unbiased estimator of $\dot{\sigma}_o$ is given by the generalised least squares procedure, when $2\dot{\Psi}_o$ is known. The GLS estimator of $\dot{\sigma}_o$ is

$$(6.26) \qquad \hat{\dot{\sigma}}_o = (G_o' \dot{\Psi}_o^{-1} G_o)^{-1} G_o' \dot{\Psi}_o^{-1} \dot{e}.$$

The variance-covariance matrix for $\hat{\dot{\sigma}}_o$ is

$$(6.27) \qquad V(\hat{\dot{\sigma}}_o) = E(\hat{\dot{\sigma}}_o - \dot{\sigma}_o)(\hat{\dot{\sigma}}_o - \dot{\sigma}_o)' = 2(G_o' \dot{\Psi}_o^{-1} G_o)^{-1}.$$

Note that in deriving (6.26) we have made use of two additional assumptions, viz.,

(6.3) (e) the rank of G_o is $K(K+1)/2 < n$

(f) the ε_{ki}'s are normally distributed.

6.2.3 The Operational Generalised Least Squares Estimators of β and $\dot{\sigma}_o$

The generalised least squares estimators (6.7) and (6.26) are nonoperational because the dispersion matrices D_o and $2\dot{\Psi}_o$ are a function of unknown parameters $\sigma_{kk'}$. An operational estimator of $\dot{\sigma}_o$ can be obtained if we use an estimated variance-covariance matrix in place of the unknown matrix of the generalised least squares (6.26). Then an operational estimator of $\dot{\sigma}_o$ can be obtained by using the estimates of $\sigma_{kk'}$ from the least squares estimator,

$$(6.28) \qquad \dot{s}_o = (G_o'G_o)^{-1}G_o'\dot{e},$$

which is a linear, unbiased and consistent estimator of $\dot{\sigma}_o$, and could be used to obtain a consistent estimator of D_o and $2\dot{\Psi}_o$ respectively from (6.6) and (6.25). Let the operational estimator of $2\dot{\Psi}_o$ be $2\hat{\dot{\Psi}}_o$ where

$$(6.29) \qquad 2\hat{\dot{\Psi}} = 2(M\hat{D}_oM)*(M\hat{D}_oM)$$

with

$$(6.30) \qquad \hat{D}_o = \text{diag.}(\hat{d}^o_{11}, \hat{d}^o_{22}, \ldots, \hat{d}^o_{nn})$$

and

$$\hat{d}^o_{ii} = \sum_{k=1}^{K} \sum_{k'=1}^{K} \dot{s}_{kk'} x_{ki} x_{k'i} \qquad (i=1,2,\ldots,n),$$

where $\dot{s}_{kk'}$'s are the least squares estimates of $\sigma_{kk'}$'s from (6.28). Then the operational generalised squares estimator of $\dot{\sigma}_o$ is given by

$$(6.31) \qquad \tilde{\dot{\sigma}}_o = (G_o'\hat{\dot{\Psi}}^{-1}G_o)^{-1}G_o'\hat{\dot{\Psi}}^{-1}\dot{e};$$

the asymptotic variance-covariance matrix of $\tilde{\dot{\sigma}}_o$ is

$$(6.32) \qquad AV(\tilde{\dot{\sigma}}_o) = 2(G_o'\dot{\Psi}^{-1}G_o)^{-1}.$$

The formal basis on which the proposed operational generalised least squares estimator (6.31) is efficient is that the elements of D_o are replaced by their consistent estimates. In deriving the operational estimator of $\dot{\sigma}_o$ in (6.31) we have replaced the unknowns in the elements of D_o and

$2\dot{\psi}_0$ with their consistent least squares estimators from (6.28). Then the estimator (6.31) is unbiased (provided its mean exists) and efficient in large samples. The important point to note is that all other operational estimators of $\dot{\sigma}_0$, obtained by using an estimated dispersion matrix whose elements are obtained by replacing its unknown by any other set of consistent estimators, will have similar large sample properties. However, an operational estimator of $\dot{\sigma}_0$ which uses more efficient initial estimates of the unknowns in the estimated dispersion matrix is likely to be more efficient in small samples. Also note that neither the least squares nor the operational generalised least squares estimates of σ_{kk}'s are restricted to being positive. Thus, the estimates of variances of the stochastically varying coefficients can sometimes be negative. A simple solution to the problem is to replace all negative estimates of the σ_{kk}'s by zeros. The truncated estimates of σ_{kk}'s so obtained are biased but will be more efficient than their untruncated counterparts on the mean squared error criterion (which equals the sum of the variance and the square of the bias of the estimators). Alternatively, one may either apply a quadratic programming method to obtain constrained estimates of σ_{kk}'s, or the Bayesian method wherein prior knowledge precludes negative estimates of variances of stochastic coefficients (see Chapter 4).

The operational estimate of β can be obtained by using either the estimated variance-covariance matrix $\hat{D}_0$ obtained by using the least squares estimates of σ_{kk}'s or the estimated variance-covariance matrix $\tilde{D}_0$ obtained by using the operational generalised least squares estimates of σ_{kk}'s, in place of the true matrix D_o in the generalised least squares estimator (6.7). It can be verified that the estimated variance-covariance matrices $\hat{D}_o$ and $\tilde{D}_o$ are consistent estimators of the matrix D_o. Then the operational generalised least squares estimators of β, viz.,

$$(6.33) \qquad \hat{\beta} = (X'\hat{D}_o^{-1}X)^{-1}X'\hat{D}_o^{-1}y$$

and

$$(6.34) \qquad \tilde{\beta} = (X'\tilde{D}_o^{-1}X)^{-1}X'\tilde{D}_o^{-1}y,$$

will have the same asymptotic variance-covariance matrix given below:

$$(6.35) \qquad AV(\hat{\beta}) = AV(\tilde{\beta}) = (X'D_o{}^{-1}X)^{-1}.$$

The 'standard errors' of estimates for the $\hat{\beta}$'s and the $\tilde{\beta}$'s respectively can be obtained by taking the square root of the diagonal elements in $(X'\hat{D}_o{}^{-1}X)^{-1}$ and $(X'\tilde{D}_o{}^{-1}X)^{-1}$ matrices. Note that the moment matrices of the limiting distributions of both $\hat{\beta}$ and $\tilde{\beta}$ are likely to underestimate their respective finite sample approximate matrix of the limiting distribution in small samples (see Chapter 5). Thus, in the applications of the model (6.5), it will be desirable to obtain the standard error of estimates of $\hat{\beta}$ and $\tilde{\beta}$ from an appropriate approximate moment matrix, which could be easily derived on the pattern of the approximate matrix of the vector of mean response coefficients derived in the last chapter. Finally, based on the results of the Monte Carlo study, in some simple situations summarized in the last chapter the estimator $\tilde{\beta}$ is likely to be preferred to estimator $\hat{\beta}$ in small samples of size larger than 20. Similarly, the truncated estimators of β corresponding to estimators $\hat{\beta}$ and $\tilde{\beta}$ are likely to be more efficient on the mean squared error criterion than their untruncated counterparts.

6.3 THE GENERAL LINEAR MODEL WITH AUTOCORRELATED RANDOM COEFFICIENTS

In Section 6.2 we discussed the problem of estimation in the general linear model with random coefficients when the coefficients are assumed to be contemporaneously correlated. Now we anlayse the problem of estimation in the general linear model when the random coefficients follow a first order autoregressive scheme. Accordingly, the general linear model with random coefficients is characterised by equation (6.1) or equation (6.4). Further, we assume that

(i) $E\varepsilon_{ki}=0$, for all k and i;

(ii) $E\varepsilon_{ki}\varepsilon_{k'i}=0$, for all i and $k\neq k'$;

(iii) $E\varepsilon_{ki}\varepsilon_{ki'}\neq 0$, for all i and $i\neq i'$.

Also, we assume that the ε_{ki} follows a first order autoregressive scheme, that is

(6.36) $$\varepsilon_{ki}= \rho_k\varepsilon_{k,i-1}+\mu_{ki},$$

where $|\rho_k| < 1$ and the disturbance term μ_{ki} satisfies the following assumptions:

$E\mu_{ki}=0$, for all k and i

$E\mu_{ki}^2=\sigma_{kk}$, for all i and k,

$E\mu_{ki}\mu_{k'i'}=0$, if either $k\neq k'$ or $i\neq i'$,

$E\varepsilon_{k,i-1}\mu_{ki}=0$, for all k and i.

Finally, we assume that the initial stochastic component ε_{ko} is distributed such that

$$\text{(iv)} \qquad E\varepsilon_{ko} = 0, E\varepsilon_{ko}^2 = \frac{\sigma_{kk}}{1-\rho_k^2} = \sigma_{kk}^o .$$

Using the assumptions (i) to (iii), (iv) and (6.36) we note that

$$(6.37) \qquad \varepsilon_{ki} = \sum_{r=0}^{\infty} \rho_k^r \mu_{k,i-r}$$

such that

$$(6.38) \qquad \begin{aligned} &E\varepsilon_{ki} = 0, \\ &E\varepsilon_{ki}^2 = \sigma_{kk}/(1-\rho_k^2), \\ &E\varepsilon_{ki}\varepsilon_{k',i-s} = \rho_k^s \sigma_{kk}/(1-\rho_k^2), \text{ if } k=k' \text{ and } s<i, \\ &\qquad\qquad = 0, \qquad\qquad \text{if } k \neq k'. \end{aligned}$$

In the relation (6.38), the term ρ_k^s defines the s-th autocorrelation coefficient of the ε_{ki} series; which is easily seen if we write (6.38) as

$$(6.39) \qquad \frac{E\varepsilon_{ki}\ \varepsilon_{k',i-s}}{E\varepsilon_{ki}^2} = \rho_k^s .$$

Further, using results (6.37) to (6.39) in (6.4), we obtain

$$(6.40a) \qquad \begin{aligned} &Eu_i = 0 \qquad \text{for all } i, \\ &Eu_i^2 = \sum_{k=1}^{K} x_{ki}^2 \sigma_{kk}/(1-\rho_k^2) = d_{ii}^o, \text{ for } i=1,2,\ldots,n, \end{aligned}$$

and

$$(6.40b) \qquad Eu_i u_{i-s} = \sum_{k=1}^{K} x_{k,i} x_{k,i-s} \sigma_{kk} \rho_k^s/(1-\rho_k^2)$$

$$= d^o_{i,i-s} \qquad \text{for } s<i.$$

Note that $x_{1i}=1$ for all i in (6.40a) and (6.40b).

In matrix notation the model can be written as

$$(6.41) \qquad y_i = x_i \beta_i,$$

where

$$(6.42) \qquad \beta_i = \beta + \varepsilon_i$$

and x_i is the i-th row vector of the matrix X and $\varepsilon_i = (\varepsilon_{1i} \ldots \varepsilon_{Ki})'$. Substituting β_i from (6.42) into (6.41), we write

$$(6.43) \qquad y_i = x_i \beta + u_i$$

where $u_i = x_i \varepsilon_i$ such that $Eu_i = 0$. Further using (6.38) we obtain

$$(6.44) \qquad Eu_i u'_{i-s} = x_i (E\varepsilon_i \varepsilon'_{i-s}) x'_{i-s} = x_i D_1^s x'_{i-s}, \quad s<i$$

where for $s=0,1\ldots,n-1$

$$(6.45) \qquad D_1^s = \begin{bmatrix} \sigma_{11}\rho_1^s/1-\rho_1^2 & . & . & 0 \\ . & & & . \\ . & & & . \\ . & & & . \\ 0 & . & . & \sigma_{KK}\rho_K^s/1-\rho_K^2 \end{bmatrix}.$$

In a more compact form we can write the model (6.43), for i=1,2,...,n as

$$(6.46) \qquad y = X\beta + u$$

where

$$Eu = 0$$

and

$$(6.47) \qquad Euu' = D_2 = \begin{bmatrix} x_1 D_1^{o} x_1' & \dots & x_1 D_1^{n-1} x_n' \\ \cdot & & \\ \cdot & & \\ x_n D_1^{n-1} x_1' & \dots & x_1 D_1^{o} x_n' \end{bmatrix}.$$

6.4 ESTIMATION OF THE VECTOR OF MEAN RESPONSES

The best, linear and unbiased estimator of β in (6.46) is

$$(6.48) \qquad \tilde{\tilde{\beta}} = (X' D_2^{-1} X)^{-1} X' D_2^{-1} y;$$

its variance-covariance matrix is

$$(6.49) \qquad Var(\tilde{\tilde{\beta}}) = E(\tilde{\tilde{\beta}} - \beta)(\tilde{\tilde{\beta}} - \beta)' = (X' D_2^{-1} X)^{-1}.$$

In a special case of the general linear model with autocorrelated stochastic coefficients where the autocorrelation coefficients $\rho_i = \rho$ for all i, the dispersion matrix (6.47) reduces to

$$D_3 = \frac{1}{1-\rho^2} \begin{bmatrix} 1 & \rho & \dots & \rho^{n-1} \\ \rho & 1 & \dots & \rho^{n-2} \\ \vdots & & & \\ \rho^{n-1} & \rho^{n-2} & \dots & 1 \end{bmatrix} * \begin{bmatrix} d_{11}^{oo} & d_{12}^{oo} & \dots & d_{1n}^{oo} \\ d_{21}^{oo} & d_{22}^{oo} & \dots & d_{2n}^{oo} \\ \cdot & & & \\ \cdot & & & \\ d_{n1}^{oo} & d_{n2}^{oo} & \dots & d_{nn}^{oo} \end{bmatrix},$$

where * represents the Hardmard matrix product, ρ is the first order autocorrelation coefficient and

$$(6.50) \qquad d^{oo}_{i,i-s} = \sum_{k=1}^{K} x_{ki} x_{k,i-s} \sigma_{kk} \qquad \text{for } s<i, \text{ and } i,s=1,2,\ldots,n.$$

The model (6.46) reduces to the contemporaneously and serially uncorrelated model considered in Chapter 4 since the dispersion matrix (6.45) reduces to $D=\text{diag}(d_{11},\ldots,d_{nn})$ when $\rho_k=0$ for all $k=1,2,\ldots,K$. Finally, the model (6.46) reduces to a general linear model with fixed coefficients and homoscedastic and nonautocorrelated variances when $\rho_k=0$ for all k and $\sigma_{kk}=0$ for all $k=2,\ldots,K$ but σ_{11} (say equal to σ_1^2)$\neq 0$, and the dispersion matrix (6.45) reduces to $\sigma_1^2 I$.

6.5 ESTIMATION OF THE ELEMENTS OF DISPERSION MATRIX

Consider the OLS residual vector e=Mu. Then using (6.47), we obtain

$$(6.51) \qquad Ee' = M(Euu')M = MD_2M.$$

It is convenient to write the matrices on both sides of (6.51) in a vector form. For this we use the Vec(A) notation which means the elements of an nxm matrix A are written as a column vector; thus the first n elements are the first column of matrix A, followed by the second set of n elements from the second column of A, and so on. A useful property associated with this notation is that for three suitably dimensioned matrices A, B and C we can write:

$$\text{Vec}(ABC) = (C'B \otimes I)\text{Vec}(A) = (C' \otimes A)\text{Vec}(B);$$

see Dhrymes (1978).[2] Using these results in (6.51) we obtain

$$(6.52) \qquad \text{Vec}(Eee') = \text{Vec}(MD_2M) = (M\otimes M)\text{Vec}(D_2),$$

where we have used the fact that

$$\text{Vec}(x_1 D_1^o x_1') = (x_1\otimes x_1)\text{Vec}(D_1^o).$$

Further we write $\text{Vec}(D_2) = W_x d_2$ where W_x is an $n^2 x nK^2$ matrix defined as

$$W_x = ((x_1\otimes x_1)', .., (x_n\otimes x_1)', (x_1\otimes x_2)', .., (x_n\otimes x_n)')'$$

and d_2 is a nK^2x1 vector defined as

$$d_2 = (\text{Vec}(D_1^o)', .., \text{Vec}(D_1^{n-1})', \text{Vec}(D_1^1)', .., \text{Vec}(D_1^o)')'.$$

We note that the vector d_2 is formed with nK^2x1 elements of the matrices $D_1^o, D_1^1, .., D_1^{T-1}$. Finally, we write

$$\text{Vec}(Eee') = (M\otimes M)W_x d_2 = G_x d_2,$$

where $G_x = (M\otimes M)W_x$ is an n^2xnK^2 matrix. Note that $\text{Vec}(Eee')$ is an n^2x1 vector. Thus if we define an nxn^2 matrix J as

$$J = \begin{bmatrix} 1 & 0 & \cdot & \cdot & \cdot & 0 \\ 0 & 0 & \cdot & 1 & \cdot & 0 \\ \vdots \\ 0 & 0 & 0 & \cdot & \cdot & 1.0 \end{bmatrix},$$

then $J\text{Vec}(Eee') = E\dot{e} = (Ee_1^2 \ldots Ee_T^2)'$, where $\dot{e}$ is the diagonal elements of ee' (or $\dot{e}=e*e$ where * is the Hadamard matrix product).

Finally, following the Hildreth and Houck (1968) procedure, we write,

$$JVec(Eee')= JG_x d_2$$

or $E\dot{e}= \dot{G}_x d_2$, where $\dot{G}_x= JG_x$. Thus $\dot{e}= \dot{G}_x d_2+\xi$ and $\hat{d}_2= (\dot{G}'_x\dot{G}_x)^{-1}\dot{G}'_x\dot{e}$, provided the rank of $\dot{G}_x$ is $nK^2<n^2$ or $K^2<n$.

We note that d_2 consists of nK^2 unknown elements which are interrelated with each other. The constraints on the elements obtained by their relationships can be directly used on d_2 and one can write a modified equation of the form

$$\hat{\dot{e}}_m= \dot{G}_{x,m}d_{2m}+\xi_m,$$

where subscript m represents that the modified vector or matrix is used.

Once the estimate of d_2 is obtained we can determine D_2 and obtain the operational GLS estimator as

$$\hat{\hat{\beta}}= (X'\hat{D}_2^{-1}x)^{-1}X'\hat{D}_2^{-1}y. \tag{6.53}$$

For further extension of the model when ε_i follows a general autoregressive moving average structure see Swamy and Tinsley (1980).

NOTES

1. Also see Swamy and Mehta (1975).

2. The $\otimes$ represents the Kronecker matrix product. If A is an mxn matrix and B is a pxk matrix then $A \otimes B$ implies the product of each element of A with the matrix B. If A and B are non singular matrices then $(A \otimes B)^{-1} = A^{-1} \otimes B^{-1}$. Further if A, B, C and D are matrices of proper orders then $(A \otimes B)(C \otimes D) = AC \otimes BD$. For further results on Kronecker matrix products see Theil (1973), pp. 303-306.

7. Multicollinearity

7.1 INTRODUCTION

In this chapter we analyse a situation where some or all of the explanatory variables in the randomly varying coefficients model

$$y_i = \sum_{k=1}^{K} \beta_{ki} x_{ki} = \sum_{k=1}^{K} \beta_k x_{ki} + u_i \quad (i=1,2,\ldots n)$$

are collinear. The term 'perfect' multicollinearity refers to a situation where perfect interrelationships exist among the explanatory variables. In this case we will not get a unique solution to the generalised least squares normal equations since the data matrix X of order nxK is of a rank less than K, and hence the matrix $X'D^{-1}X$ is singular.[1] 'High' multicollinearity refers to a situation where some or all the explanatory variables are 'highly' but not 'perfectly' collinear. In this case the assumption that the data matrix X of order nxK has a rank K is only just satisfied and a unique solution to the normal equations for the generalised least squares procedure can be obtained. Further, the estimator of the vector of the means of the randomly varying coefficients has optimal properties when the variances are known; that is the estimator is the best linear unbiased estimator. It is a serious situation nonetheless; the main consequences of 'high' multicollinearity are: a) There is a loss of precision of estimates which is reflected in large variances of estimated coefficients; and b) The coefficient estimates become very sensitive to the deletion or addition of a few observations to the data. The new sample observations can sometimes produce dramatic and unpredictable shifts in estimates of some or all the coefficients.

7.2 AN ILLUSTRATION

To illustrate some of these points we consider a simple model with randomly varying coefficients

$$(7.1) \quad y_i = (\beta_1+\varepsilon_{1i})x_{1i}+(\beta_2+\varepsilon_{2i})x_{2i}$$
$$= \beta_1 x_{1i}+\beta_2 x_{2i}+(\varepsilon_{1i}x_{1i}+\varepsilon_{2i}x_{2i})$$
$$= \beta_1 x_{1i}+\beta_2 x_{2i}+u_i,$$

where the dependent variable y_i and the independent variables x_{1i} and x_{2i} are expressed as deviations from their respective sample means so that

$$\Sigma\, y_i = \Sigma\, x_{1i} = \Sigma\, x_{2i} = 0.$$

Perfect multicollinearity may now be defined as

$$(7.2) \quad x_{1i} = a x_{2i}.$$

In this case the ranks of both the data matrix X of order nx2 and the matrix of the weighted sum of squares and cross products $X'D^{-1}X$ of order 2x2 are less than 2, that is, $X'D^{-1}X$ is singular. In the case of 'high' multicollinearity the rank condition is just satisfied and the inverse of the matrix $X'D^{-1}X$, where $D=\text{diag.}(d_{11},\ldots,d_{nn})$ and $d_{ii}= \sigma_1^2 x_{1i}^2+\sigma_2^2 x_{2i}^2 = 1/\phi_{ii}$ $(i=1,2,\ldots,n)$, can be written as

$$(7.3)\qquad (X'Dx)^{-1}=\begin{bmatrix} \Sigma x_{1i}^2\phi_{ii} & \Sigma x_{1i}x_{2i}\phi_{ii} \\ \Sigma x_{1i}x_{2i}\phi_{ii} & \Sigma x_{2i}^2\phi_{ii} \end{bmatrix}^{-1}$$

$$=\frac{1}{\Delta}\begin{bmatrix} \Sigma x_{2i}^2\phi_{ii} & -\Sigma x_{1i}x_{2i}\phi_{ii} \\ -\Sigma x_{1i}x_{2i}\phi_{ii} & \Sigma x_{1i}^2\phi_{ii} \end{bmatrix},$$

where $\Delta= \Sigma x_{1i}^2\phi_{ii}\ \Sigma x_{2i}^2\phi_{ii} - (\Sigma x_{1i}x_{2i}\phi_{ii})^2$. Defining r_{12} as the sample correlation coefficient between $x_{1i}\phi_{ii}^{1/2}$ and $x_{2i}\phi_{ii}^{1/2}$, we can write the variances and covariance of the generalised least squares estimators $\hat{\beta}_1$ and $\hat{\beta}_2$ in (7.1) as

$$(7.4)\qquad \text{var}(\hat{\beta}_1)=\frac{1}{\Sigma\ x_{1i}^2\phi_{ii}(1-r_{12}^2)},$$

$$\text{var}(\hat{\beta}_2)=\frac{1}{\Sigma\ x_{2i}^2\phi_{ii}(1-r_{12}^2)}$$

and

$$(7.5)\qquad \text{cov}(\hat{\beta}_1,\hat{\beta}_2)- \frac{-r_{12}}{\sqrt{\text{var}(\hat{\beta}_1)}\ \sqrt{\text{var}(\hat{\beta}_2)}}$$

It is easily verified from (7.4) and (7.5) that as multicollinearity, measured by the absolute value of r_{12}, increases the variances of $\hat{\beta}_1$ and $\hat{\beta}_2$ and also the absolute value of the covariance between $\hat{\beta}_1$ and $\hat{\beta}_2$ increases, making the precision of the estimates smaller. Another point to note is that large variances and covariances of estimates $\hat{\beta}_1$ and $\hat{\beta}_2$ can arise even when the explanatory variables are not collinear but the variances of the varying coefficients are large. This implies that in the context of a random coefficients model the loss of precision may not always be because of multicollinearity in the data.

7.3 MEASURES OF MULTICOLLINEARITY

All measures used for judging when multicollinearity is serious are based on the nature of the explanatory variables in the population whereas multicollinearity is a data problem. Thus, alternative ways of detecting multicollinearity are not very meaningful but can serve as guidelines.

For example, one measure is to check the determinant of the matrix $X'D^{-1}X$. If it is close to zero we say that there is a problem of multicollinearity. But this is not a good measure since the determinant value can be changed by changing the units of measurement. A better alternative is to check the ratio of the square root of the largest to the square root of the smallest eigenvalues of the matrix $D^{-1/2}X$. If this ratio is large, multicollinearity can be considered serious. Another measure is a high value of R^2 (multiple correlation) coupled with low values of partial correlation coefficients.

Yet another measure of high multicollinearity is a 'highly significant' F statistic combined with 'highly insignificant' t statistics. It is important to note, however, that the above measures may lead one to conclude that in a particular situation multicollinearity is not serious while the contrary might be true; for example, if the estimates of the regression coefficients change significantly when we drop a few observations from the sample.

7.4 SOLUTIONS FOR MULTICOLLINEARITY

The several possible methods suggested for solving multicollinearity problems are: (a) Getting more data; (b) Making use of extraneous estimates; (c) Dropping some of the explanatory variables; (d) Using principal components; (e) Using ridge regression and (f) Using **a priori** information and employing Bayesian estimation. Each of these methods have some problems. Which method to apply in any particular case depends on the nature of the problem. We now briefly outline methods (a) to (d) and the difficulties involved in applying them. Then we discuss methods (e) and (f) in greater detail.

(a) The motivation behind the method of getting more data lies in the fact that the multicollinearity problem is essentially a data problem, i.e. the information content of the sample data is weak. In principle, one can try to use disaggregated data such as quarterly data, weekly data or panel data since these data might have more informational content.[2] Several difficulties, however, could arise in practice; e.g. the disaggregated data can involve seasonality while panel data may introduce several cross-sectional variations not present in time series data.

(b) The use of the extraneous estimates method is also in the spirit of using additional data. In this we first estimate the coefficient of a collinear variable by using an independent set of data. Then the modified dependent variable (obtained by subtracting the product of the extraneous estimate of the coefficient and the collinear explanatory variable) is regressed on the remaining explanatory variables. The difficulty with this method lies in the interpretation of the extraneous estimate.

(c) The dropping of the collinear explanatory variable is a commonly used method for solving the multicollinearity problem. However, the problem with this method is that it introduces bias in the estimates of the parameters.

(d) The method of using principal components instead of original collinear variables is merely a statistical solution for the multicollinearity problem. The principal components are various linear combinations of explanatory variables and explain maximum variations in the explanatory variables. But the disadvantage is that they are subject to the normalisation and zero correlation conditions. It is therefore useful only in situations where an economic interpretation is possible.

(e) The ridge estimation method attempts to solve the multicollinearity problem by adding a fixed scalar to each of the diagonal elements of the matrix of the weighted sum of squares and cross products of the explanatory variables before inverting it. Accordingly, the ridge estimator of the vector of mean response coefficients can be written as

$$(7.6) \qquad \hat{\beta}_{RR} = (X'D^{-1}X + cI)^{-1}X'D^{-1}y,$$

where $c > 0$ is the ridge coefficient. The generalised least squares estimator is a special case of the random ridge (RR) estimator (7.6) when $c=0$. The RR estimator (7.6) exists even when the rank of X is less than K; therefore it is not subject to the multicollinearity problem. The generalised least squares estimator $\hat{\beta}_{GLS} = (X'D^{-1}X)^{-1}X'D^{-1}y$ minimises the weighted residual sum of squares $(y-X\beta)'D^{-1}(y-X\beta)$ in

$$y = X\beta + u$$

where $Euu' = D$ without any restrictions on $\hat{\beta}$'s. However, the RR estimator minimises the weighted residual sum of squares subject to the restriction that $\beta'\beta = r^2 < \infty$.[3]

Note that the RR estimator shrinks the generalised least squares estimates toward the null vector. This can be verified by writing (7.6) as

$$(7.7) \qquad \hat{\beta}_{RR} = [I + c(X'D^{-1}X)^{-1}]\hat{\beta}_{GLS} = S\hat{\beta}_{GLS},$$

where $S = [I + c(X'D^{-1}X)^{-1}]$ is the matrix of shrinkage factors. Thus, the RR estimator (7.6) is biased towards zero. The advantage in using the biased RR estimator rather than the unbiased generalised least squares estimator is that the estimates are insensitive to multicollinearity and/or data perturbations. Furthermore, for some nonstochastic positive c the mean squared error of the RR estimator is smaller than the mean squared error of the generalised least squares estimator of β.

The operational ridge estimator of the vector of mean response coefficients in a varying coefficients model can be obtained by replacing the unknown variance-covariance matrix D by its consistent estimator. Several methods of obtaining consistent estimators of unknown D are outlined in Chapter 4. The unknown ridge coefficient $c>0$ may be selected either by the graphic technique, commonly known as Ridge Trace, or by using a quantified index called the Index of Stability of Relative Magnitude (ISRM). In Ridge Trace we plot the RR estimates against the values of c and choose the lowest possible value for which the estimates of the regression coefficients have stabilised. The ISRM method uses a computer programme to evaluate the value of m and c from the definition: $m=K- \Sigma\lambda_i(\lambda_i+c)^{-1}$, where λ_i's are the eigenvalues of the matrix of regressors $D^{-1/2}X$, K is the number of regressors and m is the multicollinearity allowance. Note that m measures the deficiency in the rank of regressor matrix due to collinearity. In practice m may be approximated by the number of eigenvalues λ_i's that are small.[4]

(f) Another solution to multicollinearity lies in applying the Bayesian estimation technique to estimate the vector of mean response coefficients. This approach considers β as a random variable whose prior distribution is multivariate normal with mean vector $\delta\iota$ and variance-covariance matrix $\sigma_\beta^2 V$, where ι is a Kx1 vector of unit elements and δ is a scalar. Then the posterior distribution of β can be shown to be normal with mean,

$$(7.8) \qquad \tilde{\beta}_{RR}= (X'DX+hV^{-1})^{-1}(X'Dy+hV^{-1}\delta\iota),$$

where $h=1/\sigma_\beta^2$. The estimator (7.8) may be termed as the Bayesian random (BR) estimator of the vector of mean response coefficients. It is easily seen from (7.8) that the RR estimator can be interpreted as a Bayes estimator for $\delta=0$ and $V=I$.

If $V=I$, then (7.8) reduces to

$$(7.9) \qquad \tilde{\beta}_{BR}= (X'DX+hI)^{-1}(X'Dy+h\,\delta\iota).$$

The estimators (7.8) and (7.9) are biased but more efficient than the generalised least squares estimator under the criterion of mean squared error. More importantly, the operational BR estimator defined below has been found to continue to dominate the operational generalised least squares estimator under the criterion of mean squared error.

An operational form of (7.9), when D is unknown, can be obtained as

$$(7.10)\qquad \tilde{\beta}_{BR} = (X'\hat{D}X + \hat{h}I)^{-1}(X'\hat{D}y + \hat{h}\hat{\delta}\iota),$$

where $\hat{D}$ is a consistent estimator of D. Several methods of obtaining consistent estimators of D are discussed in Chapter 4. The choice among these consistent estimators of D is arbitrary from the point of view of asymptotic efficiency. However, this may not be so in small sample situations (see Chapter 5).

The estimates of the unknown δ and $h = 1/\sigma_\beta^2 > 0$ in the BR estimator, can be obtained by an iterative procedure. Starting with the operational generalised least squares estimates of β_k's we can define

$$\hat{\sigma} = \frac{1}{K}\sum_{k=1}^{K}\hat{\beta}_k \quad\text{and}\quad \hat{\sigma}_\beta^2 = \frac{1}{K}\sum_{k=1}^{K}(\hat{\beta}_k - \hat{\delta})^2$$

as the estimators for δ and σ_β^2 respectively. Then the new estimates of β_k's are obtained; using them revised estimates of δ and σ_β^2 are calculated. The procedure is repeated till convergence is achieved. It is important to note that the BR estimator is defined even when the matrix X does not satisfy the rank condition due to multicollinearity.

7.5 SOME APPLICATIONS

In order to illustrate the RR estimator, we briefly outline the result of a study relating to wage-price behaviour in the United Kingdom from the first quarter of 1960 to the second quarter of 1971.[5] The purely random coefficients version of an expectations-augmented Phillips curve is estimated by using an operational random ridge estimation technique outlined above. Accordingly, the following wage equation is estimated as

$$(7.11) \qquad W_i = \beta_{1i} + \beta_{2i} V_i + \beta_{3i} P_i^e,$$

where W is the four-quarter percentage change in wages and salaries per employee over previous quarters, V is the four-quarter percentage change in unfilled vacancies (as a percentage of employment) and p^e is the percentage change in expected prices. The model is based on Parkin's work and the estimation is done using Carlson-Parkin's expectations data.[6]

A motivation for specifying the wage-price behaviour with randomly varying coefficients is that the short run Phillips curve is inherently unstable; the factors generating instability are: improper characterisations of labour markets, ignoring the presence of adjustment costs, lags and erratic policy shocks to the economy, among others However, the existence of a long run inflation-unemployment tradeoff relationship suggests that the operational Phillips curve is an average relationship. Thus the approach of specifying the wage-price relationship with varying coefficients, which allows the coefficients to be different with observation, seems appropriate.

We assume that $\beta_{ki} = \beta_k + \varepsilon_{ki}$ (k=1,2,3) and that the stochastic components are contemporaneously and serially uncorrelated. Then, using the operational RR estimators of β_k's, the estimated equation is

$$(7.12) \qquad P_i = \underset{(0.6394)}{1.2010} + \underset{(0.6347)}{1.3650}\, V_i + \underset{(0.2707)}{1.0987}\, P_i^e.$$

Further, R^2=0.7404, D.W.$_4$=1.0654, m=1, c=0.4113 and n=52, where R^2 is the coefficient of determination, D.W.$_4$ is a fourth order Durbin-Watson statistic, m is the multicollinearity allowance, c is the ridge coefficient and n the number of observations. We note that even though the D.W.$_4$ value is low all coefficients have the right sign. The coefficient of p^e supports Friedman's hypothesis that the coefficient of the anticipated inflation variable is unity. Further, as reflected by the coefficient of the vacancy rate, the hypothesis that excess demand for labour will result in a more rapid rise in nominal wage appears to be tenable. Finally we note that the estimated variance of the coefficient of the price expectations variable is 1.3873, which is 27% larger than the estimate of the mean coefficient 1.0987.

It is important to point out that estimates of the vector of variances, $\dot{\sigma}$, of random coefficients are obtained from the regression relation

$$(7.13) \qquad \hat{\dot{u}} = G\dot{\sigma} + w ,$$

where $\hat{\dot{u}}$ is the vector of squared least squares residuals and G is a matrix of observations on a set of regressors, which are nonlinear transforms of the explanatory variables (see Chapter 4).

When explanatory variables x_k's are highly (linearly) related then it may be more appropriate to obtain a ridge estimator of $\dot{\sigma}$ in (7.13) instead of the least squares estimator. A ridge estimator of $\dot{\sigma}$ in (7.13) is given by

$$(7.14) \qquad \hat{\dot{\sigma}}_R = (G'G + \ell I)^{-1} G'\hat{\dot{u}},$$

where the ridge coefficient $\ell > 0$ may be determined

by one of the methods discussed earlier. Then these ridge estimates of unknown variances may be used to obtain an operational RR estimator. Note that we are applying the ridge method twice; once in obtaining the estimator of $\dot{\sigma}$ and the second time in obtaining estimates of β. This new procedure may therefore be called the two stage random ridge (2SRR) estimator.

We will now discuss an illustration of the 2SRR estimation. Consider the estimation of a nonhomogeneous Cobb-Douglas production function with purely random coefficients:[7]

$$(7.15) \qquad y_i = \beta_{1i} + \beta_{2i} x_{2i} + \beta_{3i} x_{3i},$$

where y, x_2 and x_3 represent logs of output, capital and labour inputs respectively; and β_{ki}(k=1, 2,3) are varying coefficients. We hypothesise that the efficiency parameter β_{1i} varies linearly with the log of a 'Hicks-neutral' technological change and an additive stochastic term. Further, we hypothesise that output elasticities of capital and labour β_{2i} and β_{3i} respectively vary linearly with the log of the level of each input and the additive stochastic term. Accordingly,

$$(7.16) \qquad \begin{aligned} \beta_{1i} &= \beta_1 + \beta_7 x_{7i} + \varepsilon_{1i}, \\ \beta_{2i} &= \beta_2 + \beta_5 x_{2i} + \beta_4^{*} x_{3i} + \varepsilon_{2i}, \\ \beta_{3i} &= \beta_3 + \beta_4^{**} x_{2i} + \beta_6 x_{3i} + \varepsilon_{3i}, \end{aligned}$$

where x_{7i} is the ith observation on the log of a proxy for the 'Hicks-neutral' technological change; ε's are random variables satisfying the following assumptions:

(7.17) $E\varepsilon_{ki} = 0$, for all k and i,

$E\varepsilon_{ki}\varepsilon_{k'i'} = \sigma_k^2$, for k=k' and i=i',

$= 0$, otherwise.

Also, the x's are uncorrelated with ε's.

Substituting (7.16) into (7.15), we write

$$y_i = \beta_1 + \beta_2 x_{2i} + \beta_3 x_{3i} + \beta_4 x_{4i} + \beta_5 x_{5i} + \beta_6 x_{6i} + \beta_7 x_{7i} + u_i, \tag{7.18}$$

where

(7.19) $\beta_4 = \beta_4^* + \beta_4^{**}$,

$x_{4i} = x_{2i} x_{3i}$,

$x_{5i} = x_{2i}^2$,

$x_{6i} = x_{3i}^2$,

and

$$u_i = \varepsilon_{1i} + \varepsilon_{2i} x_{2i} + \varepsilon_{3i} x_{3i}. \tag{7.20}$$

Using assumption (7.17), it is easily verified that

$Eu_i = 0$, for all i,

$Eu_i^2 = \sigma_1^2 + \sigma_2^2 x_{2i}^2 + \sigma_3^2 x_{3i}^2 = d_{ii}$,

$Eu_i u_{i'} = 0$, if $i \neq i'$.

It may be noted that production model (7.18) used in this example is a variant of the transcendental logarithmic (trans-log) production model developed by Christensen, Jorgenson and Lau (1973). The trans-log model, which specifies the log of output as a second order Taylor series expansion of the arguments in the log production function, can be interpreted as a systematically varying coefficient Cobb-Douglas production function. In the specification (7.18) we have added appropriate random components to allow for misspecifications in the functional form and omitted variables, etc. (see Chapter 1).

The estimation of β's in (7.18) can be obtained from the 2SRR estimator to account for multicollinearity among explanatory variables. The model (7.17) was estimated by Vinod and Raj (1978) using the Bell system data for 1947-1976 with n=30. The dependent variable y was log of net deflated 'value added', x_2 was log of net deflated capital stock, x_3 was log of weighted employee-hours and x_7 was log of a Poisson weighted index of technology. The proxy variable for 'Hicks neutral' technology was computed by using Research and Fundamental Developmental expenses by the Bell system telephone companies deflated by the consumer price index. The output variable was constructed from five price indices having 1967 as the base year for revenue accounts. In computing the capital stock variable 23 plant accounts with appropriate detail regarding the age of plant, depreciation and specific price indices with 1967 as base were considered. Finally, the employee hours variable was constructed from six occupational categories with three or more seniority classifications weighted by average remuneration in 1967.

The ridge estimates of the vector of variances $\dot{\sigma}= (\sigma_1^2, \sigma_2^2, \sigma^2{}_3)'$ were obtained from (7.14), where

$G=\dot{M}\dot{\underline{X}}$, $\dot{M}=M*M$, $\dot{\underline{X}}=\underline{X}*\underline{X}$, $M=I-X(X'X)^{-1}X'$, and X and $\underline{X}$ are matrices of order 30x7 and 30x3 of observations on seven and three explanatory variables on the right hand side of equations (7.18) and (7.20) respectively. The matrix G'G had eigenvalues $\lambda_1=2.7472$, $\lambda_2=0.2473$ and $\lambda_3=0.0055$. This suggests severe illconditioning of the matrix (G'G) because $\sqrt{\lambda_1}/\sqrt{\lambda_3}$ is large. The biasing ridge coefficient in (7.14) $\ell=.00348$ was numerically evaluated from the Index of Stability of Relative Magnitude for the multicollinearity allowance m=1. The ridge estimates of σ_1^2, σ_2^2 and σ_3^2 are .0033, $-1.7179\text{x}10^{-5}$ and $1.1032\text{x}10^{-5}$ respectively. We note that least squares estimates of σ_1^2, σ_2^2 and σ_3^2, for $\ell=0$ are: 0.0049, $-1.32\text{x}10^{-5}$ and $-2.96\text{x}10^{-5}$ respectively. Thus, the ridge estimate of σ_2^2 is slightly less negative than the least squares estimate. Further, the ridge estimate of σ_3^2 is positive whereas the least squares estimate is negative.

The operational two stage ridge estimators of β's in (7.17) were obtained from

$$(7.20)\qquad \hat{\beta}=(X'\hat{D}^{-1}X+cI)^{-1}X'\hat{D}^{-1}y,$$

where $\hat{D}$ is an estimator of D obtained by using the truncated estimates of σ_k^2's. The matrix of regressions $\hat{D}^{-1/2}X$ is ill-conditioned since the eigenvalues of the correlation matrix of seven regressors weighted by the inverse of the square root of heteroscedastic variances are respectively: 5.8330, 1.0000, 0.1223, $0.4455\text{x}10^{-1}$, $0.1192\text{x}10^{-3}$, $0.4805\text{x}10^{-5}$ and $0.2208\text{x}10^{-6}$. Therefore, we obtained the value of biasing coefficient c=0.0637 corresponding to multicollinearity allowance m=4 from the Index of Stability of Relative Magnitude. Finally, the two stage ridge estimates we obtained as: $\hat{\beta}_1=-13.7651$, $\hat{\beta}_2=0.2229$, $\hat{\beta}_3=0.2822$, $\hat{\beta}_4=0.0130$, $\hat{\beta}_5=0.0214$, $\hat{\beta}_6=0.0198$ and $\hat{\beta}_7=0.3169$.

The estimate of scale elasticity for the stochastic production function (7.17) may be obtained from

$$\varepsilon_t = E[\partial y_t/\partial x_{2t}+\partial y_t/\partial x_{3t}]$$

$$= \beta_2+\beta_3+\beta_4(x_{2t}+x_{3t})+2\beta_5 x_{2t}+2\beta_6 x_{3t}.$$

The average scale elasticity, evaluated at the mean value of logs of inputs $\bar{x}_2=8.5887$ and $\bar{x}_3=10.2208$, is $\bar{\varepsilon}=1.3987$. This point estimate of scale elasticity for the Bell system was found to be similar with the estimates obtained by other methods.

NOTES

1. The matrix D is the variance-covariance matrix of disturbance vector $u=(u_1, u_2,...,u_T)'$, that is $Euu'=D$, see Chapter 4.

2. Panel data represents a time series of cross-section observations.

3. See Hoerl and Kennard (1970a). The value of Kx1 vector of coefficients β is obtained by minimising the function. $S^*=(Y-X\beta)'D^{-1}(y-X\beta)+c(\beta'\beta-r^2)$ where c is a Lagrange multiplier. Differentiating S^* with respect to β and equating to zero gives

$$-2X'D^{-1}y+2X'D^{-1}X\beta+2cI\beta=0.$$

The solution to these normal equations gives the estimator in (7.6); see Swamy (1973). A critique of the ridge estimator is given in Smith and Campbell (1980).

4. See Vinod (1978). An alternative method of determining ridge coefficient c is given in Swamy, Mehta and Rappoport (1978).

5. See Parikh and Raj (1979). The data sources are also given in their paper.

6. See Carlson and Parkin (1975).

7. See Vinod and Raj (1978).

8. Polynomial Distributed Lag

8.1 INTRODUCTION

In this chapter we consider the estimation problem in a purely random coefficients model where the influence of the explanatory variable is distributed over a finite number of lagged values. Some of the estimation methods discussed in Chapter 7 are appropriate here. In addition we specify and make use of either a deterministic prior or a probabilistic prior information in the form of weights to be assigned to lagged coefficients so as to obtain a smooth lag pattern for the means of purely random coefficients in the distributed lag model and discuss estimation methods under this extraneous information. Various methods of estimation of lag coefficients are then illustrated with the help of the data set of Almon (1968).

8.2 DISTRIBUTED LAG MODEL WITH RANDOMLY VARYING COEFFICIENTS

In a distributed lag with purely random coefficients model the influence of the explanatory variable or variables is distributed over a number of periods. Accordingly, the current value of the dependent variable depends on the current as well as past values of the explanatory variable or variables. A distributed lag model with one explanatory variable with a total finite lag of length s can be written as

$$(8.1)\qquad y_i = \sum_{k=0}^{s-1} \beta_{ki} x_{i-k} + u_i, \qquad i=s,s+1,..,n,$$

where y_i is the ith observation on the dependent variable, x_{i-k} is the ith observation on the kth period lag value of the explanatory variable x, and u is the usual disturbance term in the equation. Finally, the β_k's are varying coefficients of the distributed lag model such that

$$(8.2)\qquad \beta_{ki} = \beta_k + \varepsilon_{ki}, \qquad k=0,1,..s-1,$$

where β_k and ε_{ki} are respectively the (fixed) systematic and random parts of the varying coefficients. There are in principle no additional estimation problems in the model (8.1) under the simplifying assumptions about the ε's, u and x's outlined in Chapter 4, namely:

(8.3) (a) $Eu_i = E\varepsilon_{ki} = 0,$ for all i and k;

(b) $Eu_i \varepsilon_{ki} = 0,$ for all i and k;

(c) $Eu_i u_{i'} = \sigma_u^2,$ if i=i';

$= 0$ otherwise;

(d) $E\varepsilon_{ki}\varepsilon_{k'i'} = \sigma_k^2,$ if i=i' and k=k';

(e) The x_{i-k} is either nonstochastic or, if stochastic, independent of ε_{ki} and u_i for all i and k.

Thus one could employ one of the estimation methods discussed in Chapter 4. The above point can be easily verified by substituting (8.2) into (8.1) and writing

$$(8.4) \qquad y_i = \sum_{k=0}^{s-1} \beta_k x_{i-k} + w_i,$$

where

$$(8.5) \qquad w_i = u_i + \sum_{k=0}^{s-1} \varepsilon_{ki} x_{i-k}.$$

Now, under assumption (8.3) the composite disturbance terms w_i's have zero mean and are uncorrelated with the x's. Further, the disturbances are heteroscedastic. Thus, given the knowledge about the second moments of the distribution of the stochastically varying coefficients, the best linear unbiased estimates of the regression coefficients, β's, in (8.4) can be obtained by applying the generalised least squares (GLS) procedure. However, in practice several difficulties arise. First, a choice of long distributed lag may leave very few degrees of freedom for estimation and hypothesis testing process. Second, the various lagged values of the explanatory variable will typically be highly intercorrelated, leading to a high degree of multicollinearity. This, in turn, means that the estimates of lagged coefficients will be very imprecise and useful inferences about them extremely difficult. Thus the length of lag about which a firm indication is rarely available cannot be determined precisely from the data by fitting a long lag. These difficulties can be resolved with or without imposing **a priori** assumptions about the form of the weights for β's in (8.4). Furthermore, the prior information can be deterministic or probabilistic. It is important to note that **a priori** assumptions about the form of weights, whether deterministic or probabilistic, are imposed in an attempt to produce a smooth lag pattern for the lagged coefficients, and are referred to as smoothness priors. In what follows we discuss the estimation of a lagged relationship (8.4) in three situations: (i) Without smoothness priors; (ii) With polynomial deterministic priors; and (iii) With polynomial probabilistic priors.

8.3 RANDOM RIDGE ESTIMATOR

The model (8.4) can be compactly written as

$$y = X\beta + w, \tag{8.6}$$

where

$$y = (y_s, \ldots, y_n)',$$

$$\beta = (\beta_0, \beta_1, \ldots, \beta_{s-1})',$$

$$w = (w_s, \ldots, w_n)'$$

and X is an (n-s)xs matrix of observation on the explanatory variable x and its lagged values, namely,

$$X = \begin{bmatrix} x_s & x_{s-1} & \cdots & x_1 \\ x_{s+1} & x_s & \cdots & x_2 \\ \vdots & \vdots & & \vdots \\ x_n & x_{n-1} & & x_{n-s+1} \end{bmatrix} \tag{8.7}$$

such that [under assumptions (8.3)]

$$Ew = 0, \qquad Eww' = \text{diag.}(w_{ss}, \ldots, w_{nn}) = D \tag{8.8}$$

with

$$w_{ii} = \sigma_u^2 + \sum_{k=0}^{s-1} x_{i-k}^2 \sigma_k^2, \qquad \text{for } i = s, s+1, \ldots, n.$$

Assuming $s<(n-s)$ and σ^2's are known, a simple solution to the dual problems of multicollinearity and heteroscedasticity in model (8.6) without smoothness priors requires that we minimise

$$(y-X\beta)'D^{-1}(y-X\beta)$$

subject to the condition $\beta'\beta= r^2<\infty$. This would yield an estimator

$$(8.9) \qquad \hat{\beta}_{RR}= [X'D^{-1}X+\mu I]^{-1}X'D^{-1}y,$$

which following Chapter 7 is termed as the Random Ridge (RR) estimator. As noted in Chapter 7 the RR estimator (8.9) makes allowance for the heteroscedasticity problem in model (8.6) and generalises the ordinary ridge estimator developed by Hoerl and Kennard (1970) for the standard linear regression model with fixed coefficients. Further, the estimator $\hat{\beta}_{RR}$ would exist even when the rank of X is less than s; that is when the columns of the matrix X are linearly dependent. However, the estimator $\hat{\beta}_{RR}$ is biased while the GLS estimator of β in model (8.6), which is a particular case of (8.9) for $\mu=0$, is an unbiased estimator. The estimator $\hat{\beta}_{RR}$ may be preferred over the GLS estimator because there exists some $\mu>0$ such that the mean squared error of $\hat{\beta}_{RR}$ is smaller than the mean squared error of the GLS estimator $\hat{\beta}=(X'D^{-1}X)^{-1}X'D^{-1}y$.

The RR estimator requires an estimate of μ, which may be obtained by using one of the methods discussed in Chapter 7. For example, one could use an iterative procedure suggested by Lindley and Smith (1972) with initial starting values of the GLS estimates of β_k. That is

$$\mu = \frac{1}{s-1} \sum_{k=0}^{s-1} (\hat{\beta}_k - \beta_m)^2$$

where $\beta_m = \frac{1}{s-1} \sum_{k=0}^{s-1} \hat{\beta}_k$ is the average value of $\hat{\beta}$'s. The estimate of μ is revised based on new estimates until its value converges.

It was also noted in Chapter 7 that the RR estimator (8.9) has two alternative interpretations. First, it can be interpreted as a matrix weighted average of the null vector and the vector of generalised least squares estimates. This interpretation follows from the fact that the RR estimator can be written as $\hat{\beta}_{RR} = \Delta\hat{\beta}$ where

$$\Delta = [1+\mu(X'D^{-1}X)^{-1}]^{-1}$$

is the correction factor which shrinks the GLS estimator $\hat{\beta}$ by a fixed percentage towards the null vector. Second, it can be interpreted in a Bayesian sense as the mean of the posterior distribution of β in the model (8.6) with $\mu=1/\sigma_\beta^2$ under the assumption [in addition to assumptions (8.3a) to (8.3e)] that the (sx1) vector β is a random vector whose prior distribution is normal with mean vector 0 and variance-covariance matrix $\sigma_\beta^2 I$.

The RR estimator also requires estimates of σ_u^2's and σ_k^2's for k=0,1,2,..s-1, in D. Several methods of obtaining consistent estimators of σ^2's are discussed in Chapters 4 and 5. For example, one may obtain the consistent estimators of σ^2's from the operational GLS estimator $\tilde{\dot{\sigma}}=(G'\hat{\dot{\Psi}}^{-1}G)^{-1}G'\hat{\dot{\Psi}}^{-1}\hat{\dot{w}}$ of the column vector $\dot{\sigma}=(\sigma_u^2, \sigma_0^2, .., \sigma_{s-1}^2)'$; $\hat{\dot{w}}=\hat{w}*\hat{w}$ where $\hat{w}=My$ is a vector of least squares residuals in model (8.6); $G=(M*M)(\underline{X}*\underline{X})$ and $\hat{\dot{\Psi}}=\hat{\Psi}*\hat{\Psi}$ where * represents the Hadamard matrix product; $\hat{\Psi}=M\hat{D}M$; $M=I-X(X'X)^{-1}X'$ and $\underline{X}=(\iota,X)$ where ι is a column vector of unit elements. Note that σ_u^2 is identified in model (8.6) since the model does not involve a random intercept term.

Thus, the operational RR estimator of β in (8.6) is given as

$$(8.9) \qquad \tilde{\beta}_{RR} = (X'\hat{D}^{-1}X + \mu I)^{-1}X'\hat{D}^{-1}y,$$

where $\hat{D}$ is a consistent estimator of D.

As an illustration of the methods discussed above, consider the data set of Almon, reproduced in Table 8.1, with the assumption that the lag length s=9 is known to compute the coefficients in (8.6). The Almon data consist of 60 seasonally adjusted observations for capital expenditure (y) and capital appropriations (x) on all manufacturing in the United States for the years 1953-1967 measured quarterly in millions of dollars. The generalised least squares estimates of β's from (8.9) for $\mu=0$ are: .06141, .14017, .16718, .22503, .09550, .02605, .11689, .13309, .02030. These estimated coefficients produce an erratic lag pattern, which reveals a potential difficulty in applying the generalised least squares to the model (8.6) in the presence of multicollinearity. One way to ameliorate the effects of the multicollinearity problem is to apply the (biased) RR estimation technique which is insensitive to small data revisions. The RR estimates of coefficients from (8.9) are: .12141, .12780, .13085, .13687, .11795, .09750, .09769, .08332, .06877. These estimates produce a smooth (perhaps oversmooth) lag pattern for the coefficients in model (8.6). This is not surprising since a large ridge coefficient value $\hat{\mu} = 2055$ is obtained by the iterative method discussed above. The convergence is obtained in 15 iterations.

Table 8.1: Almon's data on capital expenditure (y) and appropriations (x) for the years 1953 quarter I to 1967 quarter IV.

n	y	x	n	y	x
1	2072	1660	31	2721	2131
2	2077	1926	32	2640	2552
3	2078	2181	33	2513	2234
4	2043	1897	34	2448	2282
5	2062	1695	35	2429	2533
6	2067	1705	36	2516	2517
7	1964	1731	37	2534	2772
8	1981	2151	38	2494	2380
9	1914	2556	39	2596	2568
10	1991	3152	40	2572	2944
11	2129	3763	41	2601	2629
12	2309	3903	42	2648	3133
13	2614	3912	43	2840	3449
14	2896	3571	44	2937	3764
15	3058	3199	45	3136	3983
16	3309	3262	46	3299	4381
17	3446	3476	47	3514	4786
18	3466	2993	48	3815	4094
19	3435	2262	49	4093	4870
20	3183	2011	50	4262	5344
21	2697	1511	51	4531	5433
22	2338	1631	52	4825	5911
23	2140	1990	53	5160	6109
24	2012	1993	54	5319	6542
25	2071	2520	55	5574	5785
26	2192	2804	56	5749	5707
27	2240	2919	57	5715	5412
28	2421	3024	58	5637	5465
29	2639	2725	59	5383	5550
30	2733	2321	60	5467	5465

Source: National Industrial Board

The advantages of the RR estimator, which is biased towards zero, is that it does not produce an erratic lag pattern for the regression coefficients in the model (8.6) when there is no **a priori** assumption about smoothness priors. The disadvantage is that it oversmooths the lag pattern for the regression coefficients.

8.4 RANDOM ALMON ESTIMATOR

It is clear from the above illustrative example that on the one hand the lag shape produced by the GLS estimator technique is erratic because of the multicollinearity problem whereas the smooth lag pattern may be desirable. On the other hand, the lag pattern produced by the random ridge estimation technique, which makes allowance for the multicollinearity, can produce an oversmooth lag pattern for the lag coefficients in the model (8.6). A way out of these difficulties is to impose prior information about the form of the weights on β's in an attempt to produce more amenable estimates which are free from the multicollinearity problem and involve fewer than s parameters to estimate directly. A stronger parameterisation for the lag structure would be to assume **a priori** not just the form of the weights but the actual values. The problem with this approach may be that such strong **a priori** knowledge is not available. A weaker parameterisation might be more desirable. For example, we may assume that the weights follow a particular form. Thus, we could assume that β_k declines arithmetically over the known lag length and obtain a linear distributed lag model. More generally, we may assume that β_k follows a path described by a low degree polynomial of degree $(r-1)<s$, that is

$$\beta_k = \delta_0 + \delta_1 k + \delta_2 k^2 + \ldots + \delta_{r-1} k^{r-1},$$

for k=0,...,(s-1). These prior nonstochastic (deterministic) constraints on the lagged coefficients β_k's can be compactly written as

(8.10) $\beta = C\delta,$

where $\delta = (\delta_0, \delta_1, \ldots, \delta_{r-1})'$ and C is a sxr matrix of known values, that is

(8.11) $$C = \begin{bmatrix} 1 & 0 & \ldots & 0 \\ 1 & 1 & \ldots & 1 \\ \vdots & \vdots & & \vdots \\ 1 & (s-1) & \ldots & (s-1)^{r-1} \end{bmatrix}.$$

The estimation problem under smoothness priors (8.10) can proceed as described below. First, we substitute (8.10) into (8.6) and obtain

(8.12) $y = Z\delta + w,$

where Z=XC is an (n-s)xr matrix of observations on newly constructed variables z's, which are weighted averages of x and its lagged values. Then assuming that the ranks of matrices X and C are s and r respectively, and the dispersion matrix D is known, we can derive the GLS estimator of δ in (8.12) as

(8.13) $\hat{\delta} = (Z'D^{-1}Z)^{-1}Z'D^{-1}y,$

which is the best linear unbiased estimator of δ. Thereafter we can get the estimator of β by substituting $\hat{\delta}$ in (8.10). Thus the estimator of β under deterministic smoothness priors is

$$(8.14) \qquad \hat{\beta}_{RA} = C\hat{\delta} = C(Z'D^{-1}Z)^{-1}Z'D^{-1}y.$$

The estimator (8.14) may be termed as a random Almon (RA) estimator of β because it estimates the means of randomly varying coefficients in a distributed lag model where the means of the lagged coefficients are restricted to lie on an Almon polynomial. When the dispersion matrix D is not known, an approximate RA estimator can be obtained by replacing D in (8.14) by its consistent estimator. Several methods of obtaining the consistent estimator of D have been discussed in Chapters 4 and 5.

The point to note is that as shown in Section 5.2 of Chapter 5, all operational RA estimators such as

$$(8.15) \qquad \hat{\beta}_{RA} = C(Z'\hat{D}^{-1}Z)^{-1}Z'\hat{D}^{-1}y,$$

where different consistent estimators of D are utilised, will have identical distributions asymptotically, which in turn are equal to distribution of the RA estimator (8.14). We note that in obtaining consistent estimates of σ^2's, which are used to obtain a consistent estimator of D, one may appropriately regress the square of least squares residuals from (8.12) instead of least squares residuals from (8.6), on the transforms of regressor x and its lagged values. The motivation for using least squares residuals from (8.12), which are termed as Almon residuals, in computing estimates of σ^2's is that they incorporate smoothness prior knowledge whereas the least squares residuals do not. The Almon residuals, which are given by $\hat{w}_A=\underline{M}y$, $\underline{M}=I-Z(Z'Z)^{-1}Z'$, are used to obtain the operational GLS estimator of $\dot{\sigma}$ in the numerical example of the RA method discussed below.

We assume that the lag weights follow a quadratic polynomial so that $\beta_k=\delta_0+\delta_1 k+\delta_2 k^2$. Employing the data set of Almon with the assumption that the lag length (s=9) is known, the following operational RA estimates of β's are obtained: .12020, .13177, .13716, .13638, .12941, .11628, .09696, .07147, .03981. We note that the GLS estimator of $\dot{\sigma}=(\sigma_u^2, \sigma_o^2,..,\sigma^2_{s-1})'$ is used in computing D. Note that the imposition of deterministic priors smooth the erratic lag pattern produced by the GLS estimates. The reason for this is that the estimation of β_k's under deterministic smoothness priors removes the ill effects of multicollinearity since we regress y on a fewer number of newly-formed weighted linearly independent variables z's in the transformed model (8.12). One final point to note is that the Almon estimator of vector β of lagged coefficients in a polynomial distributed lag model with fixed obtained as a special case of the RA estimator (8.14) when $\sigma_k^2=0$ for k=0,1,2,...,s-1 and $\sigma_u^2\neq 0$, that is $D=\sigma_u^2 I$. The Almon estimator is given by

$$(8.15a) \qquad \hat{\beta}_A= C(Z'Z)^{-1}Z'y.$$

8.5 BAYESIAN RANDOM ESTIMATOR

The specification of deterministic priors (8.10) for the distributed lag model with purely random coefficients is also restrictive in the sense that the exact knowledge of the degree of polynomial is assumed whereas such prior knowledge is rarely available. Shiller (1973) has argued that deterministic smoothness priors are often specified not because we believe in them but because the lag distribution is smooth. Since our prior knowledge is actually probabilistic it would be better to formulate the prior information in probabilistic terms. Assuming that the β's lie on the stochastic polynomial priors of degree (r-1), we write

$$(8.16) \qquad \beta_k = \delta_0 + \delta_1 k + \delta_2 k^2 + \ldots + \delta_{r-1} k^{r-1} + v_k,$$

$k=0,1,2,\ldots,s-1$, where v_k is the disturbance term representing the probabilistic nature of the prior knowledge. These disturbances are assumed to be distributed with zero mean and common variance σ_v^2. We further assume that v is uncorrelated with itself and with ε's, x's and u. The stochastic (or probabilistic) smoothness priors can be compactly written as

$$(8.17) \qquad \beta = C\delta + v,$$

where β, C and δ were defined earlier and

$$v = (v_0, v_1, \ldots, v_{s-1})'$$

so that

$$Ev=0 \text{ and } Evv' = \sigma_v^2 I.$$

Further, since C is a sxr matrix of rank r, one can find a matrix R of order (s-r)xr such that RC=0 where

$$R=\begin{bmatrix} (-1)^0\binom{r}{0} & (-1)^1\binom{r}{1} \cdots & (-1)^r\binom{r}{r} & \cdots 0 \\ 0 & (-1)^0\binom{r}{0} \cdots & (-1)^r\binom{r}{r} & \cdots 0 \\ \vdots & & & \vdots \\ 0 & 0 & (-1)^0\binom{r}{0} \cdots & (-1)^r\binom{r}{r} \end{bmatrix}.$$

See Shiller (1973), p. 777; and Teräsvirta (1976). Thus we can write the stochastic smoothness priors (8.17) as

(8.18) $\quad R\beta = Rv$

such that $ERv=0$ and $ERvv'R'=\sigma_v^2 RR'=\sigma_\beta^2 RR'$.

The estimation of β in (8.6) under (8.18) may be obtained by the Bayesian method. Assuming that the prior distributions of β and δ are respectively normal(with mean $C\delta$ and dispersion matrix $\sigma_\beta^2 I = \sigma_v^2 I$) and diffused (reflecting that the prior information is weak), then applying the Bayes theorem, we can obtain the following estimator of β in (8.6) under the stochastic smoothness prior (8.18) as

(8.19) $\quad \hat{\beta}_{BR} = [X'D^{-1}X+\eta R'(RR')^{-1}R]^{-1}X'D^{-1}y,$

where $\eta=(1/\sigma_\beta^2)=(1/\sigma_v^2)$. The estimator (8.19) may be termed the Bayes Random (BR) estimator. This estimator is a ridge type estimator and can be alternatively derived by minimising the criterion function $(y-X\beta)'D^{-1}(y-X\beta)'+\eta[R'(RR')^{-1}R-h^2]$ with respect to β. That is, the criterion function is weighted residual sum of squares with weights proportional to the inverse of the dispersion matrix and the constraint is $R'(RR)'^{-1}R=h^2$, where h is a finite given constant. When D is not known one may obtain an operational BR estimator from

$$(8.20)\qquad \tilde{\beta}_{BR} = [X'\hat{D}^{-1}X+\eta R'(RR')^{-1}R]^{-1}X'\hat{D}^{-1}y,$$

where the unknown dispersion matrix D in (8.19) is replaced by its consistent estimator. Once again, from the point of large sample theory, all that is required is that D be replaced by a consistent estimator of D because all operational estimators so obtained can be shown to have identical distributions which are equal to the distribution of the BR estimator.

The Shiller (1973) estimator of the lag coefficients in a polynomial distributed lag model with fixed coefficients is a special case of the BR estimator when $D=\sigma_u^2 I$ and $RR'=I$. Shiller's formulation expresses probabilistic smoothness priors as the rth order difference equations for β_k's so that $R\beta=v$ instead of $R\beta=RV$ given in (8.18). The prior distribution of the error vector v is assumed to be normal with mean zero and the dispersion matrix $\sigma_v^2 I$.

As an illustration of the BR estimator we assume that probabilistic smoothness priors are of degree 2 and use the Almon data set referred to above to obtain the operational BR estimates from (8.20) as: .10458, .13326, .14749, .15924, .11877, .09538, .10238, .07992, .04014. The estimates of σ^2's are obtained as in the case of the RA estimator to form consistent estimator $\hat{D}$ used in (8.20). The ridge coefficient $\hat{k}$=855.060 is evaluated by using the iterative procedure of Lindley and Smith and it took only nine iterations to converge to the equilibrium value.

8.6 PURELY RANDOM VERSUS FIXED COEFFICIENT SPECIFICATIONS

The finite distributed lag with purely random coefficients model represents a class of weak specifications inthat weak prior knowledge is assumed. In order to evaluate its advantage over the specification of a distributed lag model with fixed coefficients, which is a strong specification, Ullah and Raj (1980) compared the lag patterns of the estimates obtained from various methods in Sections (8.4) and (8.5) with corresponding estimates obtained from various methods for the fixed coefficients model. Using Almon data the Almon estimates of the fixed lag coefficients for a nine period distributed lag and a second degree polynomial are obtained as: .10484, .12646, .13931, .14337, .13864, .12514, .10284, .07177, .03191. The lag pattern of the RA and Almon estimates are plotted in Figure 8.1.

Figure 8.1: LAG DISTRIBUTIONS

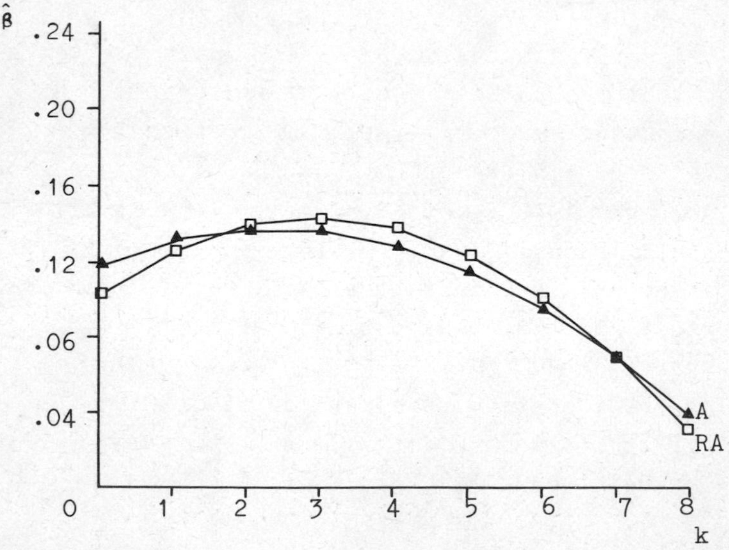

It is clear from Figure 8.1 that the lag pattern of the RA estimates is less smooth than the lag of Almon estimates. A similar conclusion was obtained when they compared the Bayesian Random estimates given above with the Shiller estimates for fixed coefficients model which are: .10225, .12721, .14132, .14484, .13854, .12355, .10091, .07120, .03463. The ridge coefficient value of 832.156 is obtained for Shiller estimator by the Lindley and Smith iterative procedure which required only four iterations to converge. Another point to note is that the lag pattern of Almon and Shiller estimates for a conventional fixed coefficient distributed lag model are almost identical. Thus, the choice between deterministic priors of Almon and the probabilistic priors of Shiller is difficult to make when strong specification of fixed coefficients is assumed. But, the lag pattern of Almon and Shiller type estimates in the distributed lag model with a weak specification of purely random coefficients can be distinguished.

8.7 EXTENSIONS

The analysis of polynomial distributed lag in a purely random coefficients model with a single explanatory variable x can be generalised to a situation where more than one explanatory variable is involved on the lines of Tinsley (1967) and Almon (1968) papers in the context of the fixed coefficients model. In Chapter 2 we considered various formulations for the randomly varying coefficients in the linear regression model. These alternative specifications for the randomly varying coefficients may be formulated instead of assuming that β's are purely random coefficients.

For example, one may assume a random and functional specification for β_{ki}. That is

$$\beta_{ki} = \beta_k + \gamma_k p_{i-k} + \varepsilon_{ki}, \tag{8.21}$$

where p is a policy variable. Under this formulation the specification (8.1) becomes a purely random coefficients model with two explanatory variables.

9. Stability of Regression Coefficients: Two Applications

9.1 INTRODUCTION

It is often difficult to justify a maintained hypothesis that the regression coefficients are stable over a sample interval. Stability(of estimated functional form) of economic relations is largely an empirical question. Stability is also closely connected with the empirical issue of choosing among appropriate definitions of the dependent and independent variables in the model. Alternative approaches to testing the stability of regression coefficients start with an assumed dynamic evolution of the regression coefficients in the model $y_i = x_i \beta_i^* + u_i$ for $i=1,2,..,n$, where y_i is a scalar observation on the dependent variable at time i, x_i is a 1xK row vector of known explanatory variables at time i and β_i^* is a Kx1 column vector of unknown coefficients at time i. The scalar disturbance u_i is assumed to be independently distributed with zero mean and constant variance. Various formulations of the evolution and tests of stability of β's are discussed below.

9.2 ALTERNATIVE FORMULATIONS

Suppose the dynamic evolution is random and functional. Then the regression model is $y_i = x_i \beta_i^*$ where a typical regression coefficient β_{ki}^*, $k=1,...,K$, is given by $\beta_{ki}^* = \beta_{k0} + \beta_{k1} f_{ki} + \varepsilon_{ki}$, such that f_{ki} is some function of time i. Thus, each coefficient is assumed to be subject to two influences that cause it to be deviated from its average value $_{ko}$. The first is the influence of factors that may vary systematically with time and the second is random influence. It is commonly assumed that the error terms ε_{ki}'s are mutually and serially independent. The function f_{ki} may represent a general form of the trend, viz., linear, parabolic, exponential, etc. This may also be specified differently for different regression coefficients. The stability test for the regression coefficients β_{ki}'s under such formulation becomes a test for the statistical significance of these coefficients. The above dynamic evolution is considered by Singh, Nagar, Choudhry and Raj (1976) (hereafter SNCR). This test has been used to test the structural change of the aggregate consumption function for Canada, Japan, Netherlands, Philippines and United Kingdom by SNCR and they are briefly discussed later in this chapter.

Another formulation of the dynamic evolution of β_{ki}'s following Cooley and Prescott (1973a) (hereafter CP) may be that they evolve adaptively. Accordingly, the regression model becomes $y_i=x_i\beta_i^*$ such that $\beta_i^*=\beta_i+u_i$ and $\beta_i=\beta_{i-1}+\varepsilon_i$ for $i=1,2,\ldots,n$ where β_i and u_i are normally distributed with zero means and the stationary covariance matrices Σ_ε^* and Σ_u^* respectively. The stability test for the regression coefficients under this formulation is a test of the null hypothesis: $\Sigma_\varepsilon^*=0$. A convenient parameterisation of Σ_ε^* and Σ_u^* and test of stability is discussed in Chapter 4. There are two drawbacks of this test. First, it is an asymptotic test and, second, it involves computations through numerical optimisation algorithms.

An exact and 'computationally well defined' test is discussed in La Motte and McWhorter (1978). The CP test is applied to testing the stability of the demand for money functions in Canada by Rausser and Laumas (1976), and it is also briefly discussed later in this chapter. Note that other more complex models of dynamic evolution of β's are possible. But, once the hypothesis of stable coefficients is rejected one might preferably consider explanation of structural instability of β's as a function of explanatory variables instead of considering more complex models of dynamic evolution of the coefficients.

Yet another formulation of the dynamic evolution of β's may be that they evolve adaptively but systematically over time, that is the hypothesis of $\Sigma^*_\varepsilon = \Sigma^*_u = 0$ in the adaptive coefficient formulation outlined above becomes a maintained hypothesis. Two methods of testing for the stability of regression coefficients under this formulation are suggested by Brown, Durbin and Evans (1975)(hereafter BDE). These tests are known as the 'cusum' (cumulative sum) test and 'cusum of squares' test.

These tests use recursive residuals which are based on least squares residuals in model $y_i = x_i \beta_{i-1} + v_i$ up to time i. It is intuitively clear and Garbade (1977) has shown that both the 'cusum' and 'cusum of squares' tests are closely related to the test based on an adaptive coefficients formulation under a true null hypothesis of $\Sigma^*_\varepsilon = 0$, that is stability of coefficients. Further, Garbade has presented some Monte Carlo evidence to suggest that it might be better to assume that coefficients followed an ARIMA (0,1,0) model and test this alternative against a null hypothesis of constancy of coefficients through the likelihood ratio (LR) test.[1]

When the evolution of β_{ki}'s is systematic and discontinuous, one could test the shift at a given point of time of β_{ki}'s by applying an F test, which is commonly referred to as Chow (1960) test. However, this test requires exact prior knowledge on how to divide the data with respect to two (or more) regimes, which is generally not available.

9.3 TWO APPLICATIONS

To provide further familiarity with the estimation and tests of stability with the randomly varying coefficients model, we shall discuss two applications in this chapter. The first involves the analysis of structural change in the consumption function for Canada, Japan, Netherlands, Philippines and United Kingdom. The second relates to stability for demand for money in Canada during the period covered.

9.3.1 The Analysis of Structural Change in Consumption Functions

To analyse the structural change in consumer behaviour SNCR utilised a randomly varying version of the consumption function

$$(9.1) \qquad y_i = \alpha_{1i} x_{1i} + \alpha_{2i} y_{i-1} \qquad i=1,2,\ldots,n,$$

where y_i and y_{i-1} respectively represent personal consumption expenditure at time i and i-1, and x_{1i} represents personal disposable income at time i. Further, the α_{1i} and α_{2i} represent the stochastically varying coefficients such that

$$(9.2) \qquad \alpha_{1i} = \beta_1 + \beta_3 i + \varepsilon_{1i}$$

and

$$(9.3) \qquad \alpha_{2i} = \beta_2 + \beta_4 i + \varepsilon_{2i}.$$

That is, the typical coefficient of the consumption function is subject to two influences that cause it to deviate from its usual fixed value. The first of these is the influence of the factors that cause the coefficient to vary systematically over time and proxied by the time variable i. The second is due to the stochastic disturbance term arising from the influence of unaccounted factors that cause the response to deviate from the systematic value. The following simplifying assumptions are made about the stochastic terms in (9.2) and (9.3). The terms ε_{1i} and ε_{2i} are normally distributed such that

$$(9.4) \qquad E\varepsilon_{1i} = E\varepsilon_{2i} = 0;$$

$$(9.5) \qquad var(\varepsilon_{1i}) = \sigma^2_{\beta_1}, \qquad var(\varepsilon_{2i}) = \sigma^2_{\beta_2};$$

$$(9.6) \qquad cov(\varepsilon_{1i}, \varepsilon_{2i'}) = 0, \qquad \text{for all i and i'}.$$

Substituting (9.2) and (9.3) into (9.1) and defining variables,

$$x_{2i} = y_{i-1},$$

$$x_{3i} = ix_{1i},$$

$$x_{4i} = iy_{i-1},$$

$$u_i = \varepsilon_{1i}x_{1i} + \varepsilon_{2i}x_{2i}$$

we write

$$(9.7) \qquad y_i = \beta_1 x_{1i} + \beta_2 x_{2i} + \beta_3 x_{3i} + \beta_4 x_{4i} + u_i .$$

The fixed coefficients β_k's (k=1,..,4) in model (9.7) may be estimated by any one of the methods discussed in Chapter 4. It is important to note that the disturbances u_i's are uncorrelated since the normal variates ε_{1i} and ε_{2i} are assumed to be serially independent. Thus, the problems associated with the use of lagged dependent variables x_{2i} and x_{4i} in conjunction with autocorrelation of disturbance terms, namely the bias and inconsistency, may not be present in estimating the coefficients in (9.7). This is especially true since the disturbances ε_{1i} and ε_{2i}, as assumed, are uncorrelated with the lagged dependent variable. Accordingly, we may estimate the parameters of the consumption function (9.7) for various countries by using the operational generalised least squares method (4.41) discussed in Chapter 4. The unknowns σ^2_β's in the variance-covariance matrix of the disturbances in (9.7) are obtained from the operational generalised least squares method (4.42). The estimated consumption equations are:

Canada (1950-1968):

$$y = \underset{(0.0790)}{0.4529^{**}} x_1 + \underset{(0.0998)}{0.5593^{**}} x_2 - \underset{(0.0124)}{0.0011} x_3 + \underset{(0.0149)}{0.0006} x_4 .$$

Estimates of $\sigma^2_{\beta_1}$ and $\sigma^2_{\beta_2}$ are:

$$\tilde{\sigma}^2_{\beta_1} = \underset{(0.0003)}{0.0008^{*}} \text{ and } \tilde{\sigma}^2_{\beta_2} = \underset{(9.0004)}{0.0012^{**}} .$$

Japan (1959-1967):

$$y = \underset{(0.1724)}{0.4866^{**}}x_1 + \underset{(0.2177)}{0.5323^{*}}x_2 + \underset{(0.0143)}{0.0307^{*}}x_3 - \underset{(0.0195)}{0.0495^{*}}x_4.$$

Estimates of $\sigma^2_{\beta_1}$ and $\sigma^2_{\beta_2}$ are:

$$\tilde{\sigma}^2_{\beta_1} = \underset{(0.0002)}{-0.0001} \text{ and } \tilde{\sigma}^2_{\beta_2} = \underset{(0.0004)}{0.0006}$$

Netherlands (1950-1966):

$$y = \underset{(0.1236)}{0.0858}x_1 + \underset{(0.1499)}{0.9908^{**}}x_2 + \underset{(0.0058)}{0.0361^{**}}x_3 - \underset{(0.0063)}{0.0484^{**}}x_4.$$

Estimates of $\sigma^2_{\beta_1}$ and $\sigma^2_{\beta_2}$ are:

$$\tilde{\sigma}^2_{\beta_1} = \underset{(0.0007)}{-0.0013} \text{ and } \tilde{\sigma}^2_{\beta_2} = \underset{(0.0013)}{0.0024}.$$

Philippines (1951-1968):

$$y = \underset{(0.1406)}{0.8946^{**}}x_1 + \underset{(0.1642)}{0.0798}x_2 - \underset{(0.0126)}{0.0448^{**}}x_3 + \underset{(0.0147)}{0.0493^{**}}x_4.$$

Estimates of $\sigma^2_{\beta_1}$ and $\sigma^2_{\beta_2}$ are:

$$\tilde{\sigma}^2_{\beta_1} = \underset{(0.0009)}{-0.0002} \text{ and } \tilde{\sigma}^2_{\beta_2} = \underset{(0.0013)}{0.0006}.$$

United Kingdom (1951-1968):

$$y = -0.2468x_1 + 1.3402^{**}x_2 + 0.0527^{**}x_3 - 0.0599^{**}x_4.$$
$$\quad (0.1911) \quad (0.2081) \quad (0.0164) \quad (0.0183)$$

Estimates of $\sigma^2_{\beta_1}$ and $\sigma^2_{\beta_2}$ are:

$$\tilde{\sigma}^2_{\beta_1} = -0.0005 \text{ and } \tilde{\sigma}^2_{\beta_2} = 0.0006.$$
$$(0.0003) \qquad (0.0003)$$

The numbers reported in the parentheses are standard errors of estimates. The statistical significance of the t-statistics of various parameter estmates at the 5 percent and 1 percent level has been indicated by a single star and double stars respectively. We now present analyses of these results in the light of the hypotheses implicit in (9.1) to (9.3).

The hypothesis that coefficients α_{1i} and α_{2i} vary stochastically for Canada during the sample period is supported by the t-statistics for esti mates of $\sigma^2_{\beta_1}$ and $\sigma^2_{\beta_2}$, which are statistically significant. In addition the t-statistics of estimates of systematic shift coefficients β_3 and β_4 in (9.2) and (9.3) are statistically insignificant. This suggests that perhaps the coefficients of consumption in Canada vary stochastically around a fixed constant rather than a linear trend. The large estimated value of the coefficient of β_2 reflects stickiness in consumer habits in the country, probably resulting from consumers' confidence in the economy, existence of a good social security system and easy availability of consumer credit.

Statistically insignificant t-statistics and sometmes wrong signs of estimates of $\sigma^2_{\beta_1}$ and $\sigma^2_{\beta_2}$

for Japan, Netherlands, Philippines and United Kingdom indicate the nonstochastic character of the coefficients of consumption functions of these countries. However, for these countries the coefficients of the consumption function appear to have undergone a systematic linear shift since the t-statistics of estimates of the trend coefficients, β_3 and β_4, in all cases are statistically significant. Furthermore, the rising and falling tendencies of the systematic components of the coefficients of x_{1i} and x_{2i} (that is, estimates of β_3 and β_4 are respectively positive and negative) for Japan, Netherlands and United Kingdom suggest that consumers in these countries are exhibiting increasing adaptability to changes in income and showing decreased reliance on the traditional habits. This suggests that there is structural change in the consumption pattern of these countries during the periods under study, resulting in increasing dependence on current income. This structural shift in consumption behaviour may have been due in part to increasing industrialisation with a consequently rising proportion of wage earners in the population in these countries. For example, workers in Japan are paid a low wage rate but enjoy a bonus scheme of a transient nature.

Finally, consumers in the Netherlands and United Kingdom may have felt an increase in urgency to conserve due to lack of confidence in their respective economies during the fifties. For example, the Netherlands experienced a recession during 1952-58 and an unstable balance of payments situation during the fifties in the heavily export dependent economy. Similarly, the British economy first faced the devaluation of the pound in 1959 and in 1967 heavy unemployment and inflation.

In the case of the Philippines the systematic component of the α_{1i} appears to be falling whereas the systematic component of α_{2i} is rising. This reflects increased confidence of the consumers in economic conditions in the Philippines resulting from vigorous industrial growth due to tax exemption, liberal credit during 1950-61 and substantial improvement in the agricultural sector following devaluation and decontrol in 1962. Moreover, the minimum wage law introduced in 1950 and of 1965, the land reform code of 1964 and a progressive welfare legislation may all have contributed to reducing uncertainty and increasing stickiness in consumer habits during the sample period.

9.3.2 Stability of the Demand for Money in Canada

The stochastically varying coefficients model, where the systematic parts vary sequentially over time, can be used to test for the stability of a functional relationship over time. In what follows we describe the stability test and then utilise it to test for stability of the aggregate demand for money function in Canada.

Consider eight alternative specifications for the short run aggregate demand for money function expressed in nominal terms:

$$\log M_i = \beta_i + \beta_{2i} \log Y_i + \beta_{3i} \log r_i, \quad (9.8)$$

where M represents money stock defined either as the value of the currency outside banks plus demand deposits at chartered banks (M_1) or as M_1 plus savings deposits at the chartered banks (M_2),

Y denotes either the gross national product (Y_1) or the permanent income (Y_2) and r represents either the treasury bill yield (r_1) or the long term government bond yield (r_2). β's are stochastically varying coefficients comprised of the sum of a permanent and a transitory component. The variation in the transitory part lasts only for a single period whereas the variation in the permanent part, once it has occurred, persists into the future. More formally the model (9.8) may be compactly written as

$$(9.9) \qquad y_i = x_i \beta_i^*,$$

where y_i represents the ith observation on the log of money stock, x_i is a three-component row vector of ith observation on the explanatory variables, the first element being one while the second and third represent the log of income and the interest rate variables respectively. The β_i^* is a three-component column vector of coefficients β_{1i}^*, β_{2i}^* and β_{3i}^* in period i. We assume that vector β_i^* varies stochastically from one period to the other such that

$$(9.10) \qquad \beta_i^* = \beta_i + u_i,$$

where u_i denotes the three-component column vector of transitory change in coefficients in time i and $_i$ represents in time i the three-component column vector of the permanent change in coefficients such that

$$(9.11) \qquad \beta_i = \beta_{i-1} + \varepsilon_i.$$

Thus, the permanent change vector in period i, β_i, differs from the permanent change vector in period i-1 by a random vector ε_i. This model is discussed in Section 4.3 of Chapter 4. We reproduce its salient features here for convenience.

We assume that the error vectors ε_i and u_i are normally distributed with zero mean - which remains the same in each period - and they are contemporaneously independent. Let Σ_ε^* and Σ_u^* be the dispersion matrices of ε_i and u_i respectively, then,

$$\varepsilon_i \sim N(0, \Sigma_\varepsilon^*), \; u_i \sim N(0, \Sigma_u^*),$$

$$E(\varepsilon_i \varepsilon_s') = E(u_i u_s') = 0 \quad \text{for } i \neq s$$

and

$$E(\varepsilon_i u'_i) = 0.$$

Further, since dispersion matrices Σ_ε^* and Σ_u^* are not independently identifiable, the following convenient reparameterisation is used. It is assumed that Σ_u^* and Σ_ε^* are known up to a scale factor such that

$$\text{(9.12)} \qquad \Sigma_u^* = \sigma^2(1-\lambda)\,\Sigma_u,$$

$$\Sigma_\varepsilon^* = \sigma^2\lambda\,\Sigma_\varepsilon ,$$

where σ^2 and $0 \leq \lambda \leq 1$ respectively represent the scaling and stability parameters to be estimated; Σ_u and Σ_ε are known matrices which may be identical if there is no reason to suspect that permanent changes are more or less important than transitory changes. Note that the stability parameter λ indicates the rate at which the varying coefficient vector β_i is adapting to structural change (or permanent change) in the demand for money function. For $\lambda=o$ the dispersion matrix $\Sigma_{\varepsilon}^{*}=o$, $\beta_i=\beta_{i-1}$ and the model (9.9) becomes $y_i=x_i\beta_i+x_iu_i$ so that the coefficients are stable but random. Thus λ is a measure of model stability and a test of the null hypothesis, $\lambda=o$, versus the alternative hypothesis, $\lambda\neq o$.

As noted in Chapter 4 the process generating the stochastically varying coefficients model (9.9) is nonstationary and thus it is impossible to specify the likelihood function and estimate the parameters of the model. However, the likelihood function conditional on the specific value of the stochastic process at some point of time is well defined. Thus, the use of the conditional likelihood function amounts to treating the unknown parameters as random but stationary. A convenient procedure is to focus on the value of the parameter process one period past the sample, so that $\beta_{n+1}^{*}=\beta$ (say) and (9.10) combined with (9.11) becomes

$$(9.13)\qquad \beta_i^{*}=\beta-\sum_{s=i+1}^{n+1}\varepsilon_s+u_i.$$

Substituting (9.13) in (9.9) yields

$$(9.14)\qquad y_i=x_i\beta+v_i,\qquad i=1,2,\dots,n,$$

where

$$(9.15)\qquad v_i=x_iu_i-x_i\sum_{s=i+1}^{n+1}\varepsilon_s$$

and $\beta_{n+1}^{*}=(\beta_{1,n+1}^{*},\beta_{2n+1}^{*},\beta_{3n+1}^{*})'=(\beta_1,\beta_2,\beta_3)'=\beta$. The n equationsin (9.14) can be compactly written as

$$(9.16) \qquad y = X\beta + v,$$

where y is an nx1 vector of observations on y, X is an nx3 matrix of observations on the explanatory variables in model (9.8) and v is an nx1 vector of observations on composite errors in (9.15).

It is easily verified that the error vector is normally distributed with mean zero and dispersion matrix (see Chapter 4).

$$(9.17) \qquad Evv' = \sigma^2[(1-\lambda)R+\lambda Q] = \sigma^2\Omega(\lambda),$$

where R is a diagonal matrix with $r_{ii} = x_i \Sigma_u^* x_i'$ and Q is a matrix whose i, jth element is $q_{ij} = \min(n-i+1, n-j+1) x_i \Sigma^* x_j'$. The concentrated likelihood is given by

$$(9.18) \qquad L_c(y;\lambda) = -\frac{n}{2}(\log 2\pi+1) - \frac{n}{2}\log s^2(\lambda) - \frac{1}{2}\log|\Omega(\lambda)|,$$

where

$$s^2(\lambda) = \frac{1}{n}[(y-X\hat{\beta})'\,\Omega^{-1}(\lambda)(y-X\hat{\beta})]$$

and

$$\hat{\beta} = [X'\Omega^{-1}(\lambda)X]^{-1}X'\Omega^{-1}(\lambda)y.$$

The strategy of maximisation in the likelihood estimation is to divide the range for λ (i.e. $0 \leq \lambda \leq 1$) into number of points and evaluate L_c for every value of λ such that the value of $L_c(y;\lambda)$ is maximised. To apply this technique Σ_u^* and Σ^* must be specified a priori. A convenient specification is that these two matrices are equal and diagonal. The equality of the matrices implies that relative importance of permanent and transitory changes in the stochastically varying coefficients are the

Table 9.1: Maximum Likelihood Estimates of Alternative Money Demand Functions for Canada

Specification	$\hat{\sigma}^2$	$\hat{\lambda}$	$Z = (\hat{\lambda}/\hat{\sigma}_{\lambda})$*
(1) $\log M_1 = -2.084 + 0.8302 \log Y_1 - 0.0689 \log r_1$ (1.863) (0.1650) (0.0232)	0.00116	0.5600 (0.1688)	3.3175**
(2) $\log M_1 = -2.188 + 0.8698 \log Y_1 - 0.2273 \log r_2$ (2.039) (0.1882) (0.1145)	0.00125	0.5800 (0.1694)	3.4238**
(3) $\log M_1 = 5.562 + 0.1527 \log Y_2 - 0.04287 \log r_1$ (1.086) (0.0960) (0.0279)	0.00167	0.9600 (0.1319)	7.2782**
(4) $\log M_1 = 5.677 + 0.1481 \log Y_2 - 0.06667 \log r_2$ (1.101) (0.0977) (0.1208)	0.00176	0.9800 (0.1274)	7.6923**
(5) $\log M_2 = -3.329 + 1.011 \log Y_1 - 0.0947 \log r_1$ (1.181) (0.1089) (0.0440)	0.00733	0.0200 (0.0192)	1.0433
(6) $\log M_2 = -2.272 + 0.9080 \log Y_1 - 0.0352 \log r_2$ (1.493) (0.1548) (0.1655)	0.00785	0.0200 (0.0192)	1.0433
(7) $\log M_2 = -2.392 + 0.9269 \log Y_2 - 0.0702 \log r_1$ (1.230) (0.1137) (0.0465)	0.00844	0.0200 (0.0192)	1.0433
(8) $\log M_2 = -0.9244 + 0.7676 \log Y_2 - 0.0953 \log r_2$ (1.464) (0.1539) (0.1644)	0.00869	0.0200 (0.0192)	1.0433

* $Z = \hat{\lambda}/\hat{\sigma}_{\lambda} \sim AN(0,1)$ under $Hc: \lambda = 0$

** denotes significantly different from zero at one percent level of significance.

same, and the diagonal property implies that structure changes in parameters are contemporaneously uncorrelated. Accordingly, we assume that $\Sigma_u^* = \Sigma_\varepsilon^*$=diag.(1,0,0), which is suitable for correcting for autocorrelation.

The maximum likelihood estimates of eight alternative specifications for demand for money in Canada are given in Table 9.1. These equations refer to a sample period covering the first quarter of 1954 through the third quarter of 1971. The base point n+1 for $\beta_{n+1}^* = \beta$ is the fourth quarter of 1971. Note that estimates of unknown parameters in both size and magnitude conform to a priori expectations. Further, the test for hypothesis =o indicates that: (i) The null hypothesis of stability of the aggregate demand function for money in Canada cannot be rejected when broad definition of money, M_2, is used as the dependent variable; (ii) The stability hypothesis, in contrast to (i) above, of the aggregate demand function for money in Canada can be rejected when the narrower definition for money, M_1 is used as the dependent variable; (iii) The short as well as the long interest rates yield stable demand functions for money in Canada; (iv) Both permanent income as well as current income appear to be valid constraints and yield almost stable demand for money functions when the broader definition is used as a dependent variable.

NOTES

1. Recently Pagan and Tanaka (1979) have proposed a Lagrange multiplier (LM) test of stability of coefficients. This test has the computational advantages of the BDE methods and the asymptotic power of the LR ratio test proposed by Garbade (1977).

Part Two
Multi Equations Varying Coefficient Models

10. Temporal Cross-Section Models

10.1 INTRODUCTION

Estimation of relationships which combine time series and cross-sectional data is a problem frequently encountered in econometrics. The problem is to specify a model which allows for differences in behaviour over such cross-sectional units as firms, households, geographical areas as well as differences in behaviour over time for a given cross-sectional unit. Once the model has been specified there are additional problems of getting efficient estimators of the parameters.

The model used in this context can be written as

$$(10.1) \qquad y_{it} = \sum_{k=1}^{K} \beta_{kit} x_{kit} + u_{it},$$

where $i=1,\ldots,n$ refers to cross-sectional units, $t=1,\ldots,T$ represents time period, y_{it} is the value of the dependent variable for i^{th} individual at time t, x_{kit} is the value of the kth explanatory variable for the ith individual at time t, and β_{kit} shows the response of y_{it} to a unit change in x_{kit}. We have n cross-section units with T observations on each.

10.2 MODEL WITH CROSS-SECTION EFFECT

For simplicity in exposition let us first consider the case of only one explanatory variable. Then (10.1) can be written as

$$y_{it} = \beta_{it} x_{it} + u_{it}. \tag{10.2}$$

We consider the Swamy-type specification for β_{it}, viz.:[1]

$$\beta_{it} = \beta_i = \beta + \varepsilon_i. \tag{10.3}$$

The disturbances u_{it} are all independent with means 0 and variances σ_i^2. The β_i's are random with means β and variances σ^2, i.e. $E\varepsilon_i = 0$ and $V(\varepsilon_i) = \sigma^2$. Also $\text{cov}(\varepsilon_i, \varepsilon_j) = 0$ for $j \neq i$, $j=1,..,n$. The ε_i and u_{it} are jointly independent.

Under these assumptions the model can be written as

$$y_{it} = \beta x_{it} + w_{it}, \tag{10.4}$$

where

$$w_{it} = u_{it} + \varepsilon_i x_{it} \tag{10.5}$$

such that $Ew_{it} = 0$, and

$$(10.6)\quad V(w_{it}) = \sigma_i^2 + \sigma^2 x_{it}^2,$$

$$\text{cov}(w_{it}, w_{jt'}) = \sigma^2 x_{it} x_{it'}, \qquad j=i$$

$$= 0, \qquad j \neq i,$$

$t'=1,\ldots,T$. If we now write the model in matrix notation for i^{th} cross-section unit as

(10.7) $$y_i = \beta x_i + w_i,$$

where $y_i = (y_{i1},\ldots,y_{iT})'$, $x_i = (x_{i1},\ldots,x_{iT})'$

and $w_i = (w_{i1},\ldots,w_{iT})'$, then

(10.8) $$Ew_i = 0,$$

$$Ew_i w_i' = \sigma_i^2 I + \sigma^2 x_i x_i' = \sigma_i^2 I + x_i(\sigma^2 I)x_i' = \Omega_{ii},$$

$$Ew_i w_j' = 0, \qquad j \neq i.$$

If we further write the model as

(10.9) $$y = x\beta + w,$$

where $y = (y_1,\ldots,y_n)'$, $x = (x_1,\ldots,x_n)'$ and $w = (w_1,\ldots,w_n)'$ then all nT disturbances are such that $Ew = 0$ and

(10.10) $$Eww' = \begin{bmatrix} \sigma_1^2 I + \sigma^2 x_1 x_1' & \cdots & 0 \\ \vdots & \ddots & \\ 0 & \cdots & \sigma_n^2 I + \sigma^2 x_n x_n' \end{bmatrix} = \Omega.$$

The ordinary least squares (OLS) estimator of β in (10.9) is

(10.11) $$b = (x'x)^{-1}x'y = \left(\sum_{i=1}^{n} x_i' x_i\right)^{-1} \sum_{i=1}^{n} x_i' y_i.$$

However, this is not efficient since $Eww' \neq I$. To get an efficient estimator we have to use the generalised least squares (GLS) estimator which is

(10.12) $$\hat{\beta} = (x'\Omega^{-1}x)^{-1}x'\Omega^{-1}y$$

$$= [\sum_{i=1}^{n} (x_i'\Omega_{ii}^{-1}x_i)]^{-1} \sum_{i=1}^{n} (x_i'\Omega_{ii}^{-1}y_i),$$

where

$$\Omega_{ii} = \sigma_i^2 I + \sigma^2 x_i x_i'.$$

Using the matrix inversion result for Ω_{ii}, we obtain[2]

(10.13) $$\Omega_{ii}^{-1} = \frac{1}{\sigma_i^2} - \frac{\sigma^2 x_i x_i'}{\sigma_i^2(\sigma_i^2 + \sigma^2 x_i'x_i)}.$$

Then we can write

(10.14) $$\hat{\beta} = \sum_{i=1}^{n} \lambda_i \hat{\beta}_i,$$

where

(10.15) $$\hat{\beta}_i = (x_i'x_i)^{-1}x_i'y_i$$

is the OLS estimator obtained from the ith cross-section unit and

(10.16) $$\lambda_i = \frac{1/(\sigma^2 + \sigma_i^2/x_i'x_i)}{\sum_{j=1}^{n} [1/(\sigma^2 + \sigma_j^2/x_j'x_j)]}.$$

In this framework $\hat{\beta}$ appears as a weighted sum of

$\hat{\beta}_i$ with weights being inversely proportional to the total variance in β_i, viz., $\sigma^2+\sigma_i^2/x_i'x_i$. We note that σ^2 is the prior variance in β_i whereas $\sigma_i^2/x_i'x_i = V(\hat{\beta}_i)$ is the sample variance. If $\sigma^2=0$ then the weights contain sample information only. On the other hand if either σ^2 is very large or $\sigma_i^2/x_i'x_i$ are almost equal for all i, then $\hat{\beta}$ will be close to a simple unweighted average. However, we note that if $\sigma_i^2/x_i'x$ are the same then $\hat{\beta}$ will be the same irrespective of the value of σ^2, including zero, but the variances will be different.

Finally, we note that λ_i in the estimator (10.15) involves unknown parameters. The estimation of these unknown parameters is discussed later in this section.

When there is more than one explanatory variable, say K, model (10.9) becomes

$$(10.17) \qquad y= X\beta+w,$$

where β is Kx1 and X is now an nTxK matrix, that is

$$(10.18) \qquad X= \begin{bmatrix} X_1 \\ \vdots \\ X_n \end{bmatrix}.$$

Each X_i, i=1,...,n is a TxK matrix. Further,

$$(10.19) \qquad Eww' = \begin{bmatrix} \sigma_1^2 I + X_1\Sigma X_1' & \cdots & 0 \\ \vdots & \ddots & \\ 0 & \cdots & \sigma_1^2 I + X_n \Sigma X_n' \end{bmatrix} = \Omega,$$

where

$$(10.20)\quad \Sigma = \begin{bmatrix} \sigma_{11} & \cdots & 0 \\ \vdots & \ddots & \\ 0 & & \sigma_{KK} \end{bmatrix}.$$

The OLS and GLS estimators respectively are

$$(10.21)\quad b = (X'X)^{-1}X'y = \left(\sum_{i=1}^{n} X_i'X_i\right)^{-1}\left(\sum_{i=1}^{n} X_i'y_i\right),$$

$$(10.22)\quad \hat{\beta} = (X'\Omega^{-1}X)^{-1}X'\Omega^{-1}y$$

$$= \left[\sum_{i=1}^{n} (X_i'\Omega_{ii}^{-1}X_i)\right]^{-1} \sum_{i=1}^{n} (X_i'\Omega_{ii}^{-1}y_i),$$

where

$$(10.23)\quad \Omega_{ii} = \sigma_i^2 I + X_i \Sigma X_i'.$$

Using the matrix inversion result for Ω_{ii}, we write

$$(10.24)\quad \Omega_{ii}^{-1} = (\sigma_i^2 I + X_i \Sigma X_i')^{-1}$$

$$= \frac{1}{\sigma_i^2} I - \frac{1}{\sigma_i^2} X_i \left(\frac{X_i'X_i}{\sigma_i^2} + \Sigma^{-1}\right)^{-1} \frac{X_i'}{\sigma_i^2}.$$

Thus

$$(10.25)\quad X_i'\Omega_{ii}^{-1}X_i = \frac{X_i'X_i}{\sigma_i^2} - \frac{X_i'X_i}{\sigma_i^2}\left(\frac{X_i'X_i}{\sigma_i^2} + \Sigma^{-1}\right)^{-1} \frac{X_i'X_i}{\sigma_i^2}$$

$$= \frac{X_i'X_i}{\sigma_i^2}\left[I - \left(\frac{X_i'X_i}{\sigma_i^2} + \Sigma^{-1}\right)^{-1} \frac{X_i'X_i}{\sigma_i^2}\right].$$

Using this,

$$(10.26)\quad \hat{\beta}=\sum_{i=1}^{n}\Lambda_i\hat{\beta}_i,$$

which is a matrix weighted combination of

$$\hat{\beta}_i=(X_i'X_i)^{-1}X_i'y_i.$$

The estimator $\hat{\beta}_i$ is the OLS estimator of β_i in the regression $y_i=X_i\beta_i+u_i$. This estimator is distributed with mean β_i and covariance matrix

$$V(\hat{\beta}_i)=E(\hat{\beta}_i-\beta_i)(\hat{\beta}_i-\beta_i)'=\sigma_i^2(X_i'X_i)^{-1}.$$

The matrix of weights is

$$(10.27)\quad \Lambda_i=[\sum_{j=1}^{n}(\Sigma+\sigma_j^2(X_j'X_j)^{-1})^{-1}]^{-1}$$

$$(\Sigma+\sigma_i^2(X_i'X_i)^{-1})^{-1}$$

such that $\sum_{i=1}^{n}\Lambda_i=I$.

The pooled estimator $\hat{\beta}$, under the assumption that the vector of coefficients for each state β_i is distributed about mean vector β and covariance matrix Σ, is best linear unbiased estimator of β.

The estimator $\hat{\beta}$ contains unknown σ_i^2's and Σ. The unknown σ_i^2 can be estimated by

$$(10.28)\quad \hat{\sigma}_i^2=\hat{u}_i'\hat{u}_i/(T-K),$$

where $\hat{u}_i=[I-X_i(X_i'X_i)^{-1}X_i']y_i=M_iy_i$,

which is an unbiased estimator of σ_i^2 obtained by dividing the sum of squares of OLS residuals for its cross-sectional regression by degress of freedom. The unknown Σ can be estimated by

$$(10.29) \qquad \hat{\Sigma} = \frac{1}{n-1}\Big[\sum_{i=1}^{n} \hat{\beta}_i \hat{\beta}_i' - \frac{1}{n} \sum_{i=1}^{n} \hat{\beta}_i \sum_{n=1}^{n} \hat{\beta}_i' \Big]$$

$$- \frac{1}{n} \sum_{i=1}^{n} \hat{\sigma}_i^2 (X_i' X_i)^{-1}.$$

Note that the estimator $\hat{\Sigma}$ may contain some negative elements because the expression (10.29) is in the form of the difference between two matrices. The estimator for Σ is obtained from the relation

$$(10.30) \qquad E(\hat{\beta}_i - \beta)(\hat{\beta}_i - \beta)' = \Sigma + \sigma_i^2 (X_i' X_i)^{-1}.$$

The operational estimator of $\hat{\beta}$ with estimated values of σ_i^2 and Σ from (10.28) and (10.29), viz.:

$$(10.31) \qquad \hat{\hat{\beta}} = \sum_{i=1}^{n} \hat{\Lambda}_i \hat{\beta}_i,$$

where

$$(10.32) \qquad \hat{\Lambda}_i = \Big[\sum_{j=1}^{n} \big(\hat{\Sigma} + \hat{\sigma}_j^2 (X_i' X_i)^{-1} \big)^{-1} \Big]^{-1}$$

$$\big[\hat{\Sigma} + \hat{\sigma}_i^2 (X_i' X_i)^{-1} \big]^{-1}$$

is asymptotically normally distributed about β and variance-covariance matrix

$$AV(\hat{\hat{\beta}}) = \Big[\sum_{j=1}^{n} \big(\Sigma + \sigma_j^2 (X_i' X_i)^{-1} \big)^{-1} \Big]^{-1}.$$

Thus the asymptotic standard errors of estimates $\hat{\hat{\beta}}$'s can be obtained as the square root of the diagonal elements of

$$(10.33) \quad \widehat{AV(\hat{\beta})} = \left[\sum_{j=1}^{n} (\hat{\Sigma} + \hat{\sigma}_j^2 (X_i' X_i')^{-1})^{-1} \right]^{-1},$$

where $\hat{\sigma}_j^2$ and $\hat{\Sigma}$ are given in (10.28) and (10.29).

Some observations about the Swamy-type model (10.1) under the random cross-sectional effect are useful. This model implies constant mean and variances for random coefficients. Hence it is in the framework of the single equation purely random coefficients model considered in Chapter 4. However, the estimation problem in the single equation case is different from Swamy's model case; whereas in the former we attempt to estimate 2K (K β's and K σ's) parameters given T observations, in the latter we estimate $[\frac{1}{2}K(K+1)+K+n]$ parameters with nT observations.

Swamy (1971) extends the model (10.1) by assuming that the disturbance u_{it} may be autoregressive with $\rho_i (0<|\rho_i|<1)$ as the coefficient of autoregression. Swamy's 1973 paper further extends the model by assuming that the covariance between individuals may be nonzero but the serial correlation between a pair of observations in different time periods declines geometrically with the distance involved. The model with these additional assumptions certainly has much wider applications to real life situations but is much more difficult to estimate because of the involvement of additional unknowns [ρ_i and $\sigma_{ij} (i \neq j)$ for $i,j=1,\ldots,n$]. If sample size is small this would create the problem of degrees of freedom. Swamy (1974) proposes efficient GLS estimators for β along with ρ_i, σ_{ij} and Σ which are consistent.

The model in (10.1) can be related with the classical models considered in the literature on pooled data estimation. In fact a special case of this model is

$$y_{it}= \beta_1+ \sum_{k=2}^{K} \beta_k x_{kit}+\varepsilon_{1i}+u_{it},$$

which is Nerlove's error component (EC) model. In this case we are only considering the intercept to be random. For example if in the model (10.1) we let $x_{1it}=1$ for all i and t, and $\varepsilon_{ki}=0$ for k=2,..,K then it reduces to the above model.[3] In addition, if we let ε_{1i} to be constant then it becomes Mundlak's fixed effect (FE) model or Dummy's variable model, also known as the analysis of covariance (ANCOVA) model. Kmenta (1971) has suggested the best estimators for this case. Maddala (1971) and Nerlove, however, indicated that the FE approach results in a substantial loss of degrees of freedom and also eliminates a major portion of variation among dependent and independent variables. Thus they concluded that the FE estimator will be less efficient compared to the GLS estimator of error component model. Mundlak (1978) has indicated, however, that the EC model is misspecified, and if one considers

$$\beta_{1i}= \beta_1+\bar{x}_{1i}\pi_1+ \bar{x}_{2i}\pi_2+ \ldots+ \bar{x}_{ki}\pi_K+\varepsilon_{1i}$$

instead of $\beta_{1i}= \beta_1+\varepsilon_{1i}$ then the unrestricted GLS estimator and FE estimator of slope coefficient will be the same, whereas the EC estimator will be the restricted GLS estimator. Thus, in his view, unless $\pi_1 = \pi_2 = .. = \pi_k = 0$ is true the FE estimator will be the efficient GLS estimator. Note that $\bar{x}$'s represent the means of x's over T values.

10.3 MODEL WITH BOTH CROSS-SECTION AND INTERACTION EFFECT

In this case we can specify the simple model as

$$(10.34) \quad y_{it} = \beta_{it} x_{it} + u_{it},$$

where

$$(10.35) \quad \beta_{it} = \beta + \varepsilon_i + \eta_t.$$

The estimation of parameters of this model are developed by Hsiao (1972, 1974).

In the general case we can write the model as

$$(10.36) \quad y_{it} = \sum_{k=1}^{K} \beta_{kit} x_{kit} + u_{it},$$

where

$$(10.37) \quad \beta_{kit} = \beta_k + \varepsilon_{ki} + \eta_{kt}.$$

We assume that

$$(10.38a) \quad E\varepsilon_{ki} = 0, \qquad E\varepsilon_{ki}^2 = \sigma_{kk},$$

$$E\varepsilon_{ki}\varepsilon_{k'j} = 0, \qquad k \neq k',\ i \neq j,$$

$k' = 1, \ldots, K$ and

$$(10.38b) \quad E\eta_{kt} = 0, \qquad E\eta_{kt}^2 = \sigma_{kk}^{*},$$

$$E\eta_{kt}\eta_{k't'} = 0, \qquad k \neq k',\ t \neq t'$$

$t'=1,\ldots,T$. Also η_{kt} is uncorrelated with u's and ε's. The assumptions made about ε_{ki} and u_{it} are as before, except that $Eu_{it}^2=\sigma^2$ instead of σ_i^2. Substituting the β_{kit} in the model we can write it as

$$(10.39) \qquad y_{it}=\sum_{k=1}^{K} \beta_k x_{kit}+w_{it},$$

where

$$(10.40) \qquad w_{it}=\sum_{k=1}^{K} x_{kit}(\varepsilon_{ki}+\eta_{kt})+u_{it}$$

such that $Ew_{it}=0$ and

$$(10.41) \qquad Ew_{it}^2=\sigma_i^2+\sum_{k=1}^{K} x_{kit}^2(\sigma_{kk}+\sigma_{kk}^*),$$

$$Ew_{it}w_{jt}=\sum_{k=1}^{K} x_{kit}x_{kjt}\,\sigma_{kk}^*,$$

$$Ew_{it}w_{it'}=\sum_{k=1}^{K} x_{kit}x_{it'}\sigma_{kk},$$

$$Ew_{it}w_{jt'}=0 \qquad \text{for } t\neq t',\ j\neq i.$$

Now write the model (10.39) for all T observations as

$$(10.42) \qquad y_i=X_i\beta+w_i,$$

where, using (10.41),

$$(10.43) \qquad Ew_i=0, \qquad Ew_iw_i'=\sigma^2 I+X_i\Sigma X_i'+D(X_i\Sigma^* X_i')$$

$D(\ )$ represents the matrix of diagonal elements of $X_i\Sigma^* X_i'$ and Σ^* is a diagonal matrix with the elements $\sigma_{11}^*,\ldots,\sigma_{KK}^*$. Further,

(10.44) $Ew_i w_j' = D(X_i \Sigma^* X_j')$.

Thus for i=1,...,n, the complete model is

(10.45) $y = X\beta + w$,

where $Ew=0$ and $Eww' = \Omega$ such that

(10.46)
$$\Omega = \begin{bmatrix} \sigma^2 + X_1 \Sigma X_1' + D(X_1 \Sigma^* X_1') & \cdots & D(X_1 \Sigma^* X_N') \\ \vdots & \ddots & \vdots \\ D(X_N \Sigma^* X_1') & \cdots & \sigma^2 + X_n \Sigma X_n' + D(X_N \Sigma^* X_1') \end{bmatrix}$$

The OLS estimator of β is

(10.47) $b = (X'X)^{-1}X'y$

and the GLS estimator

(10.48) $\hat{\beta} = (X'\Omega^{-1}X)^{-1}X'\Omega^{-1}y$.

The matrix Ω is unknown. So, to use $\hat{\beta}$ in practice, we first estimate σ^2 and the elements of Σ and Σ^*. The σ^2 and the elements of Σ and Σ^* can be estimated by using the methods discussed in Chapter 4. For example, we can write (10.36)to (10.37) as

(10.49)
$$y_{it} = \sum_{k=1}^{K} (\beta_k + \varepsilon_{ki}) x_{kit} + \sum_{k=1}^{K} \eta_{kt} x_{kit} + u_{it}$$

$$= \sum_{k=1}^{K} \beta_{ki} x_{kit} + w_{it}^*,$$

where $\beta_{ki} = \beta_k + \varepsilon_{ki}$ and $w_{it}^* = \sum_{k=1}^{K} \eta_{kt} x_{kit} + u_{it}$. In the matrix notation, for t=1,...,T, $y_i = X_i \beta_i + w_i^*$. Then for each i we can treat this as a single equation model with purely random coefficients, as considered in Chapter 4. This would give, for i=1,...,n,

$$(10.50)\qquad \hat{\dot{w}}_i^* = \dot{M}_i\dot{Z}_i\,\dot{\sigma}^* + \xi_i,$$

where $\hat{\dot{w}}_i^*$ is a Tx1 vector of the squared least squares residuals, $\dot{Z}_i$ is the Tx(K+1) matrix of the squared elements of the matrix $Z_i=[\iota, X_i]$ and $\dot{M}_i$ is the matrix of the squared elements of the matrix $M_i= I-Z_i(Z_i'Z_i)^{-1}Z_i'$. Further, $\dot{\sigma}^* = (\sigma^2,\sigma_{11}^*,\ldots,\sigma_{KK}^*)'$ is a (K+1)x1 vector and ξ_i is an error vector such that $E\xi_i=0$. The pooled least squares estimator of $\dot{\sigma}^*$ can then be written as

$$(10.51)\qquad \hat{\dot{\sigma}}^* = [\sum_{i=1}^{n}(\dot{M}_i\dot{Z}_i)'(\dot{M}_i\dot{Z}_i)]^{-1}\sum_{i=1}^{n}(\dot{M}_i\dot{Z}_i)'\hat{\dot{w}}_i^*.$$

Similarly, we can write (10.36) and (10.37) as

$$(10.52)\qquad y_{it}= \sum_{k=1}^{K}(\beta_k+\eta_{kt})x_{kit}+\sum_{k=1}^{K}\varepsilon_{ki}x_{kit}+u_{it}$$

$$= \sum_{k=1}^{K}\beta_{kt}x_{kit}+w_{it},$$

or in matrix notation, for i=1,...,n, as

$$(10.53)\qquad y_t= X_t\beta_t+w_t.$$

Then, if we define $M_t= I-Z_t(Z_t'Z_t)^{-1}Z_t'$, $Z_t= [\iota,X_t]$, we can write

$$(10.54)\qquad \hat{\dot{w}}_t= \dot{M}_t\dot{Z}_t\dot{\sigma}+\xi_t,$$

where $\dot{\sigma} = (\sigma^2, \sigma_{11}, \ldots, \sigma_{KK})'$ and $\hat{\dot{w}}_t$ is the vector of squared least squares residuals from (10.53). This would give the pooled estimator of $\dot{\sigma}$ as

$$(10.55) \qquad \hat{\dot{\sigma}} = [\sum_{t=1}^{T} (\dot{M}_t \dot{Z}_t)'(\dot{M}_t \dot{Z}_t)]^{-1} \sum_{t=1}^{T} (\dot{M}_t \dot{Z}_t)' \hat{\dot{w}}_t .$$

Note that we get two estimators of σ^2, one from (10.51) and the other from (10.55). A solution is to take the simple average of these two estimators.

Using $\hat{\dot{\sigma}}$ and $\hat{\dot{\sigma}}^*$ we can get $\hat{\Omega}$ and hence

$$(10.56) \qquad \hat{\hat{\beta}} = (X'\hat{\Omega}^{-1}X)^{-1}X'\hat{\Omega}^{-1}y.$$

The estimator $\hat{\hat{\beta}}$ is asymptotically distributed as normal with the mean β and variance-covariance matrix $(X'\Omega^{-1}X)^{-1}$, that is the asymptotic distribution of $\sqrt{T}(\hat{\hat{\beta}}-\beta)$ is the same as that of $\sqrt{T}(\hat{\beta}-\beta)$.

In the literature, some more general models than (10.36) and (10.37) have been estimated; for example, Swamy and Mehta (1975, 1977) and Swamy and Tinsley (1980). Given that individuals differ in their behaviour and change their habits over time, Swamy and Mehta specify the regression coefficients across individuals with an interaction effect term, that is

$$\beta_{kit} = \beta_k + \varepsilon_{ki} + \eta_{kit}.$$

They then discuss both Bayesian and non-Bayesian methods of estimating parameters in the model. The paper by Swamy and Tinsley considers the estimation problem of such models under a more general assumption regarding the error structure. A further extension of model (10.36), when

$$(10.57) \quad \beta_{kit} = \beta_k + \varepsilon_{ki} + \eta_{kt} + \xi_{kit}$$

remains to be explored.

It would also be useful to note the special cases of model (10.36). Hoch (1962) and Mundlak (1963) considered the following special case:

$$(10.58) \quad y_{it} = \beta_1 + \varepsilon_{1i} + \eta_{1t} + \sum_{k=2}^{K} \beta_k x_{kit} + u_{it},$$

where ε_{1i} and η_{1t} are considered as fixed parameters. Nerlove (1971) and Swamy and Arora (1972) considered the error component model by assuming ε_{1i} and η_{1t} to be random. Swamy and Arora (1972) have shown that there is a whole class of estimators of β's which perform equally well in terms of asymptotic efficiency. They therefore investigated the finite sample properties in their model and concluded that the error component estimator is less efficient than OLS if n and T and true values of σ_{11}, σ_{11}^* are small. The error component estimator is less efficient than the fixed effect estimator if n and T are small and true values of σ_{11}, σ_{11}^* are large. Bayesian analysis of the model (10.58) is given in Swamy and Mehta (1973).

10.4 AN APPLICATION

To illustrate the specification and estimation of the temporal cross-section model under simplifying assumptions outlined in this chapter, we briefly discuss the results of a study by Feige and Swamy (1974) on the demand for liquid assets in the United States.

The majority of temporal cross-section studies of the liquid assets have assumed that behaviour both across geographic units and time periods is identical. Accordingly, the coefficients in the regression relations are assumed to be fixed. It can be argued that behaviour of individuals across geographical units is not fixed but differs for a variety of reasons. First, the laws regulating financial intermediary innovations such as mutual banking, holding companies and branch banking generally differ from state to state. Second, in some states financial markets are more sophisticated than others resulting in different portfolio behavioural responses. Thus the fixed coefficient assumptions in the temporal cross-section model of demand for liquid assets may not be valid

In view of this and the fact that, using appropriate F tests, coefficients were found to be stable over time but unstable across states, Feige and Swamy formulated the purely random coefficients model, outlined in Section 10.2, for the demand for liquid assets. They assumed a log linear functional form for the demand for liquid assets, which depends upon income, the rate of return on the assets and rate of returns on competing assets. The aggregate equation was of the form

$$A_{it}=\beta_{1i}+\beta_{2i}r_{dit}+\beta_{3i}r_{eit}+\beta_{4i}r_{sit}+\beta_{5i}Y_{it}+u_{it}$$

where $i=1,...,n$ indexes cross-section behaviour for the n states and $t=1,...,T$ indexes time series observations. Further, β_{ki} was assumed to be equal to $\beta_k+\varepsilon_{ki}$ as in Section 10.2, $k=1,...,K$. The data consisted of annual observations from 48 continental states plus the District of Columbia for the period 1949-1965.

The description of the variables is given below.

A A liquid asset such as DD, TD and SD defined below.

DD Real per capita commerical bank deposits held by individuals, partnerships and corporations.

TD Real per capita savings and loan association shares.

SD Real per capita disposable income.

r_d Cost of holding deposits measured by the ratio of service charges to average demand deposits.

r_e Weighted average of actual interest yields on commercial bank time deposits and mutual savings bank deposits.

r_s Actual interest yield on savings and loan associations shares.

Y Real per capita disposable income.

The estimated equations from the pooled data of log linear demand functions for liquid assets with random coefficients are:

(a) Demand for demand deposit

$$\underset{(0.2030)}{DD=1.7942}+\underset{(0.0199)}{0.0860r_d}-\underset{(0.0091)}{0.0175r_e}-\underset{(0.0312)}{0.2063r_s}+\underset{(0.0237)}{0.6194Y}$$

(b) Demand for time deposits

$$\underset{(1.0146}{TD=-3.0037}-\underset{(0.0584)}{0.0207r_d}+\underset{(0.1168)}{0.1386r_e}-\underset{(0.2008)}{0.4828r_s}+\underset{(0.1309)}{1.0579Y}$$

(c) Demand for savings and loan associations shares

$$\underset{(1.3072)}{SD=-4.6041}-\underset{(0.0891)}{0.5270r_d}+\underset{(0.0815)}{0.4465r_e}+\underset{(0.1957)}{0.3513r_s}+\underset{(0.1589)}{1.2630Y}$$

It may be instructive to compare the results from the random coefficients model with that of the fixed coefficients model given below:

(d) Demand for demand deposits

$$DD=-3.7025+0.3674r_d-0.0670r_e+0.0766r_s+1.2659Y$$
$$(0.0331)(0.0027)\ (0.0041)\ (0.0093)\ (0.0041)$$

(e) Demand for time deposits

$$TD=-4.6324-0.2749r_d+0.1775r_e-0.4740r_s+1.4508Y$$
$$(0.0811\ (0.0058)\ (0.0114)\ (0.0226)\ (0.0107)$$

(f) Demand for savings and loan associations shares

$$SD=-9.7600-0.2631r_d-0.2562r_e+1.5603r_s+1.7985Y$$
$$(0.0763)(0.0059)\ (0.0093)\ (0.0185)\ (0.0096)$$

The estimates of fixed coefficients in (d) to (f) have been obtained after substituting $\hat{\Sigma}=I$ in (10.31), that is by using

$$\hat{\beta}=\left[\sum_{i=1}^{n}\frac{X_i'X_i}{\hat{\sigma}_i^2}\right]^{-1}\left[\sum_{i=1}^{n}\frac{X_i'A_i}{\hat{\sigma}_i^2}\right],$$

where $\hat{\sigma}_i^2$ is defined in (10.28). The asymptotic standard errors of estimates of fixed coefficients are obtained from:

$$AV(\hat{\hat{\beta}})=\left[\sum_{i=1}^{n}\frac{(X_i'X_i)}{\hat{\sigma}_i^2}\right]^{-1}.$$

Comparing results in equations (a) to (c) with the results in equations (d) to (e) we may conclude that: (i) Demand deposits and savings and loan associations shares display a stronger substitution relationship across equation in the random coefficients model compared to the fixed coefficients model; (ii) Time deposits and savings and loan shares display a substitution relation in the fixed coefficients model while they display a complementary relationship in the random coefficients model. (iii) The income elasticity for each asset is positive and larger in the fixed coefficients model than for the random coefficients model; (iv) The own elasticities have expected signs in both models but their magnitude is larger for the fixed coefficients than for the random coefficients.

The lower elasticities of income elasticity for each asset have been obtained by other researchers using covariance models where allowance is made for separate time and state intercepts. The finding of a complementary relationship between time deposits and savings and loans associations, disturbing as it is, is not supported by other studies.

The random coefficients model has also been applied to other situations with theoretically plausible results. For example, Swamy (1971) analysed the micro investment behaviour for eleven large U.S. corporations and the consumption function for 24 countries. Finally, Mehta, Narasimham and Swamy (1978) applied the random coefficients model for estimation of a dynamic demand function for gasoline.

10.5 AGGREGATION AND TEMPORAL CROSS-SECTION RANDOM COEFFICIENT MODELS

An interesting property of a random coefficients model originally shown by Zellner (1966) is that for some specifying assumptions there is no aggregation bias in the least squares estimates of coefficients in an aggregate macro equation obtained by summing over all micro units. To illustrate his point Zellner considered the following micro equation for the ith unit:

$$(10.59) \qquad y_i = X_i \beta_i + u_i,$$

where y_i is a Tx1 vector of observations on the dependent variable, X_i is a TxK matrix of observations on the K explanatory variables, β_i is a Kx1 vector of random coefficients associated with the explanatory variables in the ith micro relation and u_i is a Tx1 vector of disturbances. Further, it is assumed that:

(i) The explanatory variables are nonstochastic and linearly independent;

(ii) $Eu_i=0$; $Eu_iu_i'=\sigma^2 I$ and $Eu_iu_j'=0$ if $i \neq j$;

(iii) There are n micro units, that is $i=1,2,..,n$;

(iv) $\beta_i = \beta + \varepsilon_i$,

where ε_i is a Kx1 random vector with $E\varepsilon_i=0$.

Using assumption (iv) we can rewrite (10.59) as

$$(10.60) \qquad y_i = X_i \beta + X_i \varepsilon_i + u_i.$$

Now consider the following macro relation corresponding to (10.60) obtained by simple aggregation over i:

$$(10.61) \qquad \sum_{i=1}^{n} y_i = \sum_{i=1}^{n} X_i \beta + \sum_{i=1}^{n} X_i \varepsilon_i + \sum_{i=1}^{n} u_i.$$

Further, defining macro variables obtained by simple aggregation over i as

$$(10.62) \qquad \bar{y} = \sum_{i=1}^{n} y_i, \ \bar{X} = \sum_{i=1}^{n} X_i \text{ and } \bar{u} = \sum_{i=1}^{n} u_i,$$

we can write the macro relation (10.61) as

$$(10.63) \qquad \bar{y} = \bar{X}\beta + \sum_{i=1}^{n} X_i \varepsilon_i + \bar{u}.$$

Supposing, instead of the relation (10.63) the following relationship is postulated connecting the macro variables:

$$(10.64) \quad \bar{y} = \bar{X}\beta + v,$$

where $\bar{y}$ and $\bar{X}$ are defined in (10.62), β is a Kx1 vector of fixed coefficients and v is a Tx1 vector of macro disturbances with mean zero and variance-covariance matrix $\sigma^2 I$. Further suppose we estimate β in (10.64) by least squares and we obtain

$$(10.65) \quad b = (\bar{X}'\bar{X})^{-1}\bar{X}'\bar{y} = (\bar{X}'\bar{X})^{-1}\bar{X}' \sum_{i=1}^{n} y_i .$$

Though the least squares estimator (10.65) estimates the coefficients vector β in the aggregate macro equation (10.64) when the true aggregate relationship is given by (10.63), there is no aggregation bias in b; that is the expectation of b is equal to β. To verify this we substitute (10.63) in (10.65) and obtain

$$(10.66) \quad b = (\bar{X}'\bar{X})^{-1}\bar{X}'(\bar{X}\beta + \sum_{i=1}^{n} X_i \varepsilon_i + \bar{u}),$$

and taking expectation on both sides, we write

$$(10.67) \quad Eb = \beta + E(\bar{X}'\bar{X})^{-1}\bar{X}' \sum_{i=1}^{n} X_i \varepsilon_i + E(\bar{X}'\bar{X})^{-1}\bar{X}'\bar{u}$$

$$= \beta .$$

The second equality in (10.67) follows from the assumptions that the explanatory variables are nonstochastic and that $E\varepsilon_i = 0$ and $Eu_i = 0$. We note that Theil's (1954) case of absence of aggregation bias when micro coefficients β_i and the weights matrix $(\bar{X}'\bar{X})^{-1}\bar{X}'X_i$ are uncorrelated is built into the assumption $\beta_i=\beta+\varepsilon_i$.

Finally, we point out that if the elements of X_i are assumed to be stochastic and distributed independent of ε_i and u_i, there will still be no aggregation bias. Furthermore, if X_i contains lagged values of y_i, then $E(b)= \beta$ can be reformulated to read plim $b = \beta$ and the property of no aggregation bias will still hold. If the elements of X_i are correlated with the elements of either ε_i or u_i, then there will of course be aggregation bias. The above approach is also closely related to Theil's (1971, pp. 570-573, 580-587) convergence approach to aggregation (see Swamy [1971], pp. 15-16).

The random coefficients approach to aggregation assumes that micro coefficients vary only across micro units and remain stable over time. This may be a reasonable assumption in the Temporal Cross-Section (or panel) data provided we observe micro units over a short period of time. Examples of the above approach are discussed in Swamy (1971), Mehta, Narasimham and Swamy (1978), among other places.

NOTES

1. Rao (1965) suggested a similar model.

2. Let A and D be nonsingular matrices of orders mxm and nxn respectively and B a mxn matrix. Then,

$$[A+BDB']^{-1}= A^{-1}-A^{-1}B(B'A^{-1}B+D^{-1})^{-1}B'A^{-1}$$

Also see Maddala (1977), p. 446 and Rao (1973), p. 29.

3. The estimation of this model has been considered by Nerlove (1971), Amemiya (1971), and Wallace and Hussain (1969), among others. Kuh (1959) studied a model where ε_{1i} and u_{it} are correlated whereas Nerlove (1971) indicated that the covariance term is not identified.

11. Seemingly Uncorrelated Regressions

11.1 INTRODUCTION

In this chapter we analyse a multi regressions model, a là Zellner's (1962a) set of seemingly unrelated regressions (SUR), with the purely random coefficients. The related multi equations model discussed in Chapter 10 differs with the SUR model in three respects. First, in all the models of Chapter 10 the matrix of explanatory variables was the same across equations. Second, the set of regression coefficients on the average remained the same for different equations. Third, the correlation across equations was not considered. In contrast, in this chapter we will consider a multi regressions model without these restrictions.

11.2 THE MODEL AND ITS ASSUMPTIONS

Let us write a set of M seemingly unrelated regression equations of which the ith equation at the time point t is

$$(11.1) \qquad y_{it}=\sum_{k=1}^{K_i} \beta_{ikt}x_{ikt}+u_{it}, \quad i=1,..,M;t=1,..,T.$$

In the set of M equations (11.1), y_{it} is the tth observation on dependent variable y_i, x_{ikt} is the

t^{th} known nonrandom value of the independent variable $x_{ik}(k=1,\ldots,K_i)$, and u_{it} is the usual disturbance term in the ith equation corresponding to the tth observation. Further, β_{ikt} is the regression coefficient taking different values for each t for the reasons discussed in Chapter 1. Because of this specification of β_{ikt}, the model (11.1) differs from the conventional model of the set of regressions in which the regression coefficient is the same for each time point.

As discussed in Chapter 2 there can be various formulations for the randomly varying behaviour of regression coefficients. One can use those formulations for the coefficients of each of the M equations in (11.1) and can suitably modify the corresponding methods of estimation - discussed in Chapter 4 - in the present context. However, we shall be considering here only the purely random coefficient case.

11.3 PURELY RANDOM VARYING COEFFICIENT MODELS

In this formulation, we assume

(11.2) $$\beta_{ikt}=\beta_{ik}+\varepsilon_{ikt},$$

where β_{ik}, the deterministic component, is the mean regression coefficient and ε_{ikt}, the stochastic component, is the unobservable disturbance term. The model in (11.1), using (11.2), can then be written as

(11.3) $$y_{it}=\sum_{k=1}^{K_i}\beta_{ik}x_{ikt}+w_{it},$$

where

$$(11.4) \qquad w_{it} = \sum_{k=1}^{K_i} \varepsilon_{ikt} x_{ikt} + u_{it}.$$

Thus model (11.1) under the specification (11.2) reduces to the familiar model of a set of regression equations with fixed coefficients. However, it would be clear from the following assumptions that the nature of the disturbance term differs from the conventional model. In fact, the disturbance term within each equation becomes heteroscedastic. To see this we must first outline the simplifying assumptions that underlie this model.

<u>Assumptions</u>:

(i) $Eu_{it} = E\varepsilon_{ikt} = 0$, for i's, k's and t's,

(ii) $Eu_{it}u_{jt'} = \delta_{tt'}\sigma_{ij}$, $i, j=1,\ldots,M$,

(iii) $Eu_{it}\varepsilon_{ikt} = 0$, for i, k and t,

(iv) $E\varepsilon_{ikt}\varepsilon_{j\ell t'} = \delta_{tt'}\delta_{k\ell}\theta_{ijk\ell}$, $\ell=1,\ldots,K_j$,

where δ represents Kronecker delta, which is a scalar quantity such that for $t, t'=1,\ldots,T$

$$(11.5) \qquad \delta_{tt'} = 1, \quad \text{if } t=t'$$
$$= 0, \quad \text{if } t \neq t'.$$

Similarly, $\delta_{k\ell}=1$ for $k=\ell$ and 0 for $k\neq\ell$.

The assumption $E\varepsilon_{ikt}=0$ implies that the mean response coefficient in the model is constant over time, and it is β_{ik}. Assumption (ii) is the usual assumption of correlation in the equational errors across equations at the same time point. We have kept the error u_{it} in model (11.1) so as to have direct comparison with Zellner's SUR model without random coefficients. In this case, however, we note that the variance of u_{it} and ε_{i1t} cannot possibly be estimated separately. But we can estimate the variance of the combined disturbance $u_{it}+\varepsilon_{i1t}$. Throughout this chapter we shall consider this case only. Assumption (iii) implies that the causes which generate errors in the equation may not be the same as those introducing randomness in the coefficients. The last assumption (iv) along with (11.2) indicates that the coefficients are uncorrelated across time points, and also that the coefficients of two different variables in the system are uncorrelated. Serial correlation could also be considered on the lines of Chapter 6, but it is beyond the scope of this test.

Using the above assumptions it can now easily be verified that the expectation of the combined disturbance term w_{it} in (11.4) is zero and

$$(11.6)\quad Ew_{it}w_{jt'} = \delta_{tt'}(\sigma_{ij} + \sum_{k=1}^{K_i}\sum_{\ell=1}^{K_j} x_{ikt}x_{j\ell t'}\delta_{k\ell}\theta_{ijk\ell})$$

$$= \omega_{ijtt'}.$$

In the model where $K_i=K_j$, the expectation in (11.6) reduces to[1]

$$(11.6a)\quad Ew_{it}w_{jt'} = \delta_{tt'}(\sigma_{ij} + \sum_{k=1}^{K_i} x_{ikt}x_{jkt'}\theta_{ijkk})$$

$$= \omega_{ijtt'}.$$

Since many econometric models will be having this setup we shall take up the analysis for this case in detail. The change in analysis when $K_i \neq K_j$ and $\delta_{k\ell}=1$ for all k and ℓ is indicated later in this section. In either case we observe that the randomness in the coefficients has introduced heteroscedasticity of a specific form in each equation.

Case 1: $K_i=K_j$. Before proceeding for the estimation it would be better to present the model (11.3) to (11.4) in the matrix notation as below:

(11.7) $$y_i = X_i \beta_i + w_i,$$

$$w_i = X_i^* \varepsilon_i + u_i,$$

where

(11.8) $$y_i = (y_{i1}, \ldots, y_{iT})',$$

$$\beta_i = (\beta_{i1}, \ldots, \beta_{iKi})',$$

$$w_i = (w_{i1}, \ldots, w_{iT})',$$

$$u_i = (u_{i1}, \ldots, u_{iT})'$$

and

(11.9) $$\varepsilon_i = (\varepsilon_{i11}, \ldots, \varepsilon_{iK_i1}, \ldots, \varepsilon_{i1T}, \ldots, \varepsilon_{iK_iT})'$$

are column vectors of order Tx1, K_ix1, Tx1 and TK_ix1 respectively. Further, the matrices X_i and X_i^* of order TxK_i and $TxTK_i$ respectively are defined as

$$(11.10) \quad X_i = \begin{bmatrix} x_{i11} & \cdots & x_{iK_i1} \\ \vdots & & \vdots \\ x_{i1T} & & x_{iK_iT} \end{bmatrix}$$

and

$$(11.11) \quad X_i^* = \begin{bmatrix} x_{i11} & \cdots & x_{iK_i1} & \cdots & 0 & \cdots & 0 \\ 0 & \cdots & 0 & \ddots & 0 & \cdots & 0 \\ \vdots & & \vdots & & & \ddots & \\ 0 & \cdots & 0 & \cdots & x_{i1T} & \cdots & x_{iK_iT} \end{bmatrix}$$

respectively. Note that the matrix X_i^* is in fact a diagonal matrix of row vectors with the tth diagonal element being the tth row of the matrix X_i.

The system of M equations can then be written as

$$(11.12) \quad \begin{bmatrix} y_1 \\ \vdots \\ y_M \end{bmatrix} = \begin{bmatrix} X_1 & \cdots & 0 \\ \vdots & & \\ 0 & \cdots & X_M \end{bmatrix} \begin{bmatrix} \beta_1 \\ \vdots \\ \beta_M \end{bmatrix} + \begin{bmatrix} w_1 \\ \vdots \\ w_M \end{bmatrix}$$

or more compactly as

$$(11.13) \quad y = X\beta + w,$$

where X is a MTxK ($K = \sum_{i=1}^{M} K_i$) block diagonal matrix and y, β and w are vectors of respective orders MTx1, Kx1, MTx1. Further, using (11.6a), we obtain,

$$(11.14) \quad E(w_i w_j') = X_i^*(E\varepsilon_i \varepsilon_j')X_j^{*\prime} + Eu_i u_j'$$

$$= X_i^*(\Delta_{ij} \otimes I_T)X_j^{*\prime} + \sigma_{ij} I_T = \Omega_{ij},$$

where

$$(11.15)\quad \Omega_{ij}=\begin{bmatrix} \omega_{ij11} & \cdots & 0 \\ \vdots & \ddots & \\ 0 & & \omega_{ijTT} \end{bmatrix}$$

is a TxT diagonal matrix and Δ_{ij} is a $K_i x K_i$ matrix as

$$(11.16)\quad \Delta_{ij}=\begin{bmatrix} \theta_{ij11} & \cdots & 0 \\ \vdots & & \\ 0 & \cdots & \theta_{ijK_iK_i} \end{bmatrix}.$$

Finally, combining (11.14) to (11.16), we get

$$(11.17)\quad Eww'=\begin{bmatrix} \Omega_{11} & \cdots & \Omega_{1M} \\ \vdots & & \\ \Omega_{M1} & \cdots & \Omega_{MM} \end{bmatrix}$$

$$=\Omega= \Sigma_o \otimes I_T+X^*(\Delta \otimes I_T)X^{*\prime},$$

where

$$(11.18)\quad \Delta=\begin{bmatrix} \Delta_{11} & \cdots & \Delta_{1M} \\ \vdots & & \\ \Delta_{M1} & \cdots & \Delta_{MM} \end{bmatrix} \text{ and } X^*=\begin{bmatrix} X_1^* & \cdots & 0 \\ \vdots & & \\ 0 & \cdots & X_M^* \end{bmatrix}$$

are KxK and MTxTK matrices respectively and

$$(11.19)\quad \Sigma_o = \begin{bmatrix} \sigma_{11} & \cdots & \sigma_{1M} \\ \vdots & & \\ \sigma_{M1} & \cdots & \sigma_{MM} \end{bmatrix}$$

is a MxM matrix.

We can now verify that if $\theta_{ij11}=\ldots=\theta_{ijK_iK_i}=0$

then (11.13) reduces to the set of seemingly unrelated regressions with nonrandom coefficients as considered by Zellner (1962). In this case

$$(11.20) \quad \Omega = \Sigma_o \otimes I = \Sigma.$$

The problem of estimation is now basically the estimation of the general linear model (11.13) with the error variance-covariance matrix given by (11.17). If Ω is known then the best linear unbiased estimator of β is the GLS estimator given by

$$(11.21) \quad b = (X'\Omega^{-1}X)^{-1}X'\Omega^{-1}y;$$

its variance-covariance matrix is

$$(11.22) \quad V(b) = (X'\Omega^{-1}X)^{-1}.$$

The Zellner (1962) SUR estimator is

$$(11.23) \quad \tilde{\beta} = (X'\Sigma^{-1}X)^{-1}X'\Sigma^{-1}y,$$

where Σ is as given in (11.20). The $\tilde{\beta}$ is unbiased and its variance-covariance matrix is

$$(11.24) \quad V(\tilde{\beta}) = (X'\Sigma^{-1}X)^{-1}X'\Sigma^{-1}\Omega\ \Sigma^{-1}X(X'\Sigma^{-1}X)^{-1}.$$

Since $\Sigma = \Sigma_o \otimes I$ is rarely, if ever, known Zellner suggested replacing Σ_o by its consistent estimator $\tilde{\Sigma}_o$ whose i, jth element is

$$(11.25) \quad \tilde{\sigma}_{ij} = \tilde{u}_i'\tilde{u}_j/T,$$

where $\tilde{u}_i$ and $\tilde{u}_j$ are the ordinary least squares residuals vectors obtained from the ith and jth equation.

Likewise, the knowledge of Ω in (11.21) is not available and thus the straightforward application of b is not possible. Nevertheless, we can obtain a consistent estimator of Ω by using essentially a multi equations analogue of the estimator discussed in Chapter 4.[2] It is clear from (11.16), (11.17) and (11.19) that the estimation of Ω basically requires the estimation of

$$\sigma_{ij}, \theta_{ij11}, \ldots, \theta_{ijK_iK_i}.$$

We therefore outline below the procedure for estimating these unknowns.

First, we obtain the OLS residuals for each equation in (11.12), that is

$$(11.26) \quad \hat{w}_i = M_i w_i,$$

where $M_i = I - X_i(X_i'X_i)^{-1}X_i'$ is a TxT idempotent matrix. Further, using (11.14), we obtain

$$(11.27) \quad E\hat{w}_i\hat{w}_j' = M_i(Ew_iw_j')M_j = M_i\Omega_{ij}M_j$$

for i,j=1,...,M. Then define

$$(11.28) \quad \hat{w}_{ij} = \hat{w}_i * \hat{w}_j, \quad M_{ij} = M_i * M_j$$

and

$$(11.29) \quad X_{ij} = [\iota, X_i * X_j],$$

$$\theta_{ij} = (\sigma_{ij}, \theta_{ij11}, \ldots, \theta_{ijK_iK_i})',$$

where * represents the Hadamard matrix product.[3] Finally we can write the diagonal elements in (11.27) as

(11.30) $E\hat{w}_{ij} = M_{ij}X_{ij}\theta_{ij}$.

Further, if we write

(11.31) $e_{ij} = \hat{w}_{ij} - E\hat{w}_{ij}$,

we have

(11.32) $\hat{w}_{ij} = M_{ij}X_{ij}\theta_{ij} + e_{ij} = Z_{ij}\theta_{ij} + e_{ij}$,

where $Z_{ij} = M_{ij}X_{ij}$.

The OLS estimator of θ_{ij} is then obtained as

(11.33) $\hat{\theta}_{ij} = (Z'_{ij}Z_{ij})^{-1}Z'_{ij}\hat{w}_{ij}$.

Once $\hat{\theta}_{ij}$ is obtained, we have from (11.6a) that

(11.34) $\hat{\omega}_{ijtt} = \hat{\sigma}_{ij} + \sum_{k=1}^{K_i} x_{ikt}x_{jkt}\hat{\theta}_{ijkk}$.

Finally, substituting (11.34) for t=1,...,T in (11.15) we obtain $\hat{\Omega}_{ij}$ and hence $\hat{\Omega}$ from (11.17). Now we can write the GLS estimator b in (11.21) as

(11.35) $\hat{b} = (X'\hat{\Omega}^{-1}X)^{-1}X'\hat{\Omega}^{-1}y$.

It can easily be verified that $\hat{\theta}_{ij}$ is an unbiased estimator of θ_{ij}, and under the assumption that the ε's are normally distributed, its covariance matrix is

(11.36) $V(\hat{\theta}_{ij}) = (Z'_{ij}Z_{ij})^{-1}Z'_{ij}\dot{\Phi}_{ij}Z_{ij}(Z'_{ij}Z_{ij})^{-1}$,

where $\dot{\Phi}_{ij} = (M_i\Omega_{ij}M_j)*(M_i\Omega_{ij}M_j) + (M_i\Omega_{ii}M_i)*(M_j\Omega_{jj}M_j)$.[4] However, the OLS estimator $\hat{\theta}_{ij}$ is not efficient because $Ee_{ij}e'_{ij}=\dot{\Phi}_{ij}$ and not a scalar times an identity matrix. In this case one might use the GLS estimator of θ_{ij}. For j=i the result in (11.36) is identical with that given in Chapter 4 for the single equation case.

For large sample $\hat{\theta}_{ij}$ is a consistent estimator and its asymptotic variance-covariance matrix is

$$(X'_{ij}X_{ij})^{-1}X'_{ij}\dot{\Omega}_{ij}X_{ij}(X'_{ij}X_{ij})^{-1}$$

where

$$\dot{\Omega}_{ij}= \Omega_{ij}*\Omega_{ij}+\Omega_{ii}*\Omega_{jj}.$$

Also for large samples $\hat{b}$ is both a consistent and unbiased estimator. Further, its asymptotic distribution is normal with the mean vector β and variance-covariance matrix $(X'\Omega^{-1}X)^{-1}$.[5] However, its exact variance-covariance matrix is not known. Thus, in a small sample case one cannot calculate the standard errors of the elements of $\hat{b}$.

We will now show that estimator $\hat{b}$ is strictly more efficient than Zellner's SUR estimator $\tilde{\beta}$ if the true model is with random coefficients. Let

$$(X'\Sigma^{-1}X)^{-1}X'\Sigma^{-1}= (X'\Omega^{-1}X)^{-1}X'\Omega^{-1}+A,$$

where A is a matrix such that AX=0. Then from (11.24) we have

$$\begin{aligned} V(\tilde{\beta})&= (X'\Sigma^{-1}X)^{-1}X'\Sigma^{-1}\Omega\Sigma^{-1}X(X'\Sigma^{-1}X)^{-1} \\ &=[(X'\Omega^{-1}X)^{-1}X'\Omega^{-1}+A]\Omega[\Omega^{-1}X(X'\Omega^{-1}X)^{-1}+A'] \\ &= (X'\Omega^{-1}X)^{-1}+A\Omega A'= V(\hat{b})+A\Omega A'. \end{aligned}$$

Since Ω, being a variance-covariance matrix, is positive definite, $A\Omega A'$ will be at least positive semidefinite. Thus $|V(\hat{b})| \leq |V(\tilde{\beta})|$, i.e. the asymptotic variance of the estimator $\hat{b}$, is smaller than equal to the variance of SUR estimator $\tilde{\beta}$. The asymptotic relative efficiency of $\hat{b}$ with respect to $\tilde{\beta}$ can be written as

$$\frac{|V(\hat{b})|}{|V(\tilde{\beta})|} = \frac{|X'\ \Sigma^{-1}X|^2}{|X'\Omega^{-1}X|\ |X'\Psi X|} \leq 1,$$

where $\Psi = \Sigma^{-1}\ \Omega\Sigma^{-1}$. In a special case of two equations, $(M=2)$ and $K_1=2=K_2$, it has been shown by Singh and Ullah (1974) that higher the contemporaneous correlation (due to randomness in regression coefficients) across equations, the larger would be the gain in efficiency of $\hat{b}$ relative to $\tilde{\beta}$.

Case 2: $K_i \neq K_j$. In the situation where $K_i \neq K_j$ and the coefficients of exogenous variables are correlated in the system [that is the assumption (iv) is relaxed], then

$$(11.37) \qquad E\varepsilon_{ikt}\varepsilon_{j\ell t'} = \delta_{tt'}\theta_{ijk\ell}.$$

The analysis in this case requires minor adjustments. Now, the elements of Ω_{ij} in (11.5) are given by

$$\omega_{ijtt'} = \delta_{tt'}(\sigma_{ij} + \sum_{k=1}^{K_i}\sum_{\ell=1}^{K_j} x_{ikt}x_{j\ell t'}\theta_{ijk\ell}),$$

which can also be written as

$$\delta_{tt'}(\sigma_{ij} + \sum_{k=1}^{K^*} x_{ikt}x_{jkt'}\theta_{ijkk} + \sum_{k \neq \ell = 1}^{K_iK_j - K^*} x_{ikt}x_{j\ell t'}\theta_{ijk\ell}).$$

The number of terms in first summation are K^* and in the second one $K_iK_j-K^*$, where K^* is the number of variables appearing in both the ith and j^{th} equations.

Also, the matrix Δ_{ij} in (11.16) changes to

$$\Delta_{ij} = \begin{bmatrix} \theta_{ij11} & \cdots & \theta_{ij1K_j} \\ \vdots & & \\ \theta_{ijK_i1} & \cdots & \theta_{ijK_iK_j} \end{bmatrix}$$

and the vector θ_{ij} in (11.29) becomes

$$\theta_{ij} = (\sigma_{ij}, \theta_{ij11}, \ldots, \theta_{ij1K_j}, \ldots, \theta_{ijK_{i1}}, \ldots, \theta_{ijK_iK_j})',$$

which is a K_iK_j+1 column vector. Finally, X_{ij} is now a $Tx(K_iK_j+1)$ matrix such that its element given by t^{th} row and $(k\ell+1)^{th}$ column is

$$(11.38) \quad \begin{array}{ll} 1, & \text{for } k=0 \text{ and } \ell=1, \\ x_{ikt}x_{j\ell t}, & \text{for } k=1,\ldots,K_i \text{ and } \ell=1,\ldots,K_j. \end{array}$$

11.4 A SPECIAL CASE

To illustrate the model and some of the above mentioned points we may consider a two-equations model:

$$y_{1t} = \beta_{11}x_{11t} + w_{1t},$$

$$y_{2t} = \beta_{21}x_{21t} + \beta_{22}x_{22t} + w_{2t},$$

where

$$w_{1t} = \varepsilon_{11t}x_{11t} + u_{1t}$$

and

$$w_{2t} = \varepsilon_{21t}x_{21t} + \varepsilon_{22t}x_{22t} + u_{2t}.$$

The first exogenous variable in the second equation is the same as that in the first equation. Thus, under the assumptions (i) to (iv), $Ew_{1t} = Ew_{2t} = 0$, and

$$Ew_{1t}^2 = x_{11t}^2\theta_{11,11} + \sigma_{11} = \omega_{11tt},$$

$$Ew_{2t}^2 = x_{21t}^2\theta_{22,11} + x_{22t}^2\theta_{22,22} + \sigma_{22} = \omega_{22tt},$$

$$Ew_{1t}w_{2t} = x_{11t}x_{21t}\theta_{12,11} + \sigma_{12} = \omega_{12tt},$$

$$Ew_{1t}w_{2t'} = Ew_{1t}w_{1t'} = Ew_{2t}w_{2t'} = 0.$$

Note that these variances and covariances would also follow from the expression:

$$Ew_{it}w_{jt'} = \delta_{tt'}(\sigma_{ij} + \sum_{k=1}^{K_i}\sum_{\ell=1}^{K_j} x_{ikt}x_{j\ell t'}\delta_{k\ell}\theta_{ijk\ell})$$

given in (11.6). For example, if j=i=1 then $K_i = K_j = 1$ and we will get Ew_{1t}^2 for t=t', and so on.

Thus the matrix Ω in this case is

$$\Omega = \begin{bmatrix} \Omega_{11} & \Omega_{12} \\ \Omega_{21} & \Omega_{22} \end{bmatrix},$$

where Ω_{ij} for each i,j=1, 2 is a diagonal matrix which can be written by using (11.15) as

$$\Omega_{11} = \begin{bmatrix} x_{111}^2\theta_{11,11} + \sigma_{11} & \cdots & 0 \\ \vdots & \ddots & \\ 0 & & x_{11T}^2\theta_{11,11} + \sigma_{11} \end{bmatrix},$$

$$\Omega_{12} = \begin{bmatrix} x_{111}x_{211}\theta_{12,11} + \sigma_{12} & \cdots & 0 \\ \vdots & \ddots & \\ 0 & & x_{111}^2 x_{21T}\theta_{12,11} + \sigma_{12} \end{bmatrix},$$

$$\Omega_{22} = \begin{bmatrix} \omega_1 & \cdots & 0 \\ \vdots & \ddots & \\ 0 & & \omega_T \end{bmatrix}.$$

where

$$\omega_t = x_{21t}\theta_{22,11} + x_{22t}^2\theta_{22,22} + \sigma_{22},$$

$$\text{for } t=1,2,..,T.$$

Thus the GLS estimator of the vector $\beta=(\beta_{11}, \beta_{21}, \beta_{22})'$ can be written as $(X'\Omega^{-1}X)^{-1}X'\Omega^{-1}y$. We note that

$$X_1 = \begin{bmatrix} x_{111} \\ \vdots \\ x_{11T} \end{bmatrix}, \qquad X_2 = \begin{bmatrix} x_{211} & x_{221} \\ \vdots & \vdots \\ x_{21T} & x_{22T} \end{bmatrix}$$

so that

$$X = \begin{bmatrix} X_1 & 0 \\ 0 & X_2 \end{bmatrix}$$

is a (2Tx3) matrix. To estimate Ω matrix we would require estimation of σ_{11}, σ_{12}, σ_{22}, $\theta_{11,11}$, $\theta_{22,11}$, $\theta_{22,22}$, $\theta_{12,11}$. Thus if we form the vector $\theta_{ij} = (\sigma_{ij}, \theta_{ij,11}, \theta_{ij,22})'$, which is a 3x1 vector, then from (11.32), we obtain

$$(11.39) \qquad \hat{w}_{ij} = M_{ij}X_{ij}\theta_{ij} + \ell_{ij}; \qquad i,j=1,2,$$

where X_{ij} is a Tx3 matrix given by

$$X_{ij} = \begin{bmatrix} 1 & x_{i11}x_{j11} & x_{i11}x_{j21} \\ \vdots & & \vdots \\ 1 & x_{i1T}x_{j1T} & x_{i1T}x_{j2T} \end{bmatrix}.$$

The Tx1 vector $\hat{w}_{ij}$ of the least squares residuals has been obtained by using its definition given in (11.28). Now, the equation (11.39) can be used to obtain the least squares estimators of θ_{ij} for $i,j=1,2$ and hence the unknown elements in Ω.

NOTES

1. In the case where we have intercept in our model then

$$\omega_{ijtt'} = \delta_{tt'}(\theta^*_{ij11} + \sum_{k=2}^{K_i} x_{ikt}x_{jkt}\theta_{ijkk}),$$

$$\theta^*_{ij11} = \sigma_{ij} + \theta_{ij11}.$$

In this case we cannot estimate σ_{ij} and θ_{ij11} separately.

2. Also see Singh and Ullah (1974).

3. If A is an mxm matrix and B is another mxm matrix, then the Hadamard matrix product implies the multiplication of each element of the matrix A with the corresponding element of the matrix B, and it is written as A*B. See Rao (1973), p. 30.

4. For j=i, that is in the single equation case, this result has been derived in Chapter 4. In the SUR case Singh and Ullah (1974) have derived this result when $K_i=K_j$.

5. For proof of this follow Chapters 5 and 13. Also see Singh and Ullah (1974).

12. Simultaneous Equation Systems: Identification Problem

12.1 MODEL SPECIFICATION

This chapter is concerned with the problem of identification in the simultaneous equation model with purely random coefficients. Consider a set of M structural equations of a simultaneous equation model with varying coefficients in K predetermined variables:

$$(12.1) \qquad \begin{array}{c} \gamma_{11t}y_{1t}+\ldots+\gamma_{M1t}y_{Mt}+\beta_{11t}x_{1t}+\ldots+\beta_{K1t}x_{Kt}=0, \\ \vdots \\ \gamma_{1Mt}y_{1t}+\ldots+\gamma_{MMt}y_{Mt}+\beta_{1Mt}x_{1t}+\ldots+\beta_{KMt}x_{Kt}=0, \end{array}$$

where y_{mt} is the tth (t=1,...,T) observation on the mth (m=1,...,M) endogenous or jointly dependent variable, and x_{kt} is the tth (t=1,...T) observation on the kth (k=1,...,K) predetermined variable. The γ's and β's are randomly varying structural coefficients of the endogenous and predetermined variables. We assume that the predetermined variables are either fixed exogenous (current or lagged) or lagged endogenous variables. To give the real flavour of a simultaneous equation model with random coefficients we utilise a version of Klein's (1950) Model I of the US economy:

Klein's Model I with Varying Coefficients

(1) Consumption Equation

$$C_t = \gamma_{12t}P_t+\gamma_{13t}(W_t+W'_t)+\beta_{11t}+\beta_{12t}P_{t-1}$$

(2) Investment Equation

$$I_t = \gamma_{22t}P_t + \beta_{21t} + \beta_{22t}P_{t-1} + \beta_{23t}K_{t-1}$$

(3) Labour Equation

$$W_t = \gamma_{32t}X_t + \beta_{31t} + \beta_{32t}X_{t-1} + \beta_{33t}(t-1931)$$

(4) National Accounts: Definition 1

$$X_t = C_t + I_t + G_t$$

(5) Profit and Loss Account: Definition 2

$$P_t = X_t - W_t - T^*_t$$

(6) Change in Capital Stock = Investment: Definition 3

$$K_t - K_{t-1} = I_t$$

where

- C Aggregate consumption
- P Total profits
- W Total wages paid by private industry
- W' Government wage bill
- I Net investment
- K Capital stock
- X Total Production of private industry
- T* Taxes
- G Government expenditure
- t Time trend.

The γ's and β's vary with observations. The model is dynamic in the sense that it contains some lagged variables. It consists of three behavioural equations and three identities expressed in six endogenous or jointly dependent variables and eight predetermined variables.

The six endogenous variables are:

C, P, W, I, K, X

The eight predetermined variables are comprised of five exogenous variables:

G, Intercept, t, T*, W'

and three lagged (one period) endogenous variables:

K_{-1}, P_{-1}, X_{-1} .

The points to note in the specification of structural equations for the simultaneous equation model with varying coefficients given in model (12.1) and Klein's Model I are:

(i) The disturbance term in the behavioural equation is excluded or subsumed into the randomly varying intercept term in the equation, and it is identically equal to zero for the identities in the model.

(ii) Alternative formulations for coefficient variations discussed in Chapter 2 may be possible but we shall consider the case of purely random coefficient variation.

(iii) In most cases some of the endogenous and predetermined variables are excluded **a priori** from each behavioural equation of the simultaneous equation model. The varying structural coefficients γ's and β's of all those variables that do not appear in the equation are assumed to be zero.

(iv) The coefficients of identities in the model are assumed to be fixed and known.

(v) In each behavioural equation one of the γ's is assumed to be minus one and the endogenous variable associated with the unit coefficient is a left hand endogenous (dependent) variable. This assumption is known as a normalisation condition for the model.

The model (12.1) can be written in matrix form, at time t, as

$$(12.2) \qquad Y_t \Gamma_t + X_t B_t = 0,$$

where

$$(12.2a) \qquad Y_t = (y_{1t}, \ldots, y_{Mt}) \text{ and } X_t = (x_{1t}, \ldots, x_{Kt})$$

are the tth rows respectively of the matrices

$$(12.2b) \qquad Y = \begin{bmatrix} y_{11} & \cdots & y_{M1} \\ \vdots & & \vdots \\ y_{1T} & \cdots & y_{Mt} \end{bmatrix} \text{ and } X = \begin{bmatrix} x_{11} & \cdots & x_{K1} \\ \vdots & & \vdots \\ x_{1T} & \cdots & x_{Kt} \end{bmatrix}.$$

Further,

$$(12.2c) \qquad \Gamma_t = \begin{bmatrix} \gamma_{11t} & \cdots & \gamma_{1Mt} \\ \vdots & & \vdots \\ \gamma_{M1t} & \cdots & \gamma_{MMt} \end{bmatrix}; \quad B_t = \begin{bmatrix} \beta_{11t} & \cdots & \beta_{1Mt} \\ \vdots & & \vdots \\ \beta_{K1t} & \cdots & \beta_{KMt} \end{bmatrix},$$

and 0 is a MxM null matrix.

It should be observed that the successive columns of Γ_t and B_t provide the coefficients of different equations in (12.1); the first column of Γ_t and the first column of B_t give the coefficients in the first structural equation, and the last column of Γ_t and the last column of B_t give the coefficients of the Mth equation.

The reduced form of the equation system (12.1) is derived by solving the set of structural equations for jointly dependent variables in terms of the predetermined variables and the structural disturbances. This can be done most conveniently in matrix notation by postmultiplying both sides of (12.2) by Γ_t^{-1}. Thus we obtain

$$(12.3) \qquad Y_t = X_t \Pi_t,$$

where

$$(12.4) \qquad \Pi_t = \begin{bmatrix} \pi_{11t} & \cdots & \pi_{1Mt} \\ \vdots & & \vdots \\ \pi_{K1t} & \cdots & \pi_{KMt} \end{bmatrix} = -B_t \Gamma_t^{-1}$$

is the matrix of reduced form coefficients. The successive columns of Π_t provide the coefficients of predetermined variables in different reduced form equations corresponding to different jointly dependent variables. It should be noted that the existence of reduced form equations in (12.3) requires the matrix Γ_t of endogenous variables to be a nonsingular matrix; that is the determinant value of Γ_t should not be equal to zero. This condition is reasonable because singularity of Γ_t would imply that small changes in predetermined variables lead to very large changes in endogenous variables.

Further, note that particular equations of the model (say the first) can be compactly written as

$$(12.4a) \qquad Y_t \gamma_{.1t} + X_t \beta_{.1t} = 0,$$

where $\gamma_{.1t}$ and $\beta_{.1t}$ are the first columns of matrices Γ_t and B_t respectively.[1]

12.1.1 Assumptions of the Model

Now we may explicitly state all assumptions of the model with varying coefficients:

Assumption 1: Γ_t is a nonsingular matrix. This assumption is required for the reduced form equations of the model to exist. Some of its implications were stated above while the others are examined later in light of Assumption 2.

Assumption 2: The elements of each column of Γ_t and B_t are random such that

$$(12.5) \qquad \Gamma_t = \Gamma + V_t \text{ and } B_t = B + U_t,$$

where

$$(12.6) \qquad \Gamma = \begin{bmatrix} \gamma_{11} & \cdots & \gamma_{1M} \\ \vdots & & \vdots \\ \gamma_{M1} & \cdots & \gamma_{MM} \end{bmatrix} \text{ and } B = \begin{bmatrix} \gamma_{11} & \cdots & \gamma_{1M} \\ \vdots & & \vdots \\ \gamma_{K1} & \cdots & \gamma_{KM} \end{bmatrix}$$

are constant matrices of order MxM and KxM respectively and

$$(12.7) \qquad V_t = \begin{bmatrix} v_{11t} & \cdots & v_{1Mt} \\ \vdots & & \vdots \\ v_{M1t} & \cdots & v_{MMt} \end{bmatrix} \text{ and } U_t = \begin{bmatrix} u_{11t} & \cdots & u_{1Mt} \\ \vdots & & \vdots \\ u_{K1t} & \cdots & u_{KMt} \end{bmatrix}.$$

We now consider the following result:[2]

$$(12.8) \qquad \Gamma_t^{-1} = (\Gamma + V_t)^{-1} = (I + \Gamma^{-1} V_t)^{-1} \Gamma^{-1}$$

$$= [I - \Gamma^{-1}(I + V_t \Gamma^{-1})^{-1} V_t] \Gamma^{-1}$$

$$= \Gamma^{-1} - \theta_t,$$

where

$$(I + \Gamma^{-1} V_t)^{-1} = I - \Gamma^{-1}(I + V_t \Gamma^{-1})^{-1} V_t$$

and θ_t is a MxM matrix of stochastic elements

(12.9) $$\theta_t = \Gamma^{-1}(I+V_t\Gamma^{-1})^{-1}V_t\Gamma^{-1}.$$

Thus the reduced form equations (12.3) can be written as

(12.10) $$Y_t = -X_t(B+U_t)(\Gamma^{-1}-\theta_t) = X_t\Pi + W_t,$$

where

(12.11) $$\Pi = -B\Gamma^{-1} \text{ and } W_t = X_t(B\theta_t - U_t\Gamma^{-1} + U_t\theta_t).$$

Assumption 3: The elements of each row of the TxK matrix X are distributed independently of the structural disturbances in the columns of Γ_t and B_t. Alternatively, the elements of X are nonstochastic and fixed in repeated samples, which do not permit the presence of lagged endogenous variables in X. However, in most cases (especially in large sample analysis) the independence of predetermined variables and structural disturbances is all that is required. The assumption that the elements of X are nonstochastic and fixed is required in the small sample analysis of the following chapter.

Assumption 4: The rank of X is $K<T$. This implies that the columns of X are linearly independent and X'X is nonsingular. For most econometric models $K<T$. However, for many large econometric models it is possible that $K>T$. This case will be mentioned at proper places.

Assumption 5: If the elements of X are stochastic we would require that each individual element of

$$\underset{T\to\infty}{\text{plim}}\ (1/T)X'X$$

be finite and that this is a nonsingular matrix. When X is purely nonstochastic, we require $\lim_{T\to\infty}(1/T)X'X$ to be finite and nonsingular.

The equations of the structural system (12.2) are characterised by disturbances in Γ_t and B_t. We make the following assumption about the stochastic behaviour of these disturbances.

Assumption 6: The M column vectors of the structural disturbances

$$(12.12) \qquad v_{.it} = (v_{1it} \cdots v_{Mit})'$$

for t=1,...,T of matrix V_t, introduced in (12.5), are independent random drawings from an M-dimensional normal population with (i) means, (ii) variances and (iii) covariances as

(i) $Ev_{jit} = 0;$

(ii) $V(v_{jit}) = \sigma^*_{jj,ii};$

(iii) $\text{cov}(v_{jit}, v_{j'i't'}) = 0, \quad \text{if } t \neq t',\ j \neq j'$

$= \sigma^*_{jj,ii'}, \text{ if } t=t',\ j=j';$

where i,i', j,j'=1,...,M and t,t'=1,...,T. Also v_{jit} represents disturbance in the jth parameter of ith equation at time t. Similarly,

Assumption 7: The **M** column vectors of the structural disturbances

(12.13) $u_{.it} = (u_{1it}, \ldots, u_{Kit})'$

for $t=1,\ldots,T$, of the matrix U_t introduced in (12.7) are independent random drawings from an M-dimensional normal population with (i) means, (ii) variances and (iii) covariances as

(i) $Eu_{kit} = 0;$

(ii) $V(u_{kit}) = \sigma_{kk,ii};$

(iii) $\text{cov}(u_{kit}, u_{k'i't'}) = 0,$ if $t \neq t'$, $k \neq k'$

$= \sigma_{kk,ii'}$, if $t=t', k=k'$;

where $k,k'=1,\ldots,K$; $i,i'=1,\ldots,M$ and $t,t'=1,\ldots,T$. In addition $Ev_{jit}u_{ki't'}=0$ for all i,k,j,j',t and t'. The u_{kit} represents the disturbance in the kth parameter of ith equation at time t.

Thus the structural disturbances representing randomness in the structural coefficients have zero mean and are homoscedastic. Further, Assumptions 6 and 7 do not permit any serial correlation among disturbances. The contemporaneous disturbances of coefficients in different structural equations are, however, correlated as reflected by $\sigma_{kk,ii'}$ and $\sigma_{jj,ii'}$.

In vector form Assumptions 6 and 7 can be written as

(12.14) $Ev_{.it} = 0$ and $Eu_{.it} = 0$.

Further,

$$(12.15)\qquad Ev_{.it}v'_{.i't} = \Sigma^*_{ii'} = \begin{bmatrix} \sigma^*_{11,ii'} & \cdots & 0 \\ \vdots & \ddots & \\ 0 & & \sigma^*_{MM,ii'} \end{bmatrix},$$

$$Ev_{.it}v'_{.i't'} = 0, \qquad \text{for } t \neq t',$$

and likewise

$$(12.16)\qquad Eu_{.it}u'_{i't} = \Sigma_{ii'} = \begin{bmatrix} \sigma_{11,ii'} & \cdots & 0 \\ \vdots & & \\ 0 & \cdots & \sigma_{KK,ii'} \end{bmatrix},$$

$$Eu_{.it}u'_{.i't'} = 0, \qquad t \neq t'.$$

Also

$$Eu_{.it}v_{.i't'} = 0 \qquad \text{for all } i, i', t \text{ and } t'.$$

In the matrix form Assumptions 6 and 7 can be stated as

$$(12.17)\qquad EV_t = 0,\ EU_t = 0,$$

$$EV'_tV_t = \Sigma^* = \begin{bmatrix} \Sigma^*_{11} & \cdots & \Sigma^*_{1M} \\ \vdots & & \\ \Sigma^*_{M1} & \cdots & \Sigma^*_{MM} \end{bmatrix}$$

and

$$EU'_tU_t = \Sigma = \begin{bmatrix} \Sigma_{11} & \cdots & \Sigma_{1M} \\ \vdots & & \\ \Sigma_{M1} & \cdots & \Sigma_{MM} \end{bmatrix}.$$

With respect to the reduced form disturbance vector W_t in (12.11) we observe that though it is a linear function of U_t -- the disturbances in the coefficients of predetermined variables, it is not so with respect to V_t -- the disturbances in the coefficients of jointly dependent variables. Thus, in general, the assumption $EW_t=0$ may not hold. For this to be true we must be able to show that

$$(12.18) \quad Ew_t = X_t[BE\theta_t - EU_t\Gamma^{-1} + EU_tE\theta_t]$$

$$= X_tB(E\theta_t) = 0;$$

that is from (12.8) and (12.9)

$$(12.19) \quad E\theta_t = 0 \text{ or } E\Gamma_t^{-1} = E(\Gamma+V_t)^{-1} = \Gamma^{-1}.$$

If this would be true, then from (12.11)

$$EW_t'W_t = E[(\theta_t'B' - \Gamma'^{-1}U_t' + \theta_t'U_t')X_t'X_t(B\theta_t - U_t\Gamma^{-1} + U_t\theta_t)]$$

$$= E(\theta_t'B'X_t'X_tB\theta_t) + \Gamma'^{-1}E(U_t'X_t'X_tU_t)\Gamma^{-1} + E(\theta_t'U_t'X_t'X_tU_t\theta_t),$$

where we use the assumption that u's and v's are independent.

Unless $EW_t=0$ we cannot proceed with the identification and estimation of model (12.2). Therefore, we will consider below some special cases of model (12.2) in which this assumption will be true. We shall first consider the identification of the model in each of these special cases and then take up the estimation problem.

12.2 IDENTIFICATION IN THE FIXED COEFFICIENT MODELS

Consider the case when $\Gamma_t = \Gamma$ and $B = B + U_t$, where

$$(12.20) \qquad U_t = \begin{bmatrix} u_{11t} & u_{12t} & \cdots & u_{1Mt} \\ 0 & 0 & & 0 \\ \vdots & \vdots & & \vdots \\ 0 & 0 & & 0 \end{bmatrix};$$

the subscript 1 in u_{1it}, $i=1,\ldots,M$, represents the coefficient of the first predetermined variable x_{1t} which is considered in this case to be unity for $t=1,\ldots,T$. The U_t in (12.20) implies that each equation of the model is considered to have random intercept while the coefficients of other predetermined and jointly dependent variables are fixed.

For this case the model in (12.2) reduces to

$$(12.21) \qquad Y_t\Gamma + X_tB + U_{1.t} = 0,$$

where the 1xM vector $U_{1.t} = (u_{11t}\cdots u_{1Mt})$ is the first row of the matrix U_t in (12.7). The set of M equations (12.21) is the usual classical simultaneous equation model, at time t, with the fixed coefficients. The reduced form in this case is

$$(12.22) \qquad Y_t = X_t\Pi + W_{1.t},$$

where $\Pi = -B\Gamma^{-1}$ and $W_{1.t} = -U_{1.t}\Gamma^{-1}$ is now a linear function of structural disturbances such that

$$(12.23) \qquad EW_{1.t} = 0, \quad EW_{1.t}'W_{1.t} = \Gamma'^{-1}\Sigma\Gamma^{-1} = \Omega ,$$

where

$$(12.24)\quad \Sigma = \begin{bmatrix} \sigma_{11,11} & \cdots & \sigma_{11,1M} \\ \vdots & & \\ \sigma_{11,M1} & \cdots & \sigma_{11,MM} \end{bmatrix} = EU'_{1.t}U_{1.t}$$

The model (12.21) for t=1,...,T, can be written as

$$(12.25)\quad Y\Gamma+XB+U_{1.} = 0,$$

where Y and X are as given in (12.2b) and

$$(12.26)\quad U_{1.} = \begin{bmatrix} u_{111} & \cdots & u_{1M1} \\ \vdots & & \\ u_{11T} & \cdots & u_{1MT} \end{bmatrix}$$

is a TxM matrix such that $EU_{1.}=0$ and $\frac{1}{T}\, EU'_{1.}U_{1.}= \Sigma$. The reduced form for Y is

$$(12.27)\quad Y= X\Pi+W_{1.},$$

where $W_{1.}= -U_{1.}\Gamma^{-1}$.

If we have sufficient data available in the form of long time series of observations on y's and x's, we can determine (or estimate) parameters Π and Ω of the reduced form equation (12.22). The problem of identification is then to see whether we can determine (or estimate) the structural parameters in Γ, B and Σ from the estimates of reduced form parameters $\Pi= -B\Gamma^{-1}$ and $\Omega= \Gamma'^{-1}\Sigma\Gamma^{-1}$. The number of known values from Π and Ω are $MK+\frac{1}{2}M(M+1)$ and unknowns required to be determined in Γ, B and Σ given $\Pi\Gamma+B= 0$ are $M^2+MK+\frac{1}{2}M(M+1)-M$. Thus, the excess of unknown over known equals M(M-1). Hence without some a priori information (restrictions) on the structural parameters in Γ, B and Σ, it is impossible to determine the unknowns or identify the model. We shall therefore analyse below the identification of parameters of each equation of (12.21) under different types of linear **a priori** restrictions.

12.2.1 Identification by Zero Restrictions

One approach to identification is to impose zero restrictions, that is equating some elements of the matrix Γ and B to be zero. This approach is based on the fact that each structural equation of the complete system represents some hypothesis about the behaviour of certain groups of individuals or variables. For example, in Klein's Model I of United States economy, the first equation is an hypothesis regarding the behaviour of consumers whereas the second and third are related to investment and demand for labour. Therefore it is rather obvious that all variables of the complete system will not necessarily be represented in each equation. For example, only the variables in Klein's Model which reflect consumer behaviour would appear in a consumption function and others would appear with zero coefficients.

Let us then suppose that $m_1+1 \leq M$ jointly dependent and $K_1 \leq K$ predetermined variables enter any one (say, the first) structural equation of the system. In addition, we wish to identify one endogenous variable as the 'left hand side' variable by letting its associated coefficient equal minus one. Further, with some rearrangements we can write

$$(12.28) \qquad Y = [y_1 Y_1 Y_1^*], \qquad X = [X_1 X_1^*],$$

and

$$(12.29) \quad \gamma_{.1} = \begin{bmatrix} -1 \\ \gamma_1 \\ 0 \end{bmatrix}, \qquad \beta_{.1} = \begin{bmatrix} \beta_1 \\ \\ 0 \end{bmatrix},$$

where Y_1 and Y_1^* are matrices of T observations on m_1 included and $m_1^* = M-m_1-1$ excluded jointly dependent variables respectively. Similarly, X_1 and X_1^* are matrices of T observations on K_1 included and $K_1^* = K-K_1$ excluded predetermined variables. The vectors $\gamma_{.1}$ and $\beta_{.1}$ are the first column of Γ and B respectively with γ_1 and β_1 of order m_1x1 and K_1x1. The null vectors in $\gamma_{.1}$ and $\beta_{.1}$ are of orders m_1^*x1 and K_1^*x1 respectively.

Now the first equation of the system, from (12.25), can be written as

$$(12.30) \quad y_1 = Y_1\gamma_1 + X_1\beta_1 + u_1,$$

where u_1 is the first column of U_1.

The reduced form equation (12.27) can be correspondingly partitioned as

$$(12.31) \quad [y_1 Y_1, Y_1^*] = [X_1 X_1^*] \begin{bmatrix} \pi_{11} & \Pi_{11} & \Pi_{11}^* \\ \pi_{21} & \Pi_{21} & \Pi_{21}^* \end{bmatrix} + [w_1 W_1 W_1^*],$$

where π_{11}, π_{21} are K_1x1 and K_1^*x1 vectors, Π_{11}, Π_{21} are K_1xm_1 and K_1^*xm_1 matrices, and Π_{11}^*, Π_{21}^* are K_1xm_1^*, and K_1^*xm_1^* matrices respectively of reduced form parameters. Further, w_1, W_1 and W_1^* are respectively Tx1, Txm_1 and Txm_1^* vectors of disturbances corresponding to y_1, Y_1 and Y_1^*.

Our next aim is to obtain the relationship between the parameters of the above single equation with the reduced form parameters. For this we first write such a relationship in the complete system, viz.

$$(12.32) \qquad \Pi\Gamma + B = 0$$

and $W_1\Gamma = -U_1$. Then taking only the first columns of Γ and B we get

$$(12.33) \qquad \Pi\gamma_{.1} + \beta_{.1} = 0$$

or

$$(12.34) \qquad \begin{bmatrix} \pi_{11} & \Pi_{11} & \Pi_{11}^* \\ \pi_{21} & \Pi_{21} & \Pi_{21}^* \end{bmatrix} \begin{bmatrix} -1 \\ \gamma_1 \\ 0 \end{bmatrix} + \begin{bmatrix} \beta_1 \\ 0 \end{bmatrix} = 0.$$

This provides the following identifiability relationships between the structural parameters and the reduced form parameters for the first equation, i.e.

$$(12.35) \qquad \pi_{11} = \Pi_{11}\gamma_1 + \beta_1,$$

$$\pi_{21} = \Pi_{21}\gamma_1.$$

Also from (12.32), for the first equation in $W_{1.}\Gamma = -U_{1.}$, we write

$$[w_1 W_1 W_1^*] \begin{bmatrix} -1 \\ \gamma_1 \\ 0 \end{bmatrix} = -u_1$$

or

(12.36) $w_1 = W_1\gamma_1 + u_1$.

Note that these relationships have been obtained after using **a priori** zero restrictions. We shall now investigate the conditions under which γ_1 and β_1 can be determined.

The relation $\pi_{21} = \Pi_{21}\gamma_1$ is a set of K_1^* non-homogeneous equations in m_1 unknowns γ's. Thus a necessary and sufficient condition for its solution is that

(12.37) Rank Π_{21} = Rank $[\pi_{21}\Pi_{21}] = m_1$.

This is called the 'rank condition' for identification. Since the rank of Π_{21} cannot exceed the number of its rows or columns and Π_{21} is of order $K_1^* x m_1$, the following condition must be satisfied.

(12.38) $K_1^* \geqslant m_1$.

This is a necessary condition of the identifiability of the equation and it has been called the 'order condition'. The condition (12.38) implies that 'the number of predetermined variables excluded from the equation must not be smaller than the number of jointly dependent variables included in the equation less one'.

If $K_1^* > m_1$ we say the equation is 'overidentified' and the equation is called 'justidentified' if $K_1^* = m_1$. The equation is of course not identifiable if K_1^* is smaller than m_1. Overidentification normally provides multiple solutions whereas exact identification provides a unique and underidentification provides no solution.

The rank condition can be stated in a form that is more convenient to use in practice. Let A be a (K+M)xM matrix such that

$$(12.39)\qquad A=\begin{bmatrix}\Gamma\\ B\end{bmatrix}=\begin{bmatrix}-1 & \\ \gamma_1 & \Gamma_1\\ 0 & \Gamma_2\\ \hline \beta_1 & B_1\\ 0 & B_2\end{bmatrix},$$

where Γ_1, Γ_2, B_1 and B_2 are the submatrices of order $(m_1+1)x(M-1)$, $m_1^*x(M-1)$, $K_1x(M-1)$, $K_1^*x(M-1)$ respectively. Then the condition that Rank $\Pi_{21}=m_1$ is equivalent to

$$(12.40)\qquad \text{Rank}\begin{bmatrix}\Gamma_2\\ B_2\end{bmatrix}=M-1,$$

that is the rank of the matrix of coefficients of excluded endogenous and predetermined variables from the first equation and the remaining M-1 equations. The proof of this can be found in Hood and Koopmans (1953, Chapter VI) and other econometrics textbooks.

The above rank conditions, though equivalent, represent two different ways of looking at the identification problem. Condition (12.37) is based on the requirement that we should be able to derive the structural parameters from the reduced form parameters. Condition (12.40) requires that any linear combination of the first equation and the remaining (M-1) equations should not produce an equation similar to the first equation.

12.2.2 An Example

To illustrate these identification conditions, we consider the two-equation model for the American meat market.[3] The first equation of the system is a demand equation for meat:

$$(12.41) \qquad y_1 = \gamma_1 y_2 + \beta_1 x_1 + u_1;$$

and the second equation is the corresponding supply equation:

$$(12.42) \qquad y_1 = \gamma_2 y_2 + \beta_2 x_2 + \beta_3 x_3 + u_2,$$

where

y_1 = quantity of meat bought and sold,
y_2 = a deflated price index of meat,
x_1 = real disposable income,
x_2 = an index of the cost of processing meat,
x_3 = an index of the cost of producing agricultural products

and u_1, u_2 are the structural disturbances.

It is easy to verify that the first equation (12.41) of this system is overidentified because $K_1^* = 2$ and $m_1 = 1$, and the second equation (12.42) is justidentified because in this case $K_1^* = m_1 = 1$.

To examine the rank condition of identifiability (in terms of structural coefficients) let us observe that for (12.41) we would require that the rank of the 2x1 matrix $[\beta_2, \beta_3]$ must be unity, i.e. at least one of the coefficients β_2, β_3 must be nonzero; and for the second equation (12.42) we require that the rank of the 1x1 matrix--or a scalar --β_1 must be one, i.e. β_1 must be nonzero.

The rank condition (12.37)--in terms of reduced form coefficients--can be examined if we write the reduced form of (12.41) and (12.42) as follows:

$$(12.43) \quad y_1 = -\frac{\gamma_2\beta_1}{\gamma_1-\gamma_2}x_1 + \frac{\gamma_1\beta_2}{\gamma_1-\gamma_2}x_2 + \frac{\gamma_1\beta_3}{\gamma_1-\gamma_2}x_3 + \frac{\gamma_1 u_2-\gamma_2 u_1}{\gamma_1-\gamma_2}$$

$$(12.44) \quad y_2 = \frac{\beta_1}{\gamma_1-\gamma_2}x_1 + \frac{\beta_2}{\gamma_1-\gamma_2}x_2 + \frac{\beta_3}{\gamma_1-\gamma_2}x_3 + \frac{u_2-u_1}{\gamma_1-\gamma_2}.$$

For the first equation (12.41) the rank condition (12.37) requires

$$(12.45) \quad \text{Rank}\begin{bmatrix}\gamma_1\beta_2/\gamma_1-\gamma_2 & \beta_2/\gamma_1-\gamma_2\\ \gamma_1\beta_3/\gamma_1-\gamma_2 & \beta_3/\gamma_1-\gamma_2\end{bmatrix} = 1;$$

and we observe that the first column of the 2x2 matrix involved here is γ_1 times the second column. Therefore, the rank of this matrix will be 1, provided $\gamma_1 \neq \gamma_2$ and at least one of the coefficients β_2, β_3 is nonzero. In fact $\gamma_1 \neq \gamma_2$ is required so that the reduced form of the system exists. Similarly, for the second equation the rank condition would require

$$(12.46) \quad \text{Rank}\begin{bmatrix}-\gamma_2\beta_1/\gamma_1-\gamma_2\\ -\beta_1/\gamma_1-\gamma_2\end{bmatrix} = 1,$$

i.e. $\gamma_1 \neq \gamma_2$ and $\beta_1 \neq 0$.

12.2.3 Identification by General Linear Homogeneous and Nonhomogeneous Restrictions

General linear homogeneous restrictions on Γ and B include restrictions of the type $\gamma_{21}-\gamma_{31}=0$, $\gamma_{41}=-\beta_{41}$, etc. The zero restrictions considered above are then a special case. To develop identification by general linear homogeneous restrictions we consider again the matrix A, viz.

$$A=\begin{bmatrix}\Gamma\\ \\ B\end{bmatrix},$$

where Γ and B are as given in (12.6). Further, let $\delta_{.1}=(-1,\gamma_{21},\ldots,\gamma_{M1},\beta_{11},\ldots,\beta_{K1})'$ be the (M+K)x1 vector of elements in the first column of A related to the coefficients of the first equation. Then we may express the restriction on the first equation as

$$(12.47)\qquad \delta'_{.1}R=0,$$

where R is a (M+K)xr matrix of known elements where r columns equal the number of restrictions. For example if M=3, K=4, $\gamma_{21}-\gamma_{31}=0$ and $\gamma_{41}=-\beta_{41}$ then

$$R=\begin{bmatrix}0 & 0\\ 1 & 0\\ -1 & 0\\ 0 & 1\\ 0 & 0\\ 0 & 0\\ 0 & -1\end{bmatrix}.$$

The rank condition (necessary and sufficient)

of identification of the structural parameters of the first equation under (12.47) is then

(12.48) $\text{Rank}(A'R) = M-1.$

For proof see Fisher (1966). However, since multiplying a matrix by another cannot increase its rank, a necessary condition (also a 'general order condition') of identification is

$$\text{Rank}\ (R) \geq M-1.$$

This is easier to check in practice. A further necessary condition for identification, which is necessary for the 'general order condition' to be met, is

$$r \geq M-1.$$

Thus if Rank (R) > M-1 the equation is overidentified, if Rank (R)= M-1 it is justidentified and if Rank (R) < M-1 it is underidentified.

When the restrictions are linear nonhomogeneous we can write them as

$$\delta'_{.1}R = c,$$

where c has at least one nonzero element. These kinds of restrictions are quite common in econometric work. The restriction could be, say $\gamma_{21}+\gamma_{31}=1$ and so on. For such a case the rank condition becomes

$$\text{Rank}\ (A'R) = M.$$

12.2.4 Some Further Problems in Identification

In the above discussion the identification was achieved by a priori restrictions on the structure of B and Γ but there was no restriction imposed on Σ. Another approach to identification is through the imposition of restrictions on the covariance matrix Σ along with the restrictions on Γ and B. Once again we could impose zero restrictions, such as $\sigma_{1i'}=0$ for some $i'\neq 1$. That is, the first equation is uncorrelated with the disturbance in some other equation. Alternatively we could impose non-zero restrictions in the form of known relative sizes of variance and/or covariances in Σ.

An example of the model where we have some specific zero restrictions on both Γ and Σ is a recursive model. In this case Γ is a triangular matrix with, say, lower offdiagonal elements zero and Σ is a diagonal matrix; hence all the offdiagonal elements are zero. In this case each equation is exactly identified for the simple reason that there are then $MK+M+\frac{1}{2}M(M+1)-M$ unknown structural parameters in the normalised system which is equal to the known reduced form parameters $MK+\frac{1}{2}M(M+1)$. Thus each structural parameter can be uniquely determined from the knowledge of the reduced form parameters.

12.3 IDENTIFICATION IN THE FIXED AND RANDOM COEFFICIENT MODELS

Consider the case when $\Gamma_t=\Gamma$ and $B_t=B+U_t$, where U_t is the full disturbance matrix as given in (12.7). This case implies that we have fixed coefficients of jointly dependent variables but random coefficients for predetermined variables. This model can be justified on the grounds that the policy makers normally have control over some exogenous variables and the coefficients of exogenous variables are not invariant with respect to changes in policy. Since W_t, the reduced form disturbance in (12.10) becomes a linear function of disturbances U_t when $\Gamma_t=\Gamma$, we get $EW_t=0$. In this case, the condition under which the parameters in B and Γ are identifiable will be exactly the same as discussed in the earlier section.

12.4 IDENTIFICATION WHEN ALL THE COEFFICIENTS ARE RANDOM

We now consider $\Gamma_t=\Gamma+V_t$ and $B_t= B+U_t$. In this case, it can be noted from (12.10) that W_t is not a linear function of disturbances. Hence we have to see first whether or not $EW_t=0$. If $EW_t=0$ then the condition of identifiability for B and Γ would be the same as in the cases discussed in Sections 12.2 to 12.3. On the other hand, if $EW_t \neq 0$ then the conditions would be different. We shall take up first the situations or the models for which $EW_t=0$, i.e. $E\theta_t=0$ or $E\Gamma_t^{-1}= \Gamma^{-1}$, and then consider models when $EW_t \neq 0$.

The condition $EW_t=0$, or $E\Gamma_t^{-1}= E(\Gamma+V_t)^{-1}=\Gamma^{-1}$ would be true for all those models for which the determinant of $(\Gamma+V_t)$ does not involve any of the elements of V_t. In other words

$$(12.49) \qquad \det.(\Gamma+V_t)= f(\Gamma)$$

because $\det.(\Gamma+V_t)$ is independent of V_t and θ_t. Thus, $(\Gamma_t+\Gamma)^{-1}= \Gamma^{-1}-\theta_t$ will only be a linear function of V_t; see equation (12.8). To see this we note that in general

$$(12.50) \qquad \theta_t = G(V_t)/\det.(I+V_t\Gamma^{-1});$$

$G(V_t)$ is the MxM matrix whose elements are the functions of the elements of V_t. These functions are linear in the sense that they will not involve the square or inverse of the elements of V_t. Thus, if $\det.(\Gamma+V_t)= f(\Gamma)$ is true then $E\theta_t=0$, which implies that $EW_t=0$. Two examples of the model are given below where the above condition is satisfied.

Example 1 (Triangular System). In this system Γ_t is a triangular matrix. With M=3 equations and assuming normalisation we write

$$\Gamma_t = \Gamma+V_t,$$

where

$$\Gamma_t = \begin{bmatrix} 1 & \gamma_{12t} & \gamma_{13t} \\ 0 & 1 & \gamma_{23t} \\ 0 & 0 & 1 \end{bmatrix}, \quad \Gamma = \begin{bmatrix} 1 & \gamma_{12} & \gamma_{13} \\ 0 & 1 & \gamma_{23} \\ 0 & 0 & 1 \end{bmatrix}$$

and

$$V_t = \begin{bmatrix} 0 & v_{12t} & v_{13t} \\ 0 & 0 & v_{23t} \\ 0 & 0 & 0 \end{bmatrix}.$$

For this system

$$(I+V_t\Gamma^{-1})^{-1}V_t = \begin{bmatrix} 0 & v_{12t} & v_{13t} + v_{23t}\, v_{12t} \\ 0 & 0 & v_{23t} \\ 0 & 0 & 0 \end{bmatrix},$$

and $\det.(I+V_t\Gamma^{-1})=1$. Thus $\det.(\Gamma+V_t)= \det.(I+V_t\Gamma^{-1})$, det.$(\Gamma) = f(\Gamma)$ and the condition (12.49) is satisfied. Therefore, using Assumption 6 and (12.50)

$$E\theta_t = \Gamma^{-1}[E(I+V_t\Gamma^{-1})^{-1}V_t] = 0.$$

This gives

$$E\Gamma_t^{-1} = \Gamma.$$

The above result is true for a triangular equations system of any size because det.$(I+V_t\Gamma^{-1})=1$ for a MxM triangular equation system.

Example 2. Now consider the following equations system:

$$y_{1t} = \gamma_{21t}y_{2t}+\gamma_{31t}y_{3t}+\beta_{11t}x_{1t},$$

$$y_{2t} = \gamma_{12}y_{1t}+\gamma_{22}y_{3t}+\beta_{12t}x_{2t},$$

$$y_{3t} = \gamma_{13}y_{1t}+\gamma_{23}y_{2t}+\beta_{13t}x_{3t}.$$

This implies that

$$\Gamma_t = \begin{bmatrix} 1 & -\gamma_{12} & -\gamma_{13} \\ -\gamma_{21t} & 1 & -\gamma_{23} \\ -\gamma_{31} & -\gamma_{22} & 1 \end{bmatrix}$$

$$= \begin{bmatrix} 1 & -\gamma_{12} & -\gamma_{13} \\ -\gamma_{21} & 1 & -\gamma_{23} \\ -\gamma_{31} & -\gamma_{22} & 1 \end{bmatrix} + \begin{bmatrix} 0 & 0 & 0 \\ -v_{21t} & 0 & 0 \\ 0 & 0 & 0 \end{bmatrix}.$$

This system consists of only one random parameter viz. γ_{21t} which is the coefficient of y_{2t} in the first equation. In this case

$$|\Gamma_t| = |\Gamma+V_t| = |I+V_t\Gamma^{-1}|\ |\Gamma|$$

$$= [1-\gamma_{12}\gamma_{23}\gamma_{31}-\gamma_{13}\gamma_{31}-\gamma_{22}\gamma_{23}-\gamma_{21t}(\gamma_{13}\gamma_{22}+\gamma_{12})],$$

which is not $f(\Gamma)$ and hence in this case $E\theta_t$ may not be zero. However, if $\gamma_{13}=\gamma_{12}=0$ or $\gamma_{22}=\gamma_{12}=0$ then $|\Gamma_t|$ will be $f(\Gamma)$ and satisfies the condition in (12.49). The zero restrictions on structural parameters indicate that if y_{1t} depends upon y_{2t} by way of a random coefficient, then y_{2t} must not either directly via the second equation or indirectly through the system depend upon y_{1t}.

In general if we have an M equation system in which the only parameter that is random is the coefficient of the second endogenous variable in the first equation, and there is no feedback of y_{2t} in terms of y_{1t}, then $|\Gamma_t|$ will be a function of Γ.

Now we consider the identification problem when $E\Gamma_t^{-1}\neq\Gamma^{-1}$, i.e. $EW_t\neq 0$. In this case the usual classical identification approach discussed in 12.2 will have to be modified. This is because now $E\Gamma_t^{-1}=\Gamma^{-1}-g(\Gamma)$, where $g(\Gamma)=E\theta_t$ is a nonlinear function of the elements of Γ provided $E\theta_t$ exists. Thus $E(y_t/x_t)\neq\Pi$, but $\Pi+Bg(\Gamma)$. The reduced form (12.10) becomes

$$\text{(12.51)}\quad Y_t = X_t\Pi + X_tBg(\Gamma) + X_tU_t(\theta_t-\Gamma^{-1})$$

$$= X_t\Pi + X_t\Pi_o + X_tU_t(\theta_t-\Gamma^{-1})$$

$$= X_t\Pi^* + W_t^*,$$

where

$$(12.52) \quad W_t^* = X_t U_t(\theta_t - \Gamma^{-1}), \quad \Pi^* = \Pi_o + \Pi; \quad \Pi_o = Bg(\Gamma)$$

and $\Pi = -B\Gamma^{-1}$ as before. Also,

$$(12.52a) \quad EW_t^* = X_t E(U_t) g(\Gamma) - X_t E(U_t)\Gamma^{-1} = 0.$$

The problem of identification now is whether we can determine the mean of the random structural parameters Γ and B from the knowledge of reduced form parameters $\Pi^* = \Pi + \Pi_o$. In all the cases considered so far $\Pi_o = BE(\theta_t) = Bg(\Gamma)$ was assumed to be zero and hence Π^* was equal to Π. In the case when Π_o is not zero but any other known matrix then the problem of identification reduces to the cases considered in 12.2, 12.3 and earlier in this section. This is because now $\Pi^* = -B\Gamma^{-1} + Bg(\Gamma)$ or $\Pi^*\Gamma - Bg(\Gamma)\Gamma = -B$ or $(\Pi^* - \Pi_o)\Gamma = -B$ or $\Pi\Gamma = -B$. However, in general, Π_o is neither zero nor a known matrix. For such situations the conditions of identifiability are not known in the literature.[4]

NOTES

1. The nx1 vector $a_{.t} = (a_{11} \ldots a_{nt})'$ and the nx1 vector $a_{t.}$ implies $a_{t.} = (a_{t1} \ldots a_{tn})'$ throughout this chapter.

2. See Footnote 2 of Chapter 10 for the inverse of the matrix.

3. See Tintner (1952).

4. See Kelejian (1974).

13. Simultaneous Equation Systems: Estimation

13.1 INTRODUCTION

In this chapter we will consider the estimation problem of the complete system

$$(13.1) \qquad Y_t\Gamma_t + X_tB_t = 0, \qquad t=1,\ldots,T,$$

as given in (12.2) under the following situations. [Recall that $Y_t=(y_{1t},\ldots,y_{Mt})$, $X_t=(x_{1t},\ldots,x_{Kt})$, $\Gamma_t=\Gamma+V_t$ and $B_t=B+U_t$].

(1) Classical Model; $\Gamma_t=\Gamma$ and $B_t=B+U_t$ where

$$U_t=\begin{bmatrix} u_{1.t} \\ \\ 0 \end{bmatrix},$$

$u_{1.t}=(u_{11t},\ldots,u_{1Mt})$ is a 1xM vector and 0 is a (M-1)xM zero matrix. Further, $x_{1t}=1$, for $t=1,\ldots,T$, in each equation of (13.1).

(2) Both Fixed and Random Coefficients; $\Gamma_t=\Gamma$, $B_t=B+U_t$, where U_t is the complete matrix given in (12.7).

(3) All Random Coefficients; $\Gamma_t=\Gamma+V_t$ and $B_t=B+V_t$ as given in (12.5).

In each of the above three cases there are two ways to estimate System (13.1): (a) Estimating each equation by taking into account the identifiability restrictions on only that equation; and (b) Estimating all equations together by taking into account all the identifiability restrictions in the system. In the former case the estimators are called limited information (LI) estimators whereas in the latter case they are called full information (FI) estimators. We shall first discuss the LI estimators.

13.2 LIMITED INFORMATION ESTIMATION OF THE CLASSICAL MODEL

In this case $\Gamma_t = \Gamma$, $B_t = B + U_t$, where U_t is given in Case 1 above. Thus the structural system (13.1), at time t, becomes

$$(13.2) \qquad Y_t \Gamma + X_t B + u_{1.t} = 0,$$

where Y_t is a 1xM vector of M jointly dependent variables, X_t is a 1xK vector of K predetermined variables, and $u_{1.t}$ is a 1xM vector of disturbances. Further,

$$(13.3) \qquad \Gamma = \begin{bmatrix} \gamma_{11} & \cdots & \gamma_{1M} \\ \vdots & & \vdots \\ \gamma_{M1} & \cdots & \gamma_{MM} \end{bmatrix} \text{ and } B = \begin{bmatrix} \beta_{11} & \cdots & \beta_{1K} \\ \vdots & & \vdots \\ \beta_{K1} & \cdots & \beta_{KM} \end{bmatrix}$$

are the MxM and KxM matrices respectively of fixed structural coefficients.

Let us consider, say, the first equation of System (13.2) as

$$(13.4) \qquad Y_t \gamma_{.1} + X_t \beta_{.1} + u_{1t} = 0,$$

where $u_{1t} = u_{11t}$ is the first element of the 1xM vector $u_{1.t}$. We have dropped the subscript 1 representing the first variable from u_{11t} for the sake of convenience. Now, some elements in $\gamma_{.1}$ and $\beta_{.1}$ will generally be known to be zero; also we wish to identify one endogenous variable as the 'left hand side' variable by letting its associated coefficient equal minus one. With necessary rearrangement, we write

$$(13.5) \qquad Y_t = [y_{1t}, Y_{1t}, Y^*_{1t}], \; X_t = [X_{1t} X^*_{1t}];$$

$$(13.6) \qquad \gamma_{.1} = \begin{bmatrix} -1 \\ \gamma_1 \\ 0 \end{bmatrix}, \; \beta_{.1} = \begin{bmatrix} \beta_1 \\ 0 \end{bmatrix}.$$

Then the first equation can be written as

$$(13.7) \qquad y_{1t} = Y_{1t}\gamma_1 + X_{1t}\beta_1 + u_{1+},$$

where y_{1t} is the left hand side jointly dependent variable, Y_{1t} is a $1xm_1$ vector of right hand jointly dependent variables present in the equation under consideration, X_{1t} is a $1xK_1$ vector of included predetermined variables in the equation, γ_1 and β_1 are m_1x1 and K_1x1 coefficient vectors respectively. We also note that $m^*_1 = M - m_1 - 1$ jointly dependent and $K^*_1 = K - K_1$ predetermined variablcs are excluded from the equation and they make up the vectors Y^*_{1t} and X^*_{1t} respectively.

In a more compact matrix notation we can write equation (13.7) as

$$(13.8) \qquad y_1 = Y_1\gamma_1 + X_1\beta_1 + u_1,$$

where y_1 is a $Tx1$ vector, Y_1 is a Txm_1 matrix, X_1 is a TxK_1 matrix and u_1 is a Tx1 vector.

The reduced form of System (13.1), at time t, can be correspondingly partitioned as

$$(13.9) \quad [y_{1t} Y_{1t} Y^*_{1t}] = [X_{1t} X^*_{1t}] \begin{bmatrix} \pi_{11} & \Pi_{11} & \Pi^*_{11} \\ \pi_{21} & \Pi_{21} & \Pi^*_{21} \end{bmatrix} + [w_{1t} W_{1t} W^*_{1t}],$$

where $W_{1.t} = -U_{1.t}\Gamma^{-1} = [w_{1t} W_{1t} W^*_{1t}]$ is partitioned according to Y_t. For t=1,...,T, (13.9) is

$$(13.10) \quad [y_1 Y_1 Y^*_1] = [X_1 X^*_1] \begin{bmatrix} \pi_{11} & \Pi_{11} & \Pi^*_{11} \\ \pi_{21} & \Pi_{21} & \Pi^*_{21} \end{bmatrix} + [w_1 W_1 W^*_1]'$$

as given in (12.31). Clearly, there is such a partition for each equation. It is convenient to define

$$(13.11) \quad \pi_1 = \begin{bmatrix} \pi_{11} \\ \pi_{21} \end{bmatrix}, \ \Pi_1 = \begin{bmatrix} \Pi_{1'1} \\ \Pi_{21} \end{bmatrix}, \ \Pi^*_1 = \begin{bmatrix} \Pi^*_{11} \\ \Pi^*_{21} \end{bmatrix},$$

where π_{11} and π_{21} are K_1x1 and K^*_1x1 vectors such that π_1 is a Kx1 vector, Π_{11} and Π_{21} are $K_1 x m_1$ and $K^*_1 x m_1$ matrices such that Π_1 is a Kxm_1 matrix and Π^*_{11} and Π^*_{21} are $K_1 x m^*_1$ and $K^*_1 x m^*_1$ matrices such that Π^*_1 is a Kxm^*_1 matrix.

We shall now consider various estimation techniques for the parameters in Equation (13.8).

13.2.1 Indirect Least Squares (ILS)

Let us rewrite the relationship between the structural parameters of the first equation (13.8) with the reduced form parameters in (13.10) from (12.35) as

(13.12) $\pi_1 = J_1 \delta_1$,

where π_1 is a Kx1 vector, and

(13.13) $$J_1 = \begin{bmatrix} \Pi_1 & \vdots & I_{K_1} \\ & \vdots & 0_{K_1^* x K_1} \end{bmatrix}, \quad \delta_1 = \begin{bmatrix} \gamma_1 \\ \beta_1 \end{bmatrix}$$

are $Kx(m_1+K_1)$ and $(m_1+K_1)x1$ respectively. To determine δ_1 we first replace π_1 and J_1 by their OLS estimates. For this we note that

(13.14) $\hat{\Pi}_1 = (X'X)^{-1}X'Y_1$

and

(13.15) $\hat{\pi}_1 = (X'X)^{-1}X'y_1$

are the OLS estimators of the respective parameters. Thus we can write

(13.16) $\hat{\pi}_1 = \hat{J}_1 \delta_1$.

In the second step we solve for δ_1. If the equation is justidentified, i.e. $m_1 = K_1^*$, then $\hat{J}_1$ becomes a square nonsingular matrix and δ_1 will have a unique solution, viz.:

(13.17) $\delta_1^* = \hat{J}_1^{-1}\hat{\pi}_1$,

which gives

(13.18) $\gamma_1^* = \hat{\Pi}_{21}^{-1}\ \hat{\pi}_{21}$ and $\beta_1^* = \hat{\pi}_{11} - \hat{\Pi}_{11}\hat{\gamma}_1^*$.

This is known as the ILS estimator; for this case this is the only estimator or solution possible.

If the equation is overidentified, i.e. $m_1 < K_1^*$ or $m_1 + K_1 < K$, then $\hat{J}_1$ will not be square and there can be more than one solution for δ_1. One way to get δ_1 in this case is to use the Moore-Penrose matrix inverse[1] of $\hat{J}_1$. Since J_1 has the column rank $m_1 + K_1$ we can write

(13.19) $\delta_1^* = (\hat{J}_1'\hat{J}_1)^{-1}\hat{J}_1'\hat{\pi}_1 = \hat{J}_1^+\hat{\pi}_1$.

This is the ILS for the overidentified case and was obtained by Khazzoom (1976).

Another estimator for δ_1, in the overidentified case, can be obtained by writing (13.16) as $X\hat{\pi}_1 = X\hat{J}_1\delta_1$ and solving for δ_1. This gives

(13.20) $d_1 = (\hat{J}_1'X'X\hat{J}_1')^{-1}\hat{J}_1'X'X\hat{\pi}_1$

$= (\hat{J}_1'X'X\hat{J}_1)^{-1}\hat{J}_1'X'y$.

The estimator d_1 is in fact the two stage least squares estimator discussed in a following section. Note that for $m_1 = K_1^*$ both d_1 and δ_1^* in (13.19) will become identical with the justidentified case estimator in (13.17).

13.2.2 Two Stage Least Squares (2SLS) Estimator

If we apply the ordinary least squares (OLS) method to estimate the parameters of (13.8) we get

$$(13.21)\quad \begin{bmatrix} c_o \\ b_o \end{bmatrix} = \begin{bmatrix} \begin{pmatrix} Y_1' \\ X_1' \end{pmatrix} (Y_1 X_1) \end{bmatrix}^{-1} \begin{bmatrix} Y_1' \\ X_1' \end{bmatrix} y_1$$

$$= \begin{bmatrix} Y_1'Y_1 & Y_1'X_1 \\ X_1'Y_1 & X_1'X_1 \end{bmatrix}^{-1} \begin{bmatrix} Y_1' \\ X_1' \end{bmatrix} y_1,$$

where c_o, b_o represent the OLS estimators of γ_1 and β_1 respectively. But the OLS estimators are not consistent because

$$(13.22)\quad \text{plim } (1/T)Y_1'u_1 \neq 0,$$

i.e. the jointly dependent variables on the right hand side of (13.8) are correlated with disturbances of that equation, even asymptotically. However,

$$(13.23)\quad Y_1 - W_1 = X\Pi_1 = \bar{Y}_1$$

according to (13.10) and the elements of X are distributed independently of u_1 according to both Assumptions 2 and 3 of Section 12.2. Therefore,

$$(13.24)\quad \text{plim } (1/T)(Y_1 - W_1)'u_1 = 0;$$

hence, if we write (13.8) as

$$(13.25)\quad y_1 = (Y_1 - W_1)\gamma_1 + X_1\beta_1 + (u_1 + W_1\gamma_1)$$

and then apply the OLS method to (13.25) we would obtain consistent estimators of parameters. Essentially this amounts to applying the OLS method to (13.8) after replacing Y_1 by its mathematical expectation (or after correcting Y_1 for its stochastic component). The difficulty in this procedure is that W_1 is a matrix of the reduced form disturbances, which are not observable. Alternatively, we may replace W_1 in (13.25) by

$$\hat{W}_1 = Y_1 - X(X'X)^{-1}X'Y_1, \tag{13.26}$$

which are the OLS residuals in the reduced form corresponding to the right hand jointly dependent variables in (13.8). This amounts to replacing Y_1 in (13.8) by its estimated value:

$$\hat{Y}_1 = X(X'X)^{-1}X'Y_1 = Y_1 - \hat{W}_1. \tag{13.27}$$

The two stage least squares (2SLS) method is then outlined as follows:

(i) In the first stage we apply OLS to (13.10) to obtain $\hat{W}_1$ from (13.26);

(ii) Next, we replace Y_1 in (13.8) by $(Y_1 - \hat{W}_1)$ in the second stage and apply OLS to

$$y_1 = (Y_1 - \hat{W}_1)\gamma_1 + X_1\beta_1 + (u_1 + \hat{W}_1\gamma_1) \tag{13.28}$$

to obtain

$$\begin{bmatrix} c_1 \\ b_1 \end{bmatrix} = \left[\begin{pmatrix} Y_1' - \hat{W}_1' \\ X_1' \end{pmatrix} (Y_1' - \hat{W}_1' X_1) \right]^{-1} \begin{bmatrix} Y_1' - \hat{W}_1' \\ X_1' \end{bmatrix} y_1 \tag{13.29}$$

$$= \begin{bmatrix} Y_1'Y_1 - \hat{W}_1'\hat{W}_1 & Y_1'X_1 \\ X_1'X_1 & X_1'X_1 \end{bmatrix}^{-1} \begin{bmatrix} Y' - \hat{W}_1' \\ X_1' \end{bmatrix} y_1{}'$$

$$= \begin{bmatrix} Y_1'X(X'X)^{-1}X'Y_1 & Y_1'X_1 \\ X_1'Y_1 & X_1'X_1 \end{bmatrix}^{-1} \begin{bmatrix} Y_1'X(X'X)^{-1}X' \\ X_1' \end{bmatrix} y_1,$$

where we made use of the following results:

$$(13.30) \quad Y_1'\hat{W}_1 = \hat{W}_1'Y_1 = \hat{W}_1'\hat{W}_1, \hat{W}_1'X = 0, \quad \text{and}$$

$$Y_1'Y_1 - \hat{W}_1'\hat{W}_1 = Y_1'X(X'X)^{-1}X'Y_1.$$

This motivation of the 2SLS estimator was given originally by Theil (1961).[2]

It is clear from the above discussion that the 2SLS estimator can be derived only if the $(m_1+K_1)x(m_1+K_1)$ matrix

$$(13.31) \quad \begin{bmatrix} Y_1'Y_1 - \hat{W}_1'\hat{W}_1 & Y_1'X_1 \\ X_1'Y_1 & X_1'X_1 \end{bmatrix}$$

in (13.29) is nonsingular, that is if it has rank m_1+K_1. Since

$$(13.32) \quad \begin{bmatrix} Y_1'Y_1 - \hat{W}_1'\hat{W}_1 & Y_1'X_1 \\ X_1'Y_1 & X_1'X_1 \end{bmatrix} = \begin{bmatrix} Y_1' - \hat{W}_1' \\ X_1' \end{bmatrix} (Y_1 - \hat{W}_1 X_1)$$

is the product of two matrices, its rank cannot exceed the rank of factor matrices. Moreover,

$$(13.33) \quad [Y_1 - \hat{W}_1 X_1] = \left[X(X'X)^{-1}X'Y_1 \vdots X\left(\begin{smallmatrix} I \\ \cdots \\ 0 \end{smallmatrix}\right) \right]$$

$$= X\left[(X'X)^{-1}X'Y \vdots \left(\begin{smallmatrix} I \\ \cdots \\ 0 \end{smallmatrix}\right) \right]$$

because

(13.34) $$X_1 = [X_1 X_1^*]\binom{I}{0} = X\binom{I}{0},$$

I being a $K_1 x K_1$ unit matrix and 0 a $K_1^* x K_1$ zero matrix. Since

(13.35) $$\left[(X'X)^{-1}X'Y \vdots \binom{I}{0}\right]$$

is of order $Kx(m_1+K_1)$, its rank can, at most, be K or m_1+K_1, whichever is smaller.

Suppose,

(13.36) $$K<m_1+K_1.$$

Then, since rank X=K (according to Assumption 4 in Section 12.2), the rank of

(13.37) $$[Y-\hat{W}_1 X_1]$$

cannot exceed K, and also the rank of the matrix in (13.32) can, at most, be K and then the matrix in (13.32) becomes singular. Hence, K must not be smaller than m_1+K_1. As a matter of fact this is the same as the order condition of identifiability derived in (12.38) of Chapter 12.

13.2.3 2SLS as a Variant of the Generalised Least Squares Estimator

Suppose we premultiply (13.8) by X' and obtain

(13.38) $$X'y_1 = X'Y_1\gamma_1 + X'X_1\beta_1 + X'u_1$$

$$= (X'Y_1 X'X_1)\binom{\gamma_1}{\beta_1} + X'u_1,$$

then the transformed disturbances in $X'u_1$ have the following covariance matrix:

$$(13.39) \quad E(X'u_1u_1'X) = \sigma_1^2 X'X,$$

where $\sigma_1^2 = \sigma_{11,11}$ from Assumption 7 in Section 12.2.

Using this covariance matrix if we apply Aitken's generalised least squares method to (13.38), we get

$$(13.40) \quad \binom{c_1}{b_1} = \left[\begin{pmatrix} Y_1'X \\ X_1'X \end{pmatrix} [\sigma_1^2 X'X]^{-1} (X'Y_1 \;\; X'X_1)\right]^{-1} \begin{pmatrix} Y_1'X \\ X_1'X \end{pmatrix} [\sigma_1^2 X'X]^{-1} X'y_1$$

$$= \begin{bmatrix} Y_1'X(X'X)^{-1}X'Y_1 & Y_1'X(X'X)^{-1}X'X_1 \\ X_1'X(X'X)^{-1}X'Y_1 & X_1'X(X'X)^{-1}X'X_1 \end{bmatrix}^{-1} \begin{bmatrix} Y_1'X(X'X)^{-1}X'y_1 \\ X_1'X(X'X)^{-1}X'y_1 \end{bmatrix}$$

$$= \begin{bmatrix} Y_1'X(X'X)^{-1}X'Y_1 & Y_1'X_1 \\ X_1'Y_1 & X_1'X_1 \end{bmatrix}^{-1} \begin{bmatrix} Y_1'X(X'X)^{-1}X'y_1 \\ X_1'y_1 \end{bmatrix},$$

because σ_1^2 cancels out from the right hand side of the first equality in (13.40) and

$$(13.41) \quad X_1 = [X_1 X_1^*]\begin{pmatrix} I \\ 0 \end{pmatrix} = X\begin{pmatrix} I \\ 0 \end{pmatrix},$$

I being a $K_1 x K_1$ unit matrix and 0 a $K_1^* x K_1$ zero matrix.

This variant of the 2SLS was discovered by Zellner and Theil (1962) which led to the three stage least squares (3SLS) estimator. The expression (13.40) can be shown to be identical with that given in (13.20).

In case the equation (13.8) to be estimated is justidentified, i.e. $K=m_1+K_1$, the matrix

$$(13.42) \quad [X'Y_1 \ X'X_1]$$

is square. Then (13.40) can be written as

$$(13.43) \quad \begin{bmatrix} c_1 \\ b_1 \end{bmatrix} = (X'Y_1 \ X'X_1)^{-1} [\sigma_1^2 X'X] \begin{bmatrix} Y_1'X \\ X_1'X \end{bmatrix}^{-1} \begin{bmatrix} Y_1'X \\ X_1'X \end{bmatrix} [\sigma_1^2 X'X]^{-1} X'y_1$$

$$= (X'Y_1 \ X'X_1)^{-1} X'y_1,$$

which provides a short cut method of computing the 2SLS estimator in the case of justidentified equations.

13.2.4 Limiting Distribution of the 2SLS Estimator

First, let us define

$$(13.44) \quad e_1 = \begin{bmatrix} c_1 \\ b_1 \end{bmatrix} - \begin{bmatrix} \gamma \\ \beta \end{bmatrix}$$

as the sampling error of the 2SLS estimator and observe that by combining (13.8) with (13.29) we get

$$(13.45)\quad e_1 = \begin{bmatrix} Y_1'X(X'X)^{-1}X'Y_1 & Y_1'X_1 \\ X_1'Y_1 & X_1'X_1 \end{bmatrix}^{-1} \begin{pmatrix} Y_1'X(X'X)^{-1}X'u_1 \\ X_1'u_1 \end{pmatrix}.$$

Now

$$(13.46)\quad \sqrt{T}e_1 = T\begin{bmatrix} Y_1'X(X'X)^{-1}X_1'Y_1 & Y_1'X_1 \\ X_1'Y_1 & X_1'X_1 \end{bmatrix}^{-1} \begin{bmatrix} Y_1'X(X'X)^{-1} \\ I \vdots 0 \end{bmatrix} \frac{X'u_1}{\sqrt{T}},$$

where

$$(13.47)\quad T\begin{bmatrix} Y_1'X(X'X)^{-1}X'Y_1 & Y_1'X_1 \\ X_1'Y_1 & X_1'X_1 \end{bmatrix}^{-1}$$

converges to, say, G_1^{-1} in probability, and

$$(13.48)\quad \begin{bmatrix} Y_1'X(X'X)^{-1} \\ I \vdots 0 \end{bmatrix}$$

converges stochastically to, say, G_2 as $T\to\infty$. Therefore, writing

$$(13.49)\quad G = G_1^{-1}G_2,$$

we conclude that the limiting distribution of $\sqrt{T}e_1$ is identical with that of

(13.50) $\quad G(1/\sqrt{T})X'u_1,$

provided this latter vector has a limiting distribution. Since, according to Assumption 6 in Section 12.2, the elements of u_1 are independently normally distributed with

(13.51) $\quad Eu_1 = 0$ and $Eu_1u_1' = \sigma_1^2 I,\ \sigma_1^2 = \sigma_{11,11}.$

The elements of $\sqrt{T}e_1$, being linear functions of the elements of u_1, will tend to be normally distributed with mean zero and the covariance matrix given by

$$\text{(13.52)}\quad \text{plim}\ Te_1e_1' = \sigma_1^2\ \text{plim}\ T\begin{bmatrix}\bar{Y}_1'\bar{Y}_1 & \bar{Y}_1X_1\\ X_1'\bar{Y}_1 & X'X_1\end{bmatrix}^{-1},$$

$$\bar{Y}_1 = X\Pi_1.$$

It should be noted, however, that the normality assumption of structural disturbances is not required for proving the asymptotic normality of the 2SLS estimator, because even when the structural disturbances are not normally distributed the elements of $\sqrt{T}e_1$ still continue to approach the normal distribution asymptotically due to the Central Limit Theorem.

We have seen that the limiting distribution of the 2SLS estimator $\begin{bmatrix}c_1\\ b_1\end{bmatrix}$ is normal with mean vector $\begin{bmatrix}\gamma_1\\ \beta_1\end{bmatrix}$ and the covariance matrix given by (13.52).

13.2.5 2SLS Estimators of γ_1 and β_1 Individually

If we premultiply both sides of (13.29) by

$$(13.53)\quad \begin{bmatrix} Y_1'Y_1 - \hat{W}_1'\hat{W}_1 & Y_1'X_1 \\ X_1'Y_1 & X_1'X_1 \end{bmatrix} = \begin{bmatrix} Y_1'M^*Y_1 & Y_1'X_1 \\ X_1'Y_1 & X_1'X_1 \end{bmatrix},$$

we get

$$(13.54)\quad Y_1'M^*Y_1c_1+Y_1'X_1b_1= Y_1'M^*y_1,$$

$$(13.55)\quad X_1'Y_1c_1+X_1'X_1b_1= X_1'y_1,$$

where

$$M^*= X(X'X)^{-1}X'.$$

It follows from (13.55) that

$$(13.56)\quad b_1= (X_1'X_1)^{-1}\ X_1'(y_1-Y_1c_1),$$

and substituting this in (13.54) we get

$$(13.57)\quad c_1= (Y_1'NY_1)^{-1}Y_1'Ny_1,$$

where

$$(13.58)\quad N=M^*-M_1^*, M^*=X(X'X)^{-1}X' \text{ and } M_1^*=X_1(X_1'X_1)^{-1}X_1'.$$

13.2.6 Residual Variance Estimation According to 2SLS Procedure

In equation (13.8) we assumed that

$$Eu_1= 0 \text{ and } Eu_1u_1'= \sigma_1^2I,$$

where I is a TxT unit matrix and

$$\sigma_1^2= \text{var } u_{1t} \qquad \text{for } t=1,\dots,T,$$

u_{1t} being the tth element of u_1. This implies that the disturbances in (13.8) have zero mean, constant variance σ_1^2 and zero autocorrelations of all orders, i.e.

$$\text{cov}(u_{1t}, u_{1t'}) = 0 \quad \text{for } t \neq t'.$$

σ_1^2 is called the residual variance.

Once the coefficient vectors γ_1, β_1 in (13.8) have been estimated according to the 2SLS procedure (13.29) outlined above, we can obtain a consistent estimator s^2 of σ_1^2:

$$(13.59) \quad s^2 = (1/T)\, \hat{u}_1'\hat{u}_1,$$

where

$$(13.60) \quad \hat{u}_1 = y_1 - Y_1 c_1 - X_1 b_1.$$

13.2.7 The General k-Class Estimators

In Section 13.2.2 we obtained the 2SLS estimator and observed that this is a consistent estimator of the coefficient vector $\begin{bmatrix}\gamma_1\\ \beta_1\end{bmatrix}$ in (13.8).

The family of general k-class estimators for estimating parameters of a single equation (which is part of a complete set of structural equations) was originally proposed by Theil (1961). Let us write the general k-class estimator of the coefficient vector $\begin{bmatrix}\gamma_1\\ \beta_1\end{bmatrix}$ in (13.8) as follows:

$$(13.61) \quad \begin{bmatrix}c_k\\ b_k\end{bmatrix} = \begin{bmatrix}Y_1'Y_1 - k\hat{W}_1'\hat{W}_1 & Y_1'X_1\\ X_1'Y_1 & X_1'X_1\end{bmatrix}^{-1} \begin{bmatrix}Y_1' - k\hat{W}_1'\\ X_1'\end{bmatrix} y_1,$$

where k is an arbitrary scalar which may be stochastic or nonstochastic.

It follows immediately that for k=0 we obtain $\begin{bmatrix} c_o \\ b_o \end{bmatrix}$, which is the OLS estimator, and for k=1 we have the 2SLS estimator $\begin{bmatrix} c_1 \\ b_1 \end{bmatrix}$ of the coefficient vector $\begin{bmatrix} \gamma_1 \\ \beta_1 \end{bmatrix}$.

Thus both the OLS and 2SLS estimators are members of the family of general k-class estimators although the former is not a consistent estimator. However, if we place a restriction on k, so that

$$\text{plim}(k-1) = 0, \tag{13.62}$$

that is k-1 is of a lower order than 1 in probability, then k-class estimators arc consistent. It can be shown that (13.62) is a sufficient condition for the consistency of the general k-class estimators (Theil, 1961). Also the limiting distribution of the general k-class estimators is the same as that of the 2SLS estimator provided plim $\sqrt{T}(k-1)=0$, i.e. k-1 is of a lower order than $1/\sqrt{T}$ in probability. Thus the OLS estimator is ruled out as a member of k-class estimators.

13.2.8 The Bias and Moment Matrix of the General k-Class Estimators

In this section we shall briefly outline the procedure adopted by Nagar (1959) for deriving the bias and moment matrix of the general k-class estimator and state the results obtained. We will omit the detailed proofs of the results; the reader can find these in the original papers.

The sampling error of the general k-class estimator is given in (13.61). If we write

$$Y_1 = \overline{Y}_1 + W_1,$$

we can express $e_k = \begin{bmatrix} c_k \\ b_k \end{bmatrix} - \begin{bmatrix} \gamma_1 \\ \beta_1 \end{bmatrix}$ as

$$(13.63) \quad e_k = [Q^{-1} + Z'V_z + V_z'Z + (1-k)V_z'V_z + kV_z'M^*V_z]^{-1} [Z' + (1-k)V_z' + kV_z'M^*]u_1$$

$$= (I+Q\Delta)^{-1}Q[Z'u_1 + (1-k)V_z'u_1 + kV_z'M^*u_1],$$

where

$$(13.64) \quad \Delta = Z'V_z + V_z'Z + (1-k)V_z'V_z + kV_z'M^*V_z,$$

$$(13.65) \quad V_2 = [W_1 \ \ 0],$$

$$(13.66) \quad Q = (\overline{Z}'\overline{Z})^{-1}, \ \overline{Z} = [\overline{Y}_1 \ \ X_1];$$

0 in V_2 is a $T \times K_1$ zero matrix.

Now let us examine the matrix $I+Q\Delta$, which is to be inverted on the right hand side of (13.63). If $k-1$ is of a lower order of magnitude than $1/\sqrt{T}$ in probability, i.e.

$$\text{plim} \sqrt{T}(k-1) = 0,$$

then the elements of $Q\Delta$ are essentially of order $1/\sqrt{T}$ in probability. Thus if we expand $(I+Q\Delta)^{-1}$ as

$$(13.67) \quad I - Q\Delta + Q\Delta Q\Delta - \ldots,$$

the successive terms of the expansion (which are random variables) are of decreasing order of magnitude in probability. However, this does not necessarily ensure the convergence of the expansion to the value $(I+Q\Delta)^{-1}$.

Supposing that the expansion (3.67) of $(I+Q\Delta)^{-1}$ is valid, we can write

$$(13.68) \quad e_k \approx Q[Z'u - \frac{1}{T}\kappa V_z'u + V_z'M^*u - Z'V_zQZ'u - V_z'ZQZ'u],$$

where, for any nonstochastic κ, we write

$$(13.69) \quad k = 1 + \frac{\kappa}{T} + \ldots$$

and neglect terms of a lower order of magnitude than 1/T. We assume k to be nonstochastic.

Now we may obtain

$$(13.70) \quad Ee_k \approx Q[E(Z'u) - \frac{1}{T}\kappa \; EV_z'u + EV_z'M^*u - EZ'V_zQZ'u - EV_z'ZQZ'u]$$

by taking mathematical expectations, term by term, on the right hand side of (13.68). However, this procedure of taking mathematical expectations term by term of an infinite series is valid only under certain specific conditions. For example, a sufficient condition under which term by term expectation of an infinite series is valid is that the series must be uniformly convergent.

Let us state the following results (See Sargan [1974] about these conditions:

Theorem 1: The bias, to order 1/T, of the general k-class estimator $\begin{bmatrix} c_k \\ b_k \end{bmatrix}$, defined in (13.61), of the coefficient vector $\begin{bmatrix} \gamma_1 \\ \beta_1 \end{bmatrix}$ of (13.8) is given by

$$(13.71)\qquad Ee_k = (-\kappa+L-1)Qq,$$

where e_k is the sampling error of the k-class estimator, and

$$(13.72)\qquad L = K-(m_1+K_1) = K_1^*-m_1$$

is the number of predetermined variables in excess of the number of coefficients to be estimated. In fact, L can be interpreted as the degree of overidentification of the equation to be estimated, viz. (13.8). The matrix Q has been defined in (13.66) and the column vector q is

$$(13.73)\qquad q = \frac{1}{T}\begin{bmatrix} EW_1'u_1 \\ 0 \end{bmatrix}.$$

Corollary 1: The bias of the 2SLS estimator $\begin{matrix} c_1 \\ b_1 \end{matrix}$, to the order of 1/T is,

$$(13.74)\qquad Ee_1 = (L-1)Qq.$$

This result has been obtained from Theorem 1 by putting k=1 or $\kappa=0$.

Corollary 2: The bias, to order 1/T, of the general k-class estimator $\begin{bmatrix} c_1 \\ b_1 \end{bmatrix}$, vanishes if we let

$$(13.75)\qquad k = 1+\frac{L-1}{T}.$$

Thus we obtain a member of the family of k-class estimators which is unbiased to order 1/T. This result has also been obtained from that of Theorem 1 stated above.

We have the following results on the moment matrix of the general k-class estimators.

Theorem 2: The moment matrix, to order $1/T^2$, of the general k-class estimator $\begin{bmatrix} c_k \\ b_k \end{bmatrix}$ around the parameter vector $\begin{bmatrix} \gamma_1 \\ \beta 1 \end{bmatrix}$ is given by

$$(13.76) \quad E e_k e_k' = \sigma_1^2 Q(I+A^*),$$

where A* is a matrix the elements of which are of order 1/T in probability:

$$(13.77) \quad A^* = [(2\kappa-2L+3)\mathrm{tr}\, C_1 Q + \mathrm{tr} C_2 Q]I + [(\kappa-L+2)^2+2(\kappa+1)C_1 Q+(2\kappa-L+2)C_2 Q],$$

σ_1^2 being the residual variance, and C_1, C_2 are defined as

$$(13.78) \quad C_1 = \frac{1}{\sigma_1^2} qq',$$

$$C_2 = \frac{1}{T} EV_2'V_2 - \frac{1}{\sigma_1^2} qq'.$$

Corollary 1. The moment matrix, to order $1/T^2$, of the 2SLS estimator $\begin{bmatrix} c_1 \\ b_1 \end{bmatrix}$ around the parameter vector $\begin{bmatrix} \gamma \\ \beta \end{bmatrix}$, is given by (13.76) where[3]

$$(13.79) \quad A^* = [-(2L-3)\mathrm{tr}\, C_1 Q + \mathrm{tr} C_2 Q]I + [(L-2)^2+2]C_1 Q - (L-2)C_2 Q.$$

For the choice of the 'best' k we consider the criterion of the minimum determinant value of the moment matrix (i.e. the minimum generalised second moment). Thus we minimise

$$(13.80) \qquad |Ee_k e_k'| = \sigma_1^2 |Q| \quad |I+A^*| = \sigma_1^2 |Q| (1+\text{tr } A^*)$$

to order $1/T^2$, for variations in k or κ. We obtain the following result.

Corollary 2. The κ-value which minimises the determinant value of the moment matrix (13.76) is

$$(13.81) \qquad \kappa = K-2(m_1-K_1)-3-\frac{\text{tr } C_2 Q}{\text{tr } C_1 Q}.$$

Thus we have obtained another member of the family of general k-class estimators which possesses the optimum property of minimum generalised second moment.

13.3 LIMITED INFORMATION ESTIMATION OF BOTH FIXED AND RANDOM COEFFICIENTS[4]

In this case we consider the system of equations (13.1) for which $\Gamma_t=\Gamma$ and $B_t= B+U_t$ and U_t is the complete matrix given in (12.7), i.e. the system in which the coefficients of endogenous variables are nonstochastic whereas the coefficients of exogenous variables are stochastic. These models can be justified since usually the policy makers have some control over some exogenous variables and therefore the coefficients of exogenous variables are not invariant with respect to changes in policy.

Let us write the first equation of such a system from (12.4a) as

$$(13.82)\quad Y_t\gamma_{.1}+X_t\beta_{.1t}=0,$$

where

$$(13.83)\quad \gamma_{.1}=\begin{bmatrix}\gamma_{11}\\ \\ \gamma_{M1}\end{bmatrix};\ \beta_{.1t}=\begin{bmatrix}\beta_{11t}\\ \\ \beta_{K1t}\end{bmatrix}=\begin{bmatrix}\beta_{11}\\ \\ \beta_{K1}\end{bmatrix}+\begin{bmatrix}u_{11t}\\ \\ u_{K1t}\end{bmatrix}.$$

Now, using the normalisation rule and the fact that some of the jointly dependent and predetermined variables of the system are not present in this equation, we can write

$$(13.84)\quad Y_t=[y_{1t}Y_{1t}Y^*_{1t}],\ X_t=[X_{1t}X^*_{1t}],$$

$$\gamma_{.1}=\begin{bmatrix}-1\\ \gamma_1\\ 0\end{bmatrix},\quad \beta_{.1t}=\begin{bmatrix}\beta_1\\ \\ 0\end{bmatrix}+\begin{bmatrix}u_{.1t}\\ \\ 0\end{bmatrix},$$

where y_{1t} is 1x1, Y_{1t} is $1xm_1$, Y_1^* is $1xM-m_1-1$, X_1 is $1xK_1$, X^* is $1xK_1^*$ and $K=K_1+K_1^*$. These are as defined before. Further, β_1 is a K_1x1 parameter vector and $u_{.1}$ is a K_1x1 vector representing disturbances in β_1. The first equation can then be written as

$$(13.85)\quad y_{1t}=Y_{1t}\gamma_1+X_{1t}\beta_1+\varepsilon_{1t},$$

$$\varepsilon_{1t}=X_{1t}u_{.1t}.$$

Using Assumption 7 in 12.2,

$$(13.86)\quad E\varepsilon_{1t}=EX_{1t}u_{.1t}=X_{1t}(Eu_{.1t})=0,$$

$$E\varepsilon_{1t}\varepsilon_{1t'}=0,\qquad t\neq t'$$

$$=X_{1t}\Sigma_{11}X'_{1t}\qquad t=t'$$

where

$$(13.87)\qquad \Sigma_{11} = \begin{bmatrix} \sigma_{11,11} & \cdots & 0 \\ \vdots & \ddots & \\ 0 & & \sigma_{K_1K_1,11} \end{bmatrix}$$

is the diagonal matrix of order $K_1 x K_1$. This is essentially a subset of the matrix defined in (12.16).

In a more compact matrix notation the equation (13.85) can be written as

$$(13.88)\qquad y_1 = Y_1\gamma_1 + X_1\beta_1 + \varepsilon_1 = Z_1\delta_1 + \varepsilon_1,$$

where $Z_1 = [Y_1 X_1]$ is a $Tx(m_1+K_1)$ matrix, δ_1 is a m_1+K_1x1 vector and ε_1 is a $Tx1$ vector such that

$$(13.89)\qquad E\varepsilon_1 = 0 \qquad E\varepsilon_1\varepsilon_1' = \Omega_{11} = \begin{bmatrix} X_{11}\Sigma_{11}X_{11}' & \cdots & 0 \\ \vdots & \ddots & \\ 0 & & X_{1T}\Sigma_{11}X_{1T}' \end{bmatrix}.$$

A necessary and sufficient condition for the identifiability of δ_1 is the same as in the classical case and this has been shown in an earlier chapter. However, we should note that although the equation (13.88) is in the same form as the equation (13.8) in the classical case, the nature of ε_1 is different here. In fact, ε_1 is subject to heteroscedasticity as was the case in the random coefficient regression models. Thus the 2SLS estimator of δ_1 is

$$(13.90)\qquad d_1 = \begin{bmatrix} c_1 \\ b_1 \end{bmatrix} = (Z_1'PZ_1)^{-1}Z_1'Py_1,$$

where $P=X(X'X)^{-1}X'$. But estimator d_1 is inefficient.

To obtain an efficient 2SLS estimator we proceed as below. Given that Ω_{11} is positive definite we transform the equation (13.88) as

$$(13.91) \qquad X'\Omega_{11}^{-1}y_1 = X'\Omega_{11}^{-1}Z_1\delta_1 + X'\Omega_{11}^{-1}\varepsilon_1,$$

such that $EX'\Omega_{11}^{-1}w_1 = 0$ and $E(X'\Omega_{11}^{-1}\varepsilon_1\varepsilon_1'\Omega_{11}^{-1}X) = X'\Omega_{11}^{-1}X$. This transformation is on the lines of deriving the 2SLS estimator by using the X' transformation and then applying Aitken's GLS (see Section 13.2.3) In this case the GLS is applied on the equation (13.91) to obtain

$$(13.92) \qquad \hat{\delta}_1 = (Z_1'RZ_1)^{-1}Z_1'Ry_1,$$

where

$$(13.93) \qquad R = \Omega_{11}^{-1}X(X'\Omega_{11}^{-1}X)^{-1}X'\Omega_{11}^{-1}.$$

The estimator $\hat{\delta}_1$ can be called the generalised 2SLS random (G2SLSR) estimator.

It can be shown that the asymptotic distributions of both d_1 and $\hat{\delta}_1$ are normal with

$$(13.94) \qquad Ed_1 = E\hat{\delta}_1 = \delta_1$$

and

$$(13.95) \qquad \text{Asy.Cov}(d_1) = (Z_1'PZ_1)^{-1}Z_1'P\Omega_{11}PZ_1(Z_1'PZ_1)^{-1};$$

$$\text{Asy.Cov}(\hat{\delta}_1) = (Z_1'RZ_1)^{-1}.$$

Theoretically, it is difficult to establish conditions under which Asy.Cov($\hat{\delta}_1$)-Asy.Cov(d_1) is a negative definite matrix. However, one would expect $\hat{\delta}_1$ to be more efficient compared to d_1. The empirical example in this chapter confirms this.

Observe that $\hat{\delta}_1$ depends on unknown Ω_{11} which in turn depends on unknown Σ_{11}. If one has information about the true unknown elements of Σ_{11} then $\hat{\delta}_1$ can be calculated, given the data. In some situations one can consider, say, $\Sigma_{11}=I$. But in general this kind of information is not available. A useful solution to this problem will be to replace the elements of Σ_{11} by its sample estimate. This can be done by following the procedure discussed in Chapter 4.

Consider γ_1 to be known and write

$$(13.96) \quad y_1-Y_1\gamma_1= y_1^*= X_1\beta_1+\varepsilon_1.$$

Then by defining $\sigma= (\sigma_{11,11}\ldots\sigma_{K_1K_1,11})'$ as the K_1x1 vector of diagonal elements of Σ_{11}, the Hildreth and Houck estimator of σ is

$$(13.97) \quad \hat{\sigma}= [(\dot{M}_1\dot{X}_1)'(\dot{M}_1\dot{X}_1)]^{-1}(\dot{M}_1\dot{X}_1)'\dot{\hat{\varepsilon}}_1,$$

where

$$(13.98) \quad \dot{M}_1= M_1*M_1, \ \dot{X}_1= X_1*X_1, \ \dot{\hat{\varepsilon}}_1= \hat{\varepsilon}_1*\hat{\varepsilon}_1,$$

and the * represents the Hadamard matrix product. The matrix $M_1= I-X_1(X_1'X_1)^{-1}X_1'$ and $\hat{\varepsilon}_1= M_1y_1^*$ is the OLS residual vector. To make $\hat{\varepsilon}_1$ operational (because $y_1^*=y_1-Y_1\gamma_1$ is not known) we can now replace

γ_1 by its 2SLS estimator c_1 given in (13.57). However, since c_1 is biased for a small sample, a better alternative will be to substitute an almost unbiased estimator:

$$(13.99) \quad c_1^* = c_1 - (K-K_1-m_1-1)\hat{Q}_{11}\hat{q}_1,$$

where

$$\hat{Q}_{11} = (Y_1'[P-X_1(X_1'X_1)^{-1}X_1']Y_1')^{-1},$$

$$\hat{q}_1 = \frac{1}{T}[Y_1'(I-P)(y_1-Z_1c_1)].$$

The estimator c_1^* is in fact constructed by subtracting from c_1 a consistent estimator of bias to order $1/T$ of c_1 as given in (13.76). Thus if the degree of overidentification is at least one, such that Ec_1 exists, then c_1^* is unbiased up to order $1/T$. In practice, therefore, one could calculate $\hat{\varepsilon}_1$ by

$$(13.99a) \quad \hat{\varepsilon}_1 = M_1(y_1-Y_1c_1^*)$$

or simply by $\hat{\varepsilon}_1 = M_1(y_1-Y_1c_1)$.

The knowledge of $\hat{\sigma}$ from (13.97) provides Σ_{11}, which in turn determines $\hat{\Omega}_{11}$. The G2SLSR estimator $\hat{\delta}_1$ to be used in practice can then be

$$(13.100) \quad \tilde{\delta}_1 = (Z_1'\hat{R}Z_1)^{-1}Z_1'\hat{R}y_1,$$

$$\hat{R} = \hat{\Omega}_{11}^{-1}X(X'\hat{\Omega}_{11}^{-1}X)^{-1}X'\hat{\Omega}_{11}^{-1}.$$

The asymptotic distribution of this estimator is the same as that of $\hat{\delta}_1$, viz. normal with mean

δ_1 and covariance matrix $(Z_1'RZ_1)^{-1}$. As noted in earlier chapters, when any element of $\hat{\sigma}$ is negative we can replace it by zero. The $\hat{\Sigma}_{11}$, $\hat{\Omega}_{11}$ and $\hat{\delta}_1$ accordingly modified and the resulting estimator $\hat{\delta}_1$ is called G2SLSRM, M representing modified.

We can obtain the estimate of σ by an alternative method. According to this we first obtain the 2SLS residual vector as

$$(13.101)\quad \tilde{\varepsilon}_1 = y_1 - Z_1 d_1 = y_1 - Z_1(Z_1'PZ_1)^{-1}Z_1'Py_1 = N_1 y_1 = N_1 \varepsilon_1,$$

where

$$(13.102)\quad N_1 = I - Z_1(Z_1'PZ_1)^{-1}Z_1'P.$$

Further, it can be shown that the asymptotic distribution of ε_1 is normal, i.e.

$$(13.103)\quad \sqrt{T}\tilde{\varepsilon}_1 \sim N[0,\ \lim T(N_1\Omega_{11}N_1)]$$

This implies that

$$(13.104)\quad \text{Asy.E}(\tilde{\varepsilon}_1) = 0 \text{ and } \text{Asy.Cov}(\tilde{\varepsilon}_1) = N_1\Omega_{11}N_1.$$

Thus, for a large sample

$$(13.105)\quad \dot{\tilde{\varepsilon}}_1 = \dot{N}_1\dot{X}_1\sigma + \xi.$$

The OLS estimator of σ is then

$$(13.106)\quad \tilde{\sigma}= [\dot{N}_1\dot{X}_1)'(\dot{N}_1\dot{X}_1)]^{-1}(\dot{N}_1\dot{X}_1)'\tilde{\dot{\varepsilon}}_1,$$

which is asymptotically unbiased. Corresponding to this estimator of $\tilde{\sigma}$ we will get a new estimator of Ω_{11} and hence of δ_1.

13.3.1 Asymptotic Properties of $\tilde{\delta}_1$

Before analysing the properties of $\tilde{\delta}_1$ we first show that $\hat{\Omega}_{11}$ involved in $\tilde{\delta}_1$ (13.100), is a consistent estimator of Ω_{11}.

For this we observe first from (13.99a) that

$$\begin{aligned}(13.107)\quad \hat{\varepsilon}_1 &= M_1[y_1-Y_1c_1^*] \\ &= M_1[y_1-Y_1c_1+(K-K_1-m_1-1)Y_1\hat{Q}_{11}\hat{q}_1] \\ &= M_1[Z_1\delta_1+\varepsilon_1-Z_1\hat{\delta}_1+(K-K_1-m_1-1)Y_1\hat{Q}_{11}\hat{q}_1] \\ &= M_1[\varepsilon_1-Z_1(\hat{\delta}_1-\delta_1)+(K-K_1-m_1-1)Y_1\hat{Q}_{11}\hat{q}_1] \\ &= M_1[\varepsilon_1-Z_1(\hat{\delta}_1-\delta_1)+(K-K_1-m_1-1)Z_1\hat{Q}\binom{\hat{q}_1}{0}].\end{aligned}$$

Now using (13.107) to form $\hat{\dot{\varepsilon}}_1$ and substituting $\hat{\dot{\varepsilon}}_1$ in (13.97) we can verify that

$$(13.108)\quad \hat{\sigma}-\sigma= \eta,$$

where the elements of η are of order T^{-g}, $g \geq 1/2$, in probability.

Finally, using (13.108), we find that

$$\hat{\Omega}_{11}-\Omega_{11}= O_p(T^{-g}),\ g \geq 1/2,$$

whence $\hat{\Omega}_{11}$ is a consistent estimator of Ω.

We now make the following assumptions.

Assumption 1: (i) The elements of

$$R = \Omega_{11}^{-1}X(X'\Omega_{11}^{-1}X)^{-1}X'\Omega_{11}^{-1}$$

are functions of the parameter vector σ such that the elements of the matrices $(\frac{\partial}{\partial\sigma_k}R)$, $k=1,\ldots,K_1$, where σ_k is the kth element of σ, are continuous functions of σ in an open sphere S of σ^o, the true value of σ; (ii) The matrices Z_1 and R are such that $\underset{T\to\infty}{\text{Plim}} \frac{1}{T} Z_1' RZ_1 = M(\sigma)$ is a finite matrix, $M^{-1}(\sigma)$ exists for all σ in S, and $\underset{T\to\infty}{\text{Plim}} \frac{1}{T} Z_1'(\frac{\partial}{\partial\sigma_k}R)Z_1 = H_k(\sigma)$ is a finite matrix whose elements are continuous functions of σ, $k=1,\ldots,K_1$; and (iii) An estimator $\hat{R}\equiv R(\hat{\sigma})$ for $R\equiv R(\sigma^o)$ is available and $\hat{\sigma}$ satisfies the condition $\hat{\sigma}=\sigma^o+O_p(T^{-g})$, $g>0$.

Assumption 2: (i) Let f_r' be the rth row vector of $\Omega_{11}^{-1/2}$. Then the elements $f_r'\varepsilon_1$ $r=1,\ldots,T$, are independent and $f_r'\varepsilon_1$ has distribution function $F_r(f'w_1)$, $r=1,2,\ldots,T$, such that

$$\sup_{r=1,2,\ldots,T} \int_{|f'w_1|>c} (f'w_1)^2 d\, F_r(f'w_1) \to 0 \text{ as } c\to\infty;$$

(ii) $\underset{T\to\infty}{\text{Plim}} \max_{1\le r\le T} (\frac{x_{1jr}^{*2}}{T}) = 0$, $j=1,\ldots,K$, where x_{1jr}^* is the $(r,j)^{th}$ element of $\Omega_{11}^{-1/2}X$; and (iii)

$\underset{T\to\infty}{\text{Plim}} (\frac{X'\Omega_{11}^{-1}X}{T})$ is finite and nonsingular, and

$\underset{N\to\infty}{\text{Plim}} (\frac{Z_1'\Omega_{11}^{-1}X}{T})$ is finite.

Lemma: If Assumptions in Chapter 12 and Assumption 2 above are satisfied, then the limiting distribution of $\sqrt{T}(\tilde{\delta}_1-\delta_1)$ is normal with mean vector 0 and variance-covariance matrix $\operatorname*{Plim}_{T\to\infty} T(Z_1'RZ_1)^{-1}$.

Proof: Write

$$\sqrt{T}(\tilde{\delta}_1-\delta_1)=\left[\frac{Z_1'\Omega_{11}^{-1}X}{T}\left(\frac{X'\Omega_{11}^{-1}X}{T}\right)^{-1}\frac{X'\Omega_{11}^{-1}Z_1}{T}\right]^{-1}$$
$$\frac{Z_1'\Omega_{11}^{-1}X}{T}\left(\frac{X'\Omega_{11}^{-1}X}{T}\right)^{-1}\frac{X'\Omega_{11}^{-1}\varepsilon_1}{\sqrt{T}}\,.$$

By Assumption 2 (iii)

$$\operatorname*{Plim}_{T\to\infty}\left[\frac{Z_1'\Omega_{11}^{-1}X}{T}\left(\frac{X'\Omega_{11}^{-1}X_1}{T}\right)^{-1}\frac{X'\Omega_{11}^{-1}Z_1}{T}\right]^{-1}$$
$$\frac{Z_1'\Omega_{11}^{-1}X}{T}\left(\frac{X'\Omega_{11}^{-1}X}{T}\right)^{-1}=\bar{G},$$

a finite matrix.

It follows from Anderson's (1971, pp. 23-25, 585) Theorem 2.6.1 that under Assumptions (i) and (ii), $\frac{X'\Omega_{11}^{-1}\varepsilon_1}{\sqrt{T}}$ converges in distribution to normal mean vector 0 and variance-covariance matrix $\operatorname*{Plim}_{T\to\infty}\frac{X'\Omega_{11}^{-1}X}{T}$.

Now applying the limit theorem (x)b in Rao (1973, 2c.4, p.122), we have the result of the Lemma.

Theorem: Suppose that Assumptions in Chapter 12 and Assumption 1 above are true. Then the limiting distribution of $\sqrt{T}(\tilde{\delta}_1-\delta_1)$ is the same as that of $\sqrt{T}(\tilde{\delta}_1-\delta_1)$.

Proof: Write

$$\tilde{\delta}_1-\delta_1= [Z_1'R(\hat{\sigma})Z_1]^{-1}Z_1'R(\hat{\sigma})\varepsilon_1,$$

where

$$R(\hat{\sigma})= \hat{\Omega}_{11}^{-1}X(X'\hat{\Omega}_{11}^{-1}X)^{-1}X'\hat{\Omega}_{11}^{-1}.$$

By Taylor's expansion about the true parameter σ^o, we obtain,

$$[Z_1'R(\hat{\sigma})Z_1]^{-1}Z_1'R(\hat{\sigma})\varepsilon_1= [\frac{1}{T}Z_1'R(\sigma^o)Z_1]^{-1}$$

$$[\frac{1}{T}Z_1'R(\sigma^o)\varepsilon_1]+ \sum_{k=1}^{K_1} \{[\frac{1}{T}Z_1'R(\sigma^1)Z_1]^{-1}$$

$$[\frac{1}{T}Z_1'(\frac{\partial}{\partial\sigma_k}R(\sigma))_{\sigma=\sigma^1}\varepsilon_1]-[\frac{1}{T}Z_1'R(\sigma^1)Z_1]^{-1}$$

$$[\frac{1}{T}Z_1'(\frac{\partial}{\partial\sigma_k}R(\sigma))_{\sigma=\sigma^1}Z_1] \cdot [\frac{1}{T}Z_1'R(\sigma^1)Z_1]^{-1}$$

$$[\frac{1}{T}Z_1'R(\sigma^1)\varepsilon_1]\}(\hat{\sigma}_k-\hat{\sigma}_k^o),$$

where σ^1 is between σ^o and σ. By Assumption 1 and limit theorem (x)a in Rao (1973, 2c.4, p.122), it follows that

$$(\tilde{\delta}_1-\delta_1)= (\hat{\delta}_1-\delta_1)+O_p[T^{-(\frac{1}{2}+g)}]$$

or

$$\sqrt{T}(\tilde{\delta}_1-\delta_1)= \sqrt{T}(\hat{\delta}_1-\delta_1)+O_p(T^{-g}).$$

Thus as $T\to\infty$, $\sqrt{T}(\tilde{\delta}_1-\delta_1)= \sqrt{T}(\hat{\delta}_1-\delta_1) \sim N(0,(\frac{Z_1'RZ_1}{T})^{-1})$.

13.3.2 An Example: Klein Model I

To illustrate the G2SLSR and G2SLSRM estimators developed in the previous section, we utilise Klein's (1950) Model I. The model was described in the previous chapter but we reproduce it here again for convenience. The random coefficients version of the model is briefly described below:

$$C_t= \gamma_1P_t+\gamma_2(W_t+W_t')+\beta_{1t}+\beta_{2t}P_{t-1}$$

$$I_t= \gamma_1'P_t+\beta_{1t}'+\beta_{2t}'P_{t-1}+\beta_{3t}'K_{t-1}$$

$$W_t= \gamma_1''X_t+\beta_{1t}''+\beta_{2t}''X_{t-1}+\beta_{3t}''(t-1931)$$

$$X_t= C_t+I_t+G_t$$

$$P_t= X_t-W_t-T_t^*$$

$$K_t= K_{t-1}+ I_t$$

where

C_t = aggregate consumption in year t,

P_t = total profits in year t,

W_t = total wages paid by private industry in year t,

I_t = net investment in year t,

K_t = capital stock in year t,

X_t = total production of private industry in year t,

T_t^* = taxes in year t,

G_t = government expenditures in year t,

W_t' = government wage bill in year t,

P_{t-1} = total profits lagged one period,

K_{t-1} = capital stock lagged one period,

X_{t-1} = total production of private industry lagged one period,

t = time trend.

Our objective is to estimate the β's and the means of γ's on the basis of the US data for the period 1921-41. It may be noted that in the above model a time trend and lagged endogenous variables appear. Thus, the exogenous variables contain time trends and our Assumptions 1(ii) and (iii), and 2(ii) and (iii) are not satisfied. However, these assumptions can be easily modified and the Lemma and Theorem in Section 13.3.1 can be reformulated as in Anderson (1971, pp. 23-25, 572, 585) so that they are true and even when the time trends are present among the exogenous variables. Further, the results of the Lemma and the Theorem will continue to hold when lagged endogenous variables are included in the model, provided the lagged endogenous variables are independent of the disturbances and random coefficients.

The fixed coefficients version of the model was estimated by Rothenberg and Leenders (1964) and others. We present the G2SLSR and G2SLSRM estimates for the above random coefficients version of Klein's Model I in Table 13.1, along with the usual 2SLS estimates and also with standard errors or parameter estimates.

A comparison of the standard errors in columns 3 and 4 of Table 13.1 reveals that the conventional estimator of the variance of the 2SLS estimator may be an underestimator if the model above with random coefficients is true. Similarly, a comparison of the standard errors of 2SLS estimates in column 4 with those of G2SLSR estimates in column 5 shows that the G2SLSR estimator can be more efficient than the 2SLS estimator. The G2SLSR and G2SLSRM estimates and their standard errors in columns 5 and 6 are identical for the consumption and labour equations because, in these cases, all estimates of the variances of random coefficients are positive. However, the G2SLSR and G2SLSRM estimates differ for the investment equation because the estimates of the variances of some random coefficients are negative. For this equation the G2SLSRM estimator appears to be less efficient than the G2SLSR estimator. This is somewhat surprising because in the Monte Carlo results published by Froehlich (1973a) the truncated estimators of coefficient variances are found to be preferable to untruncated estimators in terms of mean square error.

In order to provide a further quantitative comparison of the efficiency of alternative estimators considered we have estimated the asymptotic

TABLE 13.1: Alternative Estimates of the Fixed Coefficients and the Means of Random Coefficients in Klein's Model I: 1921-41

Eq.	Variables	Coefficient Estimates (Standard Errors) TSLS[a]	TSLS[b]	GTSLSR	GTSLSRM
C	P	0.0173 (0.1180)	0.0173 (0.1305)	0.0206 (0.1300)	0.0206 (0.1300)
	(W+W')	0.8102 (0.0402)	0.8102 (0.0447)	0.8125 (0.0447)	0.8125 (0.0447)
	Intercept	16.5548 (1.3208)	16.5548 (1.4563)	16.4780 (1.4561)	16.4780 (1.4561)
	P_{-1}	0.2162 (0.1073)	0.2162 (0.1192)	0.2115 (0.1184)	0.2115 (0.1184)
I	P	0.1502 (0.1732)	0.1502 (0.2707)	0.1251 (0.2233)	0.1403 (0.2764)
	Intercept	20.2782 (7.5427)	20.2782 (11.3435)	20.1388 (8.7280)	19.9946 (11.2188)
	P_{-1}	0.6159 (0.1628)	0.6159 (0.2555)	0.6422 (0.2104)	0.6246 (0.2590)
	K_{-1}	-0.1578 (0.0361)	-0.1578 (0.0546)	-0.1571 (0.0421)	-0.1562 (0.0539)
W	X	0.4389 (0.0356)	0.4389 (0.0371)	0.4288 (0.0317)	0.4288 (0.0317)
	Intercept	1.5003 (1.1478)	1.5003 (1.1527)	1.8343 (1.0413)	1.8343 (1.0413)
	X_{-1}	0.1467 (0.0388)	0.1467 (0.0380)	1.1528 (0.0334)	1.1528 (0.0334)
	(t-1931)	0.1304 (0.0291)	0.1304 (0.0323)	0.1324 (0.0314)	0.1324 (0.0314)

a The standard errors are computed from the matrix $\hat{\sigma}^2[Z_1'PZ_1]^{-1}$ where $\hat{\sigma}^2 = \frac{1}{T}(y_1-Z_1d_1)'(y_1-Z_1d_1)$.

b The standard errors are obtained from the matrix $[Z_1'PZ_1]^{-1}Z_1'P\hat{\Omega}_{11M}PA_1[Z_1'PZ_1]^{-1}$ where $\hat{\Omega}_{11M}$ is a modified estimator of Ω_{11} used in the G2SLSRM.

variance-covariance matrix of each of these estimators. The determinant and sum of all the elements of each of the estimated variance-covariance matrices for each equation are given in Table 13.2. Comparing these two measures of efficiency, given in columns 4 and 5 of Table 13.2, suggests that the 2SLS estimator can be less efficient than the G2SLSR estimator. A similar comparison of efficiencies between G2SLSR and G2SLSRM estimators in columns 5 and 6 suggests that the G2SLSR estimator can be more efficient than the G2SLSRM estimator.

13.4 LIMITED INFORMATION ESTIMATION WHEN ALL THE COEFFICIENTS ARE RANDOM

It was noted in Chapter 12 that when the system (13.1) has all of its coefficients random then the conditions for its identifiability are unknown. Thus the problem of estimation remains unsolved for this case. However, in some special cases like recursive systems or systems with no feedback among endogenous variables it was noted that the problem of identification reduces to that of classical cases. For such models the results of earlier sections can be applied.

13.5 FULL INFORMATION ESTIMATION OF BOTH FIXED AND RANDOM COEFFICIENTS

In the full information case we write all equations in a 'stacked' form and apply generalised least squares methods (after a transformation) to the system as a whole as in Zellner's 'Seemingly Unrelated Regression' model discussed in Chapter 11. Suppose we normalise the first equation with respect to y_1 the second with respect to y_2, etc. We can write the ith equation, corresponding to (13.88) as

TABLE 13.2: Variability Measures for Klein's Model I: 1921-41

Equations	Scalar measures for the Variance-Covariance Matrix	Methods of Estimation			
		TSLS[a]	TSLS[b]	GTSLSR	GTSLSRM
Consumption	Sum of All the Elements	1.6426	1.9990	2.0003	2.0003
	Determinant	3.2389×10^{-9}	7.2702×10^{-9}	7.2090×10^{-9}	7.2090×10^{-9}
Investment	Sum of All the Elements	56.0668	126.8102	75.0810	124.0147
	Determinant	6.0667×10^{-9}	2.1554×10^{-7}	3.6886×10^{-8}	2.2126×10^{-7}
Labour	Sum of All the Elements	1.3051	1.2932	1.0552	1.0552
	Determinant	6.6761×10^{-12}	1.1142×10^{-11}	6.1459×10^{-12}	6.1459×10^{-12}

a See footnote a in Table 13.1.
b See footnote b in Table 13.1.

$$(13.109)\quad y_i = Y_i\gamma_i + X_i\beta_i + \varepsilon_i = Z_i\delta_i + \varepsilon_i, \qquad i=1,\ldots,M,$$

where Y_i is a $T\times m_i$ matrix of observations on m_i right-hand jointly dependent variables, X_i is a $T\times K_i$ matrix of observations on K_i predetermined variables, $Z_i = [Y_i X_i]$ and $\delta_i = [\beta_i \gamma_i]'$. Further, the tth element of $T\times 1$ vector ε_i is $X_{it}u_{.it}$ such that, by using Assumption 7 in 12.2,

$$(13.110)\quad E\varepsilon_i = 0 \text{ and } E\varepsilon_i\varepsilon_i' = X_{it}\Sigma_{ii'}X_{i't}' = \Omega_{ii'},$$

where,

$$(13.111)\quad \Sigma_{ii'} = \begin{bmatrix} \sigma_{11,ii'} & \cdots & 0 \\ \vdots & \ddots & \\ 0 & & \sigma_{K_iK_i,ii'} \end{bmatrix}$$

for $i, i'=1,\ldots,M$. Note that we assume for simplicity that each equation has the same number of predetermined variables K_i. As discussed in Chapter 11, the analysis can be extended to the case where $K_i \neq K_{i'}$.

The system of equations (13.109) can be written in a more compact form as

$$(13.112)\quad y = Z\delta + \varepsilon,$$

where

$$y = \begin{bmatrix} y_1 \\ \vdots \\ y_M \end{bmatrix}, \quad \varepsilon = \begin{bmatrix} \varepsilon_1 \\ \vdots \\ \varepsilon_M \end{bmatrix}, \quad \delta = \begin{bmatrix} \delta_1 \\ \vdots \\ \delta_M \end{bmatrix} \text{ and } Z = \begin{bmatrix} Z_1 & \cdots & 0 \\ \vdots & \ddots & \\ 0 & & Z_M \end{bmatrix}$$

are respectively MTx1, MTx1, MKx1 ($K=\sum_{i=1}^{M} K_i$) and $MTx(\sum_{i=1}^{M} m_i+K)$. Further, $E\varepsilon=0$ and

$$E\varepsilon\varepsilon'=\Omega=\begin{bmatrix}\Omega_{11} & \cdots & \Omega_{1M}\\ \vdots & & \\ \Omega_{M1} & \cdots & \Omega_{MM}\end{bmatrix}.$$

As was done in the case of single equation (13.91), we can transform (13.112) as

$$(13.113)\quad X^{*\prime}\Omega^{-1}y= X^{*\prime}\Omega^{-1}Z\delta+X^{*\prime}\Omega^{-1}\varepsilon, \qquad X^{*}= I\otimes X,$$

where $EX^{*\prime}\Omega^{-1}\varepsilon=0$, $E(X^{*\prime}\Omega^{-1}\varepsilon\varepsilon'\Omega^{-1}X^{*})= X^{*\prime}\Omega^{-1}X^{*}$ and $\otimes$ represents Knonecker matrix product.

Now we can apply the GLS estimation method in (13.113) to obtain

$$\hat{\delta}= (Z'R^{*}Z)^{-1}Z'R^{*}y,$$

where

$$R^{*}= \Omega^{-1}X^{*}(X^{*\prime}\Omega^{-1}X^{*})^{-1}X^{*\prime}\Omega^{-1}$$
$$= \Omega^{-1}(I\otimes X)[(I\otimes X')\Omega^{-1}(I\otimes X)]^{-1}(I\otimes X')\Omega^{-1}.$$

We can call this estimator the generalised three stage least squares random estimator (G3SLSR).

In this case when all the coefficients of predetermined variables (except intercept) are also nonstochastic as considered in Section 13.2, the Ω matrix reduces to

$$\Omega=\begin{bmatrix}\sigma_{11,11}I & \cdots & \sigma_{11,1M}I\\ \vdots & & \\ \sigma_{11,M1}I & \cdots & \sigma_{11,MM}I\end{bmatrix}= \Sigma\otimes I,$$

where Σ is a matrix of elements $\sigma_{11,ii'}$ for $i,i'=1,\ldots,M$. Then

$$R^* = (\Sigma^{-1}\otimes I)(I\otimes X)[(I\otimes X')(\Sigma^{-1}\otimes I)(I\otimes X)]^{-1}$$

$$(I\otimes X')(\Sigma^{-1}\otimes I)$$

$$= (\Sigma^{-1}\otimes X)[\Sigma^{-1}\otimes X'X]^{-1}(\Sigma^{-1}\otimes X')$$

$$= (\Sigma^{-1}\otimes X)[\Sigma\otimes(X'X)^{-1}](\Sigma^{-1}\otimes X')$$

$$= \Sigma^{-1}\otimes X(X'X)^{-1}X'.$$ [5]

Substituting this in $\hat{\delta}$, the G3SLSR becomes the 3SLS estimator.

The estimator $\hat{\delta}$ is consistent and distributed as asymptotic normal with the mean vector δ and covariance matrix $(Z'R^*Z)^{-1}$. In practice $\hat{\delta}$ is not operational since it depends on the unknown matrix Ω. However, one can estimate the elements of the Ω matrix by using the methods discussed in Chapter 11. In that case we can get $\tilde{\delta}= (Z'R^*Z)^{-1}Z'R^*y$.

NOTES

1. This is commonly known as the generalised matrix inverse and denoted by A^+. This is determined for any mxn matrix A by the following four properties: (i) $A A^+ A= A$; (ii) $A^+ A A^+ = A^+$; (iii) $(A A^+)'= A A^+$; and (iv) $(A^+ A)'= A^+ A$. The generalised inverse matrix A is then of order nxm. Some useful properties of the generalised inverse are: (i) There is a unique generalised inverse; (ii) The generalised inverse of A' is A^+; (iii) If A is symmetric and idempotent (i.e. $A'= A$, A is square and $A A= A$), then $A^+= A$; (iv) If A is nonsingular then $A^{-1}= A^+$; and (v) If A is of rank m then $A^+ = (A'A)^{-1} A'$ such that $A^+ A= I$. Alternatively, if A is of rank n, then $A^+ = (A'A)^{-1}A'$ such that $A^+ A = I$. For a further discussion see Theil (1971), pp. 268-274; and Dhrymes (1978), pp. 501-507.

2. See Klein (1955) and Basmann (1957).

3. Mariano (1972) has shown that the moment matrix of the 2SLS estimator exists if $L \geq 2$ or $K_1^* \geq m_1+2$. Also see Sawa (1972).

4. See Raj, Srivastava and Ullah (1980).

5. See Theil (1971), pp. 303-306 and Footnote 2 in Chapter 6.

Appendix A

A.1 LINEAR REGRESSION

An estimator of a parameter is usually regarded as a random variable with a certain distribution. Thus the properties of the estimator can be discussed in terms of usual theory of probability distributions.

Consider a triplet notation $(y, X\beta, \sigma^2 I)$ for the usual regression model. Depending on the context, we usually assume that y is a multivariate normal variable with mean

$$(A.1) \qquad E(y) = X\beta$$

and variance-covariance matrix

$$(A.2) \qquad V(y) = E[y-E(y)][y-E(y)]' = \sigma^2 I,$$

where X is an nxK matrix of observations on the explanatory variables and the regression coefficient vector β is of order Kx1. The 'ordinary least squares (OLS) principle' minimises the sum of squared deviation of y's from their expected value, that is $[y-E(y)]'[y-E(y)]$. The OLS estimator b in (A.1) is

$$(A.3) \qquad b = (X'X)^{-1}X'y.$$

Clearly, the OLS estimator b is a linear transformation of an n-variate normal variable y. A known fact is that linear transformations on normal variables are also normal. Hence the ith element b_i of b is normally distributed with mean β_i, which is the ith element of the vector β. The variance of b_i is

$$(A.4) \qquad V(b\ ) = \sigma^2 (X'X)_i^{-1},$$

where $(X_i'X_i)^{-1}$ represents the ith diagonal element, i=1,2,..,K, of the matrix $(X'X)^{-1}$. The estimator b_i is only one of several probable realisations of a random variable, which is centred near the true unknown parameter β_i. Also the vector b is multivariate normal with mean vector β and variance-covariance matrix $\sigma^2(X'X)^{-1}$.

A.2 SMALL SAMPLE PROPERTIES OF ESTIMATORS

(a) Univariate Concepts

A.2.1 Definition: Univariate Unbiasedness

An estimator b_i of β_i is said to be unbiased if its expected value coincides with the true unknown parameter β_i, that is $E(b_i) = \beta_i$.

If $E(b_i) \neq \beta_i$ then b_i is a biased estimator and the magnitude of bias b_i is equal to $E(b_i) - \beta_i$.

A.2.2 Definition: Univariate Efficiency

One unbiased estimator is said to be more efficient than another if its variance is smaller than the variance of the other. For example, consider two unbiased estimators b_{i1} and b_{i2} of β_i satisfying $E(b_{1i}) = E(b_{i2}) = \beta_i$. Further, let

$$(A.5) \qquad V(b_{i1}) = E(b_{i1} - Eb_{i1})^2 = E(b_{i1} - \beta_i)^2,$$

$$V(b_{i2}) = E(b_{i2} - \beta_i)^2;$$

then the estimator b_{i1} is more efficient than b_{i2} if $V(b_{i1}) < V(b_{i2})$. When $V(b_{i1}) = V(b_{i2})$ then both estimators are equally efficient.

The concept of efficiency is simpler when we consider only unbiased estimators since we need only compare the variances of unbiased estimators. However, for 'biased' estimators comparing variances alone would lead to erroneous conclusions. To understand this point clearly, consider an arbitrary estimator,

$$(A.6) \qquad b_i = 4,$$

where 4 is a known constant. Since the estimator (A.6) is a fixed constant and not a random variable, its variance is zero. Thus, $b_i = 4$ is the most efficient among all estimators given the definition of efficiency for unbiased estimators. We have clearly obtained an erroneous conclusion. The reason is that $b_i = 4$ is a biased estimator. An appropriate concept of efficiency for biased estimators is discussed later.

A.2.3 Definition: Univariate **Mean** Squared Error

Now suppose that b_i^* is a biased estimator of β_i, then its mean squared error (MSE) is defined as

(A.7) $$MSE(b_i^*) = E(b_i^* - \beta_i)^2 = E(b_i^* - Eb_i^* + Eb_i^* - \beta_i)^2$$
$$= E(b_i^* - Eb_i^*)^2 + [E(b_i^*) - \beta_i]^2$$
$$+ 2E(b_i^* - Eb_i^*)(Eb_i^* - \beta_i).$$

Now since the third term is zero because $E(b_i^* - Eb_i^*) = 0$, we get

(A.8) $$MSE(b_i^*) = V(b_i^*) + [Bias\ (b_i^*)]^2,$$

where

(A.9) $$Bias(b_i^*) = Eb_i^* - \beta_i.$$

A.2.4 Definition: Univariate MSE Efficiency

Suppose b_{i1}^* and b_{i2}^* are two biased estimators of β_i, then b_{i1}^* is said to be more efficient than b_{i2}^* if $MSE(b_{i1}^*) < MSE(b_{i2}^*)$.

b) Multivariate Concepts

A.2.5 Definition: Multivariate Unbiasedness

A vector estimator b of a Kx1 parameter vector β is said to be unbiased if $E(b) = \beta$.

A.2.6 Definition: Multivariate Efficiency

If the two unbiased vector estimators b_1 and b_2 of a Kx1 vector β have variance-covariance matrices V_1 and V_2 respectively, then b_1 is more efficient than b_2 if $V_2 - V_1$ is a positive semidefinite matrix.

A.2.7 Definition: Moment Matrix

Denote the MSE of a biased estimator b^* of β by $MSE(b^*)$ which is defined as

$$(A.10)\quad MSE(b^*) = E(b^*-\beta)(b^*-\beta)'$$

$$= E(b^*-Eb^*+Eb^*-\beta)(b^*-Eb^*+Eb^*-\beta)'$$

$$= E(b^*-Eb^*)(b^*-Eb^*)'+(Eb^*-\beta)(Eb^*-\beta)'$$

$$= V(b^*)+[\text{Bias }(b^*)]\,[\text{Bias }(b^*)]'.$$

In the statistical decision theory $E(b^*-\beta)'(b^*-\beta)$ is known as expected squared loss function or risk function.

A.2.8 Gauss-Markov Theorem: b is BLUE of β

The Gauss-Markov theorem states that the OLS estimator b, which is linear and unbiased, is more efficient than any other estimator which is both linear and unbiased. In other words, b is 'best' in the class of 'linear unbiased estimators' (BLUE).

Proof: Consider any estimator linear in y, say $\tilde{\beta}=Cy$. Let $C= (X'X)^{-1}X'+Z$ where Z is any nonstochastic matrix. Then using the fact that $E(y)= X\beta$ we write

$$(A.11)\quad E(\tilde{\beta}) = E[(X'X)^{-1}X'+Z][X\beta]$$

$$= \beta+ZX,$$

so that for $\tilde{\beta}$ to be unbiased we require $ZX=0$. Under this condition, moment matrix of $\tilde{\beta}$ is equal to its variance-covariance matrix, which is given below:

$$(A.12)\quad E(\tilde{\beta}-\beta)(\tilde{\beta}-\beta)' = MSE(\tilde{\beta})$$

$$= E[(X'X)^{-1}X'+Z]yy'[(X'X)^{-1}X'+Z]'$$

$$=\sigma^2[(X'X)^{-1}X'IX(X'X)^{-1}+ZIX(X'X)^{-1}$$

$$+(X'X)^{-1}X'IZ'+ZIZ']$$

$$= \sigma^2(X'X)^{-1}+\sigma^2 ZZ'.$$

But ZZ' is a positive semidefinite matrix, which proves that the variance-covariance matrix of $\tilde{\beta}$ equals the variance-covariance matxrix of b plus a positive semidefinite matrix. Hence the OLS estimator is most efficient or best among all linear unbiased estimators of β.

Finally, we note that the Gauss-Markov theorem implies that any linear combinations of b, that is Lb are BLUE for the linear combinations $L\beta$, where L is a 1xK vector of fixed constants.

A.2.9 Multivariate MSE Efficiency

Consider two competing estimators b_1^* and b^*_2. Then, b_1^* is more efficient than b_2^* if the difference ∇= $MSE(b_2^*)-MSE(b_1^*)$ is positive definite. Further, to check up positive definiteness of the difference ∇ it is easier in practice to verify whether the scalar $\eta'\nabla\eta>0$ for all $\eta\neq 0$, where η is any nonzero column vector. If $\eta'\nabla\eta>0$ for all $\eta\neq 0$ is true, then it is implied that $MSE(\eta'b_2^*)>MSE(\eta'b_1^*)$ for all η. On the other hand, if $MSE(\eta'b_2^*) > MSE(\eta'b_1^*)$ for all $\eta\neq 0$, then $\eta'\nabla\eta>0$.

Definition: Probability Limit (

ny arbitrary ε>0, lim

P[|b

Let b_i ... an ...

vations with mean $Eb_i^{(n)}$ and variance $V(b_i^{(n)}) = E[b_i^{(n)}-Eb_i^{(n)}]^2$. As n increases in value from n to n+1, n+2, n+3,..., etc., we obtain sequences of set $(b_i^{(n)}$, $Eb_i^{(n)}$ and $V(b_i^{(n)}))$.

A.3.1 Definition: Asymptotic Expectation

If for any ε there is an n_o such that $|Eb_i^{(n)}-\beta_i| < \varepsilon$ for all $n \geq n_o$ then β_i is an asymptotic expectation of $b_i^{(n)}$, which is written as

$$(A.13) \quad AE[b_i^{(n)}]= \beta_i.$$

A.3.2 Definition: Asymptotic Variance

Asymptotic variance of $b_i^{(n)}$ is defined as

$$(A.14) \quad AV[b_i^{(n)}]= AE[b_i^{(n)}- Eb_i^{(n)}]^2.$$

The AE and AV are summary statistics describing the distribution of $b_i^{(n)}$ as sample size increases. If $AV[b_i^{(n)}]=0$, then the distribution of $b_i^{(n)}$ is getting more and more concentrated around its mean as $n \to \infty$. An estimator $b_i^{(n)}$ of β_i satisfying both conditions $AE[b_i^{(n)}]=\beta_i$ and $AV[b_i^{(n)}]=0$ is intuitively desirable.

However, these are large sample properties and may be irrelevant in small samples.

A.3.3 D

If for a ... $n \to \infty$ P[| b_i ... $\beta_i| \geq \varepsilon]=0$,
then we write $\operatorname{plim}_{n \to \infty} b_i^{(n)} = \beta_i$.

A.3.4 Definition: Consistency

An estimator $b_i^{(n)}$ of β_i is said to be consistent if $\operatorname{plim}_{n \to \infty} b_i^{(n)} = \beta_i$. A multivariate estension is straightforward with vectors $b^{(n)}$ and β replacing the scalars $b_i^{(n)}$ and β_i.

A convenient check for consistency is $AE[b_i^{(n)}] = \beta_i$ and $AV[b_i^{(n)}] = 0$. For example the OLS estimator b is a consistent estimator of β because $AE(b) = \beta$ and $AV(b) = 0$. To prove this, we first note that $X'X$ is a positive definite (nonsingular) matrix. Also $\lim_{n \to \infty}(\frac{1}{n} X'X) = Q$ is a finite nonsingular matrix. Hence the inverse Q^{-1} is also finite. Thus, the $\lim_{n \to \infty} (X'X)^{-1}$ is equal to

$$\text{(A.15} \qquad \lim_{n \to \infty} \frac{n}{n}(X'X)^{-1} = \lim_{n \to \infty} \frac{1}{n}\left(\frac{X'X}{n}\right)^{-1}$$

$$= 0 \,.\, Q^{-1} = 0.$$

A.4 SOME MISCELLANEOUS CONCEPTS

A.4.1 Definition: Regular Density

A density $f(.,\beta)$ is regular with respect to its first derivative if

$$\left[\frac{\partial \log f(.,\beta)}{\partial \beta_i}\right] = 0 \qquad (i=1,2,\ldots).$$

A.4.2 Definition: Information Matrix

Let $y = (y_1 \ldots y_n)$ be a random sample from a population with density $f(.,\beta)$, which is regular with respect to its first two derivatives. Let the likelihood function be

$$L(y,\beta) = \sum_{i=1}^{n} f(y_i,\beta),$$

then the information matrix is defined as

$$I = -E\left[\frac{\partial^2 \log L(y,\beta)}{\partial\beta\ \partial\beta'}\right],$$

with the i,jth element given by

$$I_{ij} = -E\left[\frac{\partial^2 \log L(y,\beta)}{\partial\beta_i\ \partial\beta_j}\right].$$

A.5 MAXIMUM LIKELIHOOD ESTIMATOR

Consider a random sample $y_1,\ldots,y_n$ of n observations represented by a n-dimensional random variable y. Suppose a known probability distribution of y is $f(y)=f(y/\theta)$, which depends on some unknown parameters θ. For example, in a regression model, θ may refer to K+1 fixed parameters β and σ^2.

For fixed value of θ, $f(y/\theta)=f(y_1,\ldots,y_n/\theta)$ represents the joint density of n random outcomes. However, suppose a given set of n observations are available and we are searching for some possible values of θ, which might have generated the fixed set of n data values on the random variable y.

Then, for this purpose, an appropriate function to look at is the likelihood function $L(\theta/y)$ wherein the n data values of y are treated as fixed while the unknown parameters θ are treated as variable. The likelihood function has the same terms as $f(y/\theta)$, so that $L(\theta/y)=f(y/\theta)$. Further, in the case when y_i's are independent

$$(A.16) \qquad L(\theta/y)= f(y_1,\ldots,y_n/\theta)= \prod_{i=1}^{n} f(y_i/\theta),$$

where $f(y_i/\theta)$ is the density of the random variable y_i. Thus, the maximum likelihood estimator of θ can be obtained by maximising the likelihood function with respect to θ. According to the 'likelihood principle' the likelihood function contains all the data information about the unknown parameters.

Given the likelihood function, we can maximise it or equivalently maximise its log (which is a 'monotonic transformation' of the likelihood function) to determine the 'most likely' value of the unknown parameter for the given data. For this, calculus methods may be used to differentiate $L(\theta/y)$ with respect to θ and setting the derivative equal to zero. Thus, the first order condition for the likelihood function to be at its maximum is given by $\frac{\partial}{\partial\theta} L(\theta/y)=0$. The second order condition requires that the Hessian matrix of second derivatives is negative definite. The values of parameters θ which maximise the likelihood function are called the maximum likelihood estimators. We note that this procedure will give sensible results if the likelihood function is

Day, N.E. (1969), 'Estimating the Components of a Mixture of Normal Distributions', Biometrika, 56, 463-74.

Dent, W.T. and C. Hildreth (1977), 'Maximum Likelihood Estimation in Random Coefficient Models', Journal of the American Statistical Association, 72, 69-72.

Dhrymes, P.J. (1978), Introductory Econometrics. (Berlin-Heidelberg - New York: Springer-Verlag).

Duffy, W.J. (1969), 'Parameter Variation in a Quarterly Model of the Post-War U.S. Economy', unpublished PhD thesis, University of Pittsburg.

Duncan, D.B. and S.D. Horn (1972), 'Linear Dynamic Recursive Estimation from the viewpoint of Regression Analysis', Journal of the American Statistical Association, 67, 815-21.

Durbin, J. (1953), 'A Note on Regression When There is Extraneous Information About One of the Coefficients', Journal of the American Statistical Association, 48, 799-808.

——— (1970) 'Testing for Serial Correlation in Least-Squares Regression When Some of the Regressors are Lagged Dependent Variables', Econometrica, 38, 410-21.

Dwyer, P.S. (1967), 'Some Applications of Matrix Derivatives in Multivariate Analysis', Journal of the American Statistical Association, 62, 607-25.

Edwards, A.W.F. (1969), 'Statistical Methods in Scientific Inference', Nature, Land, 222, 1233-37.

Efron, B. and C. Morris (1971), 'Limiting the Risk of Bayes and Empirical Bayes Estimators, Part I: The Bayes Case', Journal of the American Statistical Association, 66, 807-15.

——— (1972), 'Limiting the Risk of Bayes and Empirical Bayes Estimators, Part II: The Empirical Bayes Case', Journal of the American Statistical Association, 67, 130-9.

Enns, P.G. (1978), 'Decision Theory in the Analysis of Varying Parameter Regression Models', Proceedings of the 1978 Annual Meeting, Business and Economic Statistics Sector, American Statistical Association, 446-49.

Farley, J.U. and M.J. Hirsch (1970), 'A Test for a Shifting Slope Coefficient in a Linear Model' Journal of the American Statistical Association, 65, 1320-29.

Fearn, T. (1975), 'A Bayesian Approach to Groth Curves', _Biometrica_, 62, 89-100.
Feige, E.L. (1964), _The Demand for Liquid Assets: A Temporal Cross-Section Analysis_ (Englewood Cliffs, New Jersey: Prentice-Hall).
_____ and P.A.V.B. Swamy (1974), 'A Random Coefficient Model of the Demand for Liquid Assets', _Journal of Money, Credit, and Banking_, 6, 241-52.
Fisher, F.M. (1966), _The Identification Problem in Econometrics_ (New York: McGraw-Hill Book Company).
Fisk, P.R. (1967), 'Models of the Second Kind in Regression Analysis', _Journal of the Royal Statistical Society_, Series B, 28, 266-81.
Friedman, M. (1957), _A Theory of the Consumption Function_ (Princeton: Princeton University Press).
Froehlich, B.R. (1971), 'Estimation for a Random Coefficient Regression Model', unpublished PhD thesis, University of Minnesota, Minneapolis.
_____ (1973a), 'Some Estimators for a Random Coefficient Regression Model', _Journal of the American Statistical Association_, 68, 329-35.
_____ (1973b), 'A Note on Some Monte Carlo Results on Non-negative Variance Estimators for a Random Coefficient Regression Model', _American Journal of Agricultural Economics_, 55, 231-34.
Fuller, W.A. and B.E. Battese (1973), 'Transformations for Estimation of Linear Models with Nested-Error Structure', _Journal of the American Statistical Association_, 68, 626-32.
_____ and _____ (1974), 'Estimation of Linear Models with Crossed-Error Structure', _Journal of Econometrics_, 2, 67-78.

Gallant, A.R. and W.A. Fuller (1973), 'Fitting Segmented Polynomial Regression Models Whose Join Points Have to be Estimated', _Journal of the American Statistical Association_, 68,-144-47.
Garbade, K. (1975), 'The Initialization Problem in Variable Parameter Regression', working paper 75-61, Graduate School of Business Administration, New York University.
_____ (1977), 'Two Methods for Examining the Stability of Regression Coefficients', _Journal of the American Statistical Association_, 72, 54-63.

Geary, R.C. (1966), 'A Note on Residual Heterovariance and Estimation Efficiency in Regression', *American Statistician*, 20, 30-31.

Gleiser, H. (1969), 'A New Test for Heteroscedasticity', *Journal of the American Statistical Association*, 64, 316-23.

Goldberger, A.S. (1962), 'Best Linear Unbiased Prediction in the Generalized Linear Regression Model', *Journal of the American Statistical Association*, 57, 369-75.

——— (1964), *Econometric Theory* (New York: John Wiley & Sons).

Goldfeld, S.M., H.H. Kelejian, and R.E. Quandt (1971), 'Least Squares and Maximum Likelihood Estimation of Switching Regressions', research memorandum no. 130, Econometric Research Program, Princeton University.

——— and R.E. Quandt (1965), 'Some Tests for Homoscedasticity', *Journal of the American Statistical Association*, 60, 539-47.

——— and ——— (1972), *Nonlinear Methods in Econometrics* (Amsterdam: North-Holland Publishing Co.), ch.9.

——— and ——— (1973a), 'A Markov Model for Switching Regressions', *Journal of Econometrics*, 1, 3-16.

——— and ——— (1973b), 'The Estimation of Structural Shifts by Switching Regressions', *Annals of Economic and Social Measurement*, 2, 475-85.

——— and ——— (1976), *Studies in Non-linear Estimation* (Cambridge, Massachusetts: Ballinger).

Gordon, D.F. and A. Hynes (1970), 'On the Theory of Price Dynamics', in E. Phelps (ed.), *Microeconomic Foundations of Employment and Inflation Theory* (New York: Norton), 369-93.

Gordon, R.J. (1972), 'Wage Price Controls and the Shifting Phillips Curve', *Brookings Papers on Economic Activity* 2, 385-430.

Graybill, F.A. (1961), *An Introduction to Linear Statistical Models*, vol. 1 (New York: McGraw-Hill Book Company).

Griffiths, W.E. (1971a), 'Estimation of Regression Coefficients which Change Over Time', unpublished PhD thesis, University of Illinois.

——— (1971b), 'Generalized Least Squares with an Estimated Covariance Matrix - A Sampling Experiment', paper presented at the Econometric Society Winter Meetings, New Orleans.

_____ (1972), 'Estimation of Actual Response Coefficients in the Hildreth-Houck Random Coefficient Model', Journal of the American Statistical Association, 67, 633-35.

_____ (1974), 'Combining Time Series Cross-Section Data: Alternative Models and Estimators', paper presented at Fourth Conference of Economists, Canberra.

_____, R.G. Dryman and S. Prakash (1979), 'Bayesian Estimation of a Random Coefficient Model', Journal of Econometrics, 10, 201-20.

Hammermesh, D.S. (1970), 'Wage Bargains, Threshold Effects and the Phillips Curve', Quarterly Journal of Economics, 84, 501-17.

Hartley, H.O. and J.N.K. Rao (1967), 'Maximum Likelihood Estimation for the Mixed Analysis of Variance Model', Biometrika, 54, 89-108.

Harvey, A.C. (1976), 'Estimating Regression Models with Multiplicative Heteroscedasticity', Econometrica, 44, 461-66.

_____ (1978), 'The Estimation of Time-Varying Parameters from Panel Data', Annales de L'Insee, 30-31, 203-26.

Havenner, A. and P.A.V.B. Swamy (1978), 'A Random Coefficient Approach to Seasonal Adjustment of Economic Time Series', special studies paper no. 124, Federal Reserve Board, Washington D.C.

Henderson, C.R., Jr. (1971), 'Comment on the Use of Error Components Model in Combining Cross Section with Time Series Data', Econometrica, 39, 397-401.

Hendricks, W., R. Koenker and D.J. Poirier (1979), 'Stochastic Parameter Models for Panel Data: An Application to the Connecticut Peak Load Pricing Experiment', International Economic Review, 20, 707-24.

Hildreth, C. and J.P. Houck (1968), 'Some Estimators for a Linear Model with Random Coefficients', Journal of the American Statistical Association, 63, 584-95.

Himmelblau, D.M. (1972), Applied Nonlinear Programming (New York: McGraw-Hill Book Co.).

Hinkley, D.V. (1969), 'Inference About the Intersection in Two-Phase Regression', Biometrika, 56, 495-504.

_____ (1971), 'Inference in Two-Phase Regression', Journal of the American Statistical Association, 66, 736-43.

Ho, Y.C. and R.C.K. Lee (1964), 'A Bayesian Approach to Problems in Stochastic Estimation and Control', IEEE Transactions on Automatic Control, AC-9, 333-39.

Hoch, I. (1962), 'Estimation of Production Function Parameters Combining Time-Series and Cross-Section Data', Econometrica, 30, 34-53.

Hoerl, A.E. and R.W. Kennard (1970a), 'Ridge Regression: Biased Estimation for Non-Orthogonal Problems', Technometrics, 12, 55-67.

______ and ______ (1970b), 'Ridge Regression: Applications to Non-Orthogonal Problems', Technometrics, 12, 69-82.

Hood, W.C., and T.C. Koopmans (eds.)(1953), Studies in Econometric Methods (New York: John Wiley & Sons).

Horn, S.D., R.A. Horn, and D.B. Duncan, (1975), 'Estimating Heteroscedastic Variances in Linear Models', Journal of the American Statistical Association, 70, 380-85.

Hsiao, C. (1972), 'The Combined Use of Cross-Section and Time-Series Data in Econometric Analysis', unpublished PhD thesis, Stanford University.

______ (1974), 'Statistical Inference for a Model with Both Random Cross-Sectional and Time Effects', International Review, 15, 12-30.

______ (1975), 'Some Estimation Methods for a Random Coefficient Model', Econometrica, 43, 305-25.

Hudson, D.J. (1966), 'Fitting Segmented Curves Whose Join Points Have to be Estimated', Journal of the American Statistical Association, 61, 1097-129.

Hurwicz, L. (1950), 'Systems with Nonadditive Disturbances', in T.C. Koopmans (ed.), Statistical Inference in Dynamic Economic Models (New York: John Wiley & Sons), 410-18.

Jeffreys, H. (1961), Theory of Probability, 3rd ed. (Oxford: Clarendon Press, 1961 and 1966.

Johnson, K.H. (1974), 'On Estimating Models with Random Coefficients', Proceedings of the 1974 Annual Meeting, Business and Economics Statistics Section, American Statistical Association, 420-25.

______ and H.L. Lyon (1973), 'Experimental Evidence on Combining Cross-Section and Time Series Information', Review of Economics and Statistics, 55, 465-74.

Johnson, L.W. (1974), 'The Linear Expenditure System with Random Marginal Budget Shares', presented at Eastern Economic Association Meeting, Albany.

__________ (1975), 'A Note on Testing for Intraregional Economic Homogeneity', Journal of Regional Science, 15, 365-69.

__________ (1976), 'The Small Sample Properties of Estimators in Random Parameter Regression Models: A Survey', research paper no. 119, School of Economic and Financial Studies, Macquarie University.

__________ (1977), 'Fixed vs. Random Coefficients in Econometric Research', presented at Sixth Conference of Economists, Economic Society of Australia and New Zealand, Hobart.

__________ (1977), 'Stochastic Parameter Regression: An Annotated Bibliography', International Statistical Review, 45, 257-72.

Johnson, S.R. and G.C. Rausser (1975), 'An Estimating Method for Models with Stochastic, Time Varying Parameters', Proceedings of the 1975 Annual Meeting, Business and Economic Statistics Section, American Statistical Association, 356-61.

Kadane, J.B. (1970), 'Testing Overidentifying Restrictions when the Disturbances are Small', Journal of the American Statistical Association, 65, 182-85.

__________ (1971), 'Comparison of K-Class Estimators when the Disturbances are Small', Econometrica, 39, 723-37.

Kakwani, N.C. (1967), 'The Unbiasedness of Zellner's Seemingly Unrelated Regression Equations Estimators', Journal of the American Statistical Association, 62, 141-2.

Kalman, R.E. (1960), 'A New Approach to Linear Filtering and Prediction Problems', transactions of ASME, Series D, Journal of Basic Engineering, 82, 35-45.

__________ and R.S. Bucy (1961), 'New Results in Linear Filtering and Prediction Theory', transaction of ASME, Series D, Journal of Basic Engineering, 83, 95-108.

Kashyap, R.L. (1970), 'Maximum Likelihood Identification of Stochastic Linear Systems', IEEE Transactions on Automatic Control, AC-15, 25-34

Kau, J.B. and C.F. Lee (1977), 'A Random Coefficient Model to Estimate a Stochastic Density Gradiant', Regional Science and Urban Economics, 7, 169-77.

Kelejian, H.H. (1974), 'Random Parameters in a Simultaneous Equation Framework: Identification and Estimation', Econometrica, 42, 517-27.

Kendall, M. and A. Stuart (1973), The Advanced Theory of Statistics, vol. 2, 3rd ed (New York: Hafner Publishing Co.).

Khan, M.S. (1974), 'The Stability of the Demand-for-Money Function in the United States 1901-1965', Journal of Political Economy, 82, 1205-19.

Khazzoom, J.D. (1976), 'An Indirect Least Squares Estimator for Overidentified Equations', Econometrica, 44, 741-50.

Kiefer, J. and J. Wolfowitz (1956), 'Consistency of the Maximum Likelihood Estimator in the Presence of Infinitely Many Nuisance Parameters', Annals of Mathematical Statistics, 27, 887-906.

Klein, L.R. (1950), Economic Fluctuations in the United States, 1921-1941 (New York: John Wiley & Sons).

——— (1953), A Textbook of Econometrics (Evanston: Row Peterson), 216-18.

——— (1955), 'On the Interpretation of Theil's Method of Estimating Economic Relationships', Metroeconomica, 7, 147-53.

——— and M.K. Evans (1967), The Wharton Econometric Forecasting Model (Philadelphia: Wharton School, University of Pennsylvania Press).

Kmenta, J. (1971), Elements of Econometrics (New York: Macmillan and Co.).

Knuth, D.E. (1968), Seminumerical Algorithms - The Art of Computer Programming, vol. 2 (Reading, Massachusetts: Addison-Wesley Publishing Company), 25-31, 103-05.

Kraft, J. and M. Rodekohr (1976), 'A Regional Analysis of the Demand for Gasoline Using a Random Coefficient Regression Approach', presented at Econometric Fall North American Meeting, Atlantic City.

Kuh, E. (1959), 'The Validity of Cross-Sectionally Estimated Behavioral Equations in Time Series Application', Econometrica, 27, 197-214.

La Motte, L.R. and A. McWhorter (1976), 'A Test for the Presence of Random Coefficients in a Linear Regression Model', Proceedings of the 1976 Annual Meeting, Business and Economic Statistics Section, American Statistical Association, 400-05.

Laumas, G.S. and Y.P. Mehra (1976), 'The Stability of the Demand for Money Function: The Evidence from Quarterly Data', _Review of Economics and Statistics_, 58, 464-68.

Lee, L. and W.E. Griffiths (1979), 'The Prior Likelihood and Best Linear Unbiased Prediction in Stochastic Coefficent Linear Models', unpublished manuscript, Department of Economics, University of Minnesota, Minneapolis.

Lemke, C.E. (1965), 'Bimatrix Equilibrium Points and Mathematical Programming', _Management Science_, 11, 681-89.

Lindley, D.V. (1971), _Bayesian Statistics, A Review_ (Philadelphia: SIAM).

____________ and A.F.M. Smith (1972), 'Bayes Estimates for the Linear Model', _Journal of the Royal Statistical Society_, Series B, 34, 1-41.

Liu, Lon-Mu, and G.C. Tiao (1980), 'Random Coefficients First-order Autoregressive Models', _Journal of Econometrics_, 13, 305-25.

Lucas, R.E., Jr. (1976), 'Econometric Policy Evaluation: A Critique', in Karl Brunner and Alan Meltzer (eds.), _The Phillips Curve and Labour Markets_, vol. 1, Carnegie-Rochester Conferences on Public Policy, _Journal of Monetary Economics_, Suppl., 19-46.

Maddala, G.S. (1971), 'The Use of Variance Components Models in Pooling Cross Section and Time Series Data', _Econometrica_, 39, 341-58.

____________ (1977), _Econometrics_ (New York: McGraw-Hill Book Co.), 390-404.

Mahajan, Y.L. (1974), 'Predictive Performance and Stability of Econometric Models', paper presented at the Western Economic Association, Las Vegas.

____________ (1977), 'Estimation of the Montetarist Model Using Varying Parameter Framework and its Implication', _Proceedings of the 1977 Annual Meeting_, Business and Economic Statistics Section, American Statistical Association, 595-99.

Mariano, R.S. (1972), 'The Existence of Moments of the Ordinary Least Squares and Two-Stage Least Squares Estimators', _Econometrica_, 40, 643-52.

____________ (1976), 'Estimation and Hypothesis Testing in Time-Varying Models', presented at Econometric Society Fall North American Meeting, Atlantic City.

McGee, V.E. and W.T. Carleton (1970), 'Piecewise Regression', Journal of the American Statistical Association, 65, 1109-24.
McWhorter, A. Jr., W.A. Spivey and W.J. Wrobleski (1973), 'Computer Simulation in Varying Parameter Regression Models', Proceedings of the 1973 Annual Meeting, Business and Economics Statistics Section, American Statistical Association, 497-502.
________, ______ and ______ (1974), 'Varying Parameter Econometric Models for Interrelated Time Series', Proceedings of the 1973 Annual Meeting, Business and Economics Statistics Section, American Statistical Association, 480-85.
________, ______ and ______ (1976), 'A Sensitivity Analysis of Varying Parameter Econometric Models', International Statistical Review, 44, 265-82.
________, G.V.L. Narasimham and R.R. Simonds (1977), 'An Empirical Examination of the Predictive Performance of an Econometric Model with Random Coefficients', International Statistical Institute, 45, 243-55.
Mehra, R.K. (1972), 'Approaches to Adaptive Filtering', IEEE Transactions on Automatic Control, AC-17, 693-98.
________ (1974), 'Identification in Control and Econometrics: Similarities and Differences', Annals of Economic and Social Measurement, 3, 21-47.
Mehta, J.S., G.V.L. Narasimham and P.A.V.B. Swamy (1978), 'Estimation of a Dynamic Demand Function for Gasoline with Different Schemes of Parameter Variation', Journal of Econometrics 7, 263-79.
Mullineaux, D. (1980), 'Inflation Expectations and, Money Growth in the United States', American Economic Review, 70, 149-61.
Mundlak, Y. (1961), 'Empirical Production Functions Free of Management Bias', Journal of Farm Economics, 43, 44-56.
________ (1963), 'Estimation of Production and Behavioral Functions from a Combination of Cross-Section and Time-Series Data', in Carl F. Crist, et al. (eds.), Measurement in Economics (Stanford: Stanford University Press).
________ (1978), 'On the Pooling of Time Series and Cross Section Data', Econometrica, 46, 69-85.
Muth, J.F. (1960), 'Optimal Properties of Exponentially Weighted Forecasts', Journal of the American Statistical Association, 55, 299-306.

Nagar, A.L. (1959), 'The Bias and Moment Matrix of the General K-Class Estimators of the Parameters in Simultaneous Equations', Econometrica, 27, 575-95.
Nelder, J.A. (1972), discussion of a paper by D.V. Lindley and A.F.M. Smith on Bayes Estimates, J.R. Statistical Society B, 34, 18-20.
Nerlove, M. (1965), Estimation and Identification of Cobb-Douglas Production Functions (Chicago Rand McNally & Co.), 34-5, 61-85.
_______ (1967), 'Experimental Evidence on the Estimation of Dynamic Economic Relations from a Time Series of Cross Sections', Economic Studies Quarterly, 18, 42-74.
_______ (1971), 'Further Evidence on the Estimation of Dynamic Economic Relations from a Time Series of Cross Section Data', Econometrica, 39, 359-82.
_______ (1971), 'A Note on Errors Components Models', Econometrica, 39, 383-96.

Ozkan, T. and M. Athans, (1975), 'Application of Kalman Filter to Parameter Estimation of Macroeconomic Models', presented at NBER Stochastic Control Conference, Cambridge, Mass.

Pagan, A.R. (1975), 'Varying Parameter Regression: Theory and Applications', unpublished mimeograph, Australian National University.
_______ (1980), 'Some Identification and Estimation Results for Regression Models with Stochastically Varying Coefficients', Journal of Econometrics, 13, 341-63.
_______ and K. Tanaka (1979), 'A Further Test for Assessing the Stability of Regression Coefficients', working paper no. 016, Australian National University.
Page, E.S. (1955), 'A Test for Change in a Parameter Occurring at an Unknown Point', Biometrika, 42, 523-27.
Parikh, A. and P.K. Trivedi (1979), 'Estimation of Returns to Inputs in Indian Agriculture', working paper no. 008, Australian National University.
_______ and B. Raj (1979), 'Variable Coefficients Approach to Wage-Price Behaviour in the United Kingdom', Applied Economics, 11, 389-403.
Park, R.E. (1966), 'Estimation with Heteroscedastic Error Terms', Econometrica, 34, 888.

Parzen, E. (1961), 'An Approach to Time Series Analysis', Annals of Mathematical Statistics, 32, 951-89.

Peers, H.W. (1971), 'Likelihood Ratio and Associated Test Criteria', Biometrika, 58, 577-87.

Perlman, M.D. (1972), 'On the Strong Consistency of Approximate Maximum Likelihood Estimators' Proceedings of the Sixth Berkeley Symposium on Mathematical Statistics and Probability, 1, (Berkeley and Los Angeles: California University Press), 263-81.

Pesaran, M.H. (1973), 'Exact Maximum Likelihood Estimation of a Regression Equation with a First-Order Moving-Average Error', The Review of Economic Studies, 40, 529-35.

Poirier, D.J., 'A Switching Simultaneous Equation Model of Physician Behaviour in Ontario', unpublished manuscript.

______ (1976), The Econometrics of Structural Change (Amsterdam: North-Holland Publishing Co.).

Porter, R.D. (1973), 'On the Use of Sample Survey Weights in the Linear Models', Annals of Economic and Social Measurement, 2, 141-58.

Quandt, R.E. (1958), 'The Estimation of the Parameters of a Linear Regression System Obeying Two Separate Regimes', Journal of the American Statistical Association, 53, 873-80.

______ (1960), 'Tests of the Hypothesis That a Linear Regression System Obeys Two Separate Regimes', Journal of the American Statistical Association, 55, 324-30.

______ (1972), 'A New Approach to Estimating Switching Regressions', Journal of the American Statistical Association, 67, 306-10.

______ and S. Goldfeld (1973), 'The Estimation of Structural Shifts by Switching Regressions', Annals of Economic and Social Measurement, 2, 475-86.

Raj, B. (1973), 'The Finite Sampling Properties of Several Estimators of the Linear Regression Model with Random Coefficients', unpublished PhD thesis, University of Western Ontario, London.

______ (1975), 'Linear Regression with Random Coefficients: The Finite Sample and Convergence Properties', Journal of the American Statistical Association, 70, 127-37.

——— and V.K. Srivastava (1979), 'Asymptotic Bounds of the Probability of Non-Positive Variance Estimators in the Random Coefficient Model', unpublished manuscript, Wilfrid Laurier University, Waterloo, Ontario.

———, ——— and A. Ullah (1980), 'Generalized Two Stage Least Squares Estimators for a Structural Equation with Both Fixed and Random Coefficients', *International Economic Review*, 21, 171-83.

———, ——— and S. Upadhyaya (1976), 'The Efficiency of Estimating a Stochastic Coefficient Regression Model', research report no. 76-12, Department of Economics, Wilfrid Laurier University, Waterloo, Ontario.

———, ——— and ——— (1980), 'The Efficiency of Estimating A Random Coefficient Model', *Journal of Econometrics*, 12, 285-99.

——— and H.D. Vinod (1980), 'Varying Coefficient Approach to Interregional Comparison of Production', unpublished manuscript, Wilfrid Laurier University, Waterloo, Ontario.

Rao, C.R. (1965), 'The Theory of Least Squares When the Parameters Are Stochastic and its Application to the Analysis of Growth Curves', *Biometrika*, 52, 447-58.

——— (1970), 'Estimation of Heteroscedastic Variances in Linear Models', *Journal of the American Statistical Association*, 65, 161-72.

——— (1971a), 'Minimum Variance Quadratic Unbiased Estimation of Variance Components', *Journal of Multivariate Analysis*, 1, 257-75.

——— (1971b), 'Unified Theory of Linear Estimation', *Sankhya*, Series A, 33, 371-94.

——— (1972), 'Estimation of Variance and Covariance Components in Linear Models', *Journal of the American Statistical Association*, 67, 112-15.

——— (1973), *Linear Statistical Inference and Its Applications*, 2nd ed (New York: John Wiley and Sons), 192-93.

——— and S.K. Mitra (1971), *Generalized Inverse of Matrices and its Applications* (New York: John Wiley & Sons).

Rao, J.N.K. and K. Subrahmaniam (1971), 'Combining Independent Estimators and Estimation in Linear Regression with Unequal Variances', *Biometrics*, 27, 971-90.

Rappoport, P.N. and N.J. Kniesner (1974), 'The Illusion of the Shifting Phillips Curve: A Model with Random Coefficients', *Proceedings of the 1974 Annual Meeting*, Business and Economics Statistics Section, American Statistical Association, 535-39.

Rausser, G.C. and P.S. Laumas (1976), 'The Stability of the Demand for Money in Canada', *Journal of Monetary Economics*, 3, 367-80.

Ravindran, A. (1972), 'Algorithm 431, A Computer Routine for Quadratic and Linear Programming Problems [H]', *Communications of the ACM*, 5, 818-20.

Reinsel, G. (1976a), 'Maximum Likelihood Estimation of Stochastic Linear Difference Equations with Autoregressive Moving Average Errors', technical report no. 112, Department of Statistics, Carnegie-Mellon University.

________ (1976b), 'Maximum Likelihood Estimation of Vector Autoregressive Moving Average Models', technical report no. 117, Department of Statistics, Carnegie-Mellon University.

________ (1979), 'A Note on the Estimation of the Adaptive Regression Model', *International Economic Review*, 20, 193-202.

Roll, R. (1972), 'Interest Rates on Monetary Assets and Commodities Price Index Changes', *Journal of Finance*, 27, 251-77.

Rosenberg, B. (1968), 'Varying-Parameter Estimation', unpublished PhD thesis, Department of Economics, Harvard University.

________ (1972), 'The Estimation of Stationary Stochastic Regression Parameters Re-examined', *Journal of the American Statistical Association*, 67, 650-54.

________ (1973a), 'Linear Regression with Randomly Dispersed Parameters', *Biometrika*, 60, 65-72.

________ (1973b), 'The Analysis of A Cross Section of Time Series by Stochastically Convergent Parameter Regression', *Annals of Economic and Social Measurement*, 2, 399-428

________ (1973c), 'A Survey of Stochastic Parameter Regression', *Annals of Economic and Social Measurement*, 2, 381-97.

________ and W. McKibben (1973), 'The Prediction of Systematic and Specific Risk in Common Stocks', *Journal of Financial and Quantitative Analysis*, 8, 317-33.

Rothenberg, T.J. (1971), 'Identification in Parametric Models', *Econometrica*, 39, 577-92.

________ and C. Leenders (1964), 'Efficient Estimation of Simultaneous Equation Systems', *Econometrica*, 32, 57-76.

Rubin, H. (1950), 'Note on Random Coefficients', in T.C. Koopmans (ed.) *Statistical Inference in Dynamic Models*, Cowles Commission monograph, 10, 419-21.

Rusteem, V. and J.H. Westcott (1976), 'Recursive Parameter Estimation Using Kalman Filter: An Application to Analyze Time Varying Model Parameters and Structural Change', presented at Econometric Society European Meeting, Helsinki.

Rutemiller, H.C. and D.A. Bowers (1968), 'Estimation in a Heteroscedastic Regression Model', Journal of the American Statistical Association, 63, 552-57.

Sage, A.P. and J.L. Melsa (1971), Estimation Theory With Applications to Communications and Control (New York: McGraw Hill Book Co.).

Sant, D.T. (1977), 'Generalized Least Squares Applied to Time Varying Parameter Models', Annals of Economic and Social Measurement, 3, 301-11.

Sargent, T.J. (1976), 'The Observation Equivalance of Natural and Unnatural Rate Theories of Macro-economics', Journal of Political Economy, 84, 631-40.

Sarris, A. (1973), 'A Bayesian Approach to Estimation of Time Varying Regression Coefficients', Annals of Economic and Social Measurement, 2, 501-23.

________ (1974), 'A General Algorithm for Simultaneous Estimation of Constant and Randomly-Varying Parameters in Linear Regressions', working paper no. 38, National Bureau of Economics Research, Cambridge, Massachusetts.

Sawa, T. (1972), 'Finite Sample Properties of the K-class Estimators', Econometrica, 40, 653-80

Schaefer, S., R. Brealey, S. Hodges, and H. Thomas (1975), 'Alternative Models of Systematic Risk', in E.J. Elton and M.J. Gruber (eds.) International Capital Markets (Amsterdam: North-Holland Publishing Co.), 150-61.

Schmalensee, R. (1972), 'Variance Estimation in a Random Coefficient Regression Model', discussion paper 72-10, Department of Economics, University of California, San Diego.

Schulman, J. (1973), 'A Varying Parameter Regression Study of the Trade-off Between Inflation and Unemployment', unpublished PhD thesis, University of Michigan, Ann Arbor.

Sclove, S.L. (1973), 'Least Squares Problems with Random Coefficents', technical report no. 87, Institute of Mathematical Studies in the Social Sciences, Stanford University.

Searle, S.R. (1971), 'Topics in Variance Components Estimation', Biometrics, 27, 1-76.

Sharpe, W.F. (1964), 'Capital Asset Prices: A Theory of Market Equilibrium Under Conditions of Risk', Journal of Finance, 19, 425-42.

______ (1970), Portfolio Theory and Capital Markets (New York: McGraw Hill Book Co.).

Shiller, R.J. (1973), 'A Distributed Lag Estimator Derived from Smoothness Priors', Econometrica 41, 775-88.

Silvey, S.D. (1959), 'The Lagrangian Multiplier Test', Annals of Mathematical Statistics, 30, 389-407.

Sims, C. (1971), 'Discrete Approximation to Continuous Time Distributed Lags in Econometrics', Econometrica, 39, 545-64.

Singh, B., A.L. Nagar, N.K. Choudhry, and B. Raj (1976), 'On the Estimation of Structural Change: A Generalization of the Random Coefficients Regression Model', International Economic Review, 17, 340-61.

______ and P. Vashishtha (1974), 'Mechanization and Technological Progress in Indian Agriculture--A Farm Level Production Function Analysis', working paper no. 132, Delhi School of Economics.

______ and A. Ullah (1974), 'Estimation of the Seemingly Unrelated Regression with Random Coefficients', Journal of the American Statistical Association, 69, 191-95.

Smith, G. and F. Campbell (1980), 'A Critique of Some Ridge Regression Methods', (invited paper), Journal of the American Statistical Association, 75, 74-80. Also comments, 81-100.

Styan, George P.H. (1973), 'Hadamard Products and Multivariate Statistical Analysis', Linear Algebra and Its Applications, 6, 217-40.

Suits, D. et al.(1978), 'Spline Functions Fitted by Standard Regression Models', Review of Economics and Statistics, 50, 132-39.

Sunder, S. (1973), An Empirical Study of Stock Prices and Risk as They Relate to Accounting Changes in Inventory Valuation Methods, unpublished PhD thesis, Carnegie-Mellon University.

______ (1975), 'Stock Price and Risk Related to Accounting Changes in Inventory Valuation', The Accounting Review, 50, 305-15.

Swamy, P.A.V.B. (1968), "Statistical Inference in Random Coefficient Regression Models', unpublished PhD thesis, University of Wisconsin.

______ (1970), 'Efficient Inference in a Random Coefficient Regression Model', Econometrica, 38, 311-23.

——— (1971), Statistical Inference in Random Coefficient Regression Models (Berlin-Heidelberg-New York: Springer-Verlag).

——— (1973), 'Criteria, Constraints, and Multicollinearity in Random Coefficient Regression Models', Annals of Economic and Social Measurement, 2, 429-50.

——— (1974), 'Linear Models with Random Coefficients', in Paul Zarembka (ed.) Frontiers of Econometrics (New York: Academic Press), 143-68.

——— (1976), 'Linear Prediction and Estimation Methods for Regression with Stationary Stochastic Coefficients', special studies paper 78, Board of Governors of the Federal Reserve System, Washington, D.C.

——— and S.S. Arora (1972), 'The Exact Finite Sample Properties of the Estimators of Coefficients in the Error Components Regression Models', Econometrica, 40, 261-76.

——— and J. Holmes (1971), 'The Use of Undersize Samples in Estimation of Simultaneous Equation Systems', Econometrica, 39, 455-59.

——— and J.S. Mehta (1973), 'Bayesian Analysis of Error Components Regression Models', Journal of the American Statistical Association, 68, 648-58.

——— and ——— (1975), 'Bayesian and Non-Bayesian Analysis of Switching Regressions and of Random Coefficient Regression Models', Journal of the American Statistical Association, 70, 593-602.

——— and ——— (1977), 'Estimation of Linear Models with Time and Cross-Sectionally Varying Coefficients', Journal of the American Statistical Association, 72, 890-98.

———, ——— and P.N. Rappoport (1978), 'Two Methods of Evaluating Hoerl and Kennard's Ridge Regression', Communication in Statistics, A7, 12, 1133-55.

——— and P.A. Tinsley (1980), 'Linear Prediction and Estimation Methods for Regression Models with Stationary Stochastic Coefficients', Journal of Econometrics, 12, 103-42.

Tanaka, K. (1979), 'Analysis of Time Varying Parameter Models', unpublished PhD thesis, Australian National University.

Telser, L. (1964), 'Iterative Estimation of a Set of Linear Regression Equations', Journal of the American Statistical Association, 59, 845-62.

Terasvirta, T. (1976), 'A Note on Bias in the Almon Distributed Lag Estimator', Econometrica, 44, 1317-22.
Theil, H. (1954), Linear Aggregation of Economic Relations (Amsterdam: North-Holland Publishing Co.).
________ (1961), Economic Forecasts and Policy, 2nd ed (first edition 1958) (Amsterdam: North-Holland Publishing Co.)
________ (1968), 'Consistent Aggregation of Micromodels with Random Coefficients', report 6816, Center for Mathematical Studies in Business and Economics, University of Chicago.
________ (1971), Principles of Econometrics (New York: John Wiley & Sons), 570-73, 580-87, 622-28.
________ and A.S. Goldberger (1961), 'On Pure and Mixed Statistical Estimation in Economics', International Economic Review, 2, 65-78.
________ and L.B.M. Mennes (1959), 'Multiplicative Randomness in Time Series Regression Analysis', report 5901, Econometric Institute of the Netherlands School of Economics, Rotterdam.
Tiao, G.C. and A. Zellner (1964), 'Bayes's Theorem and the Use of Prior Knowledge in Regression Analysis', Biometrika, 44, 315-27.
Tinsley, P.A. (1967), 'An Application of Variable Weight Distributed Lags', Journal of the American Statistical Association, 62, 1277-89.
Tintner, G. (1952), Econometrics (New York: John Wiley & Sons).
Trivedi, P.K. (1980), 'Small Samples and Collateral Information: An Application of the Hyper-Parameter Model', Journal of Econometrics, 12, 301-18.

Ullah, A. and B. Raj (1979), 'A Distributed Lag Estimator Derived From Shiller's Smoothness Priors: An Extension', Economics Letters, 2, 219-23.
________ and ______ (1980), 'A Polynomial Distributed Lag Model with Stochastic Coefficients' forthcoming in Empirical Economics.

Vinod, H.D. (1978), 'A Survey of Ridge Regression and Related Techniques for Improvements over Ordinary Least Squares', Review of Economics and Statistics, 60, 121-31.
________ and A. Ullah (1980), Recent Advances in Regression Methods, forthcoming (New York: Marcel Dekkar).

___________ and B. Raj (1978), 'Bell System Economies Estimated from a Randomly Varying Parameter Model', Proceedings of the 1978 Annual Meeting, Business and Economic Statistics Section, American Statistical Association, 596-99.

Wald, A. (1947), 'A Note on Regression Analysis', Annals of Mathematical Statistics, 18, 586-89.

Wall, K. and T.F. Cooley (1975), 'On the Identification of Time-Varying Structures', paper presented at NBER Stochastic Control Conference, Cambridge, Mass.

Wallace, T.D. and A. Hussain (1969), 'The Use of Error Components Models in Combining Cross Section with Time Series Data', Econometrica, 3, 55-72.

Wilton, D.A. (1972), 'Structural Shift with an Inter-structural Transition Function', discussion paper no. 92, Institute for Economic Research, Queen's University.

Winkler, R.L. (1967), 'The Assessment of Prior Distributions in Bayesian Analysis', Journal of the American Statistical Association, 62, 776-800.

___________ (1975) 'Varying Parameters: A Bayesian Approach', paper presented at the tenth NBER-NSF Seminar on Bayesian Inference in Econometrics, Chicago.

Wright, R.L. (1977), 'Analysis of Stock Repurchases with a Random Coefficient Regression Model', Proceedings of the 1977 Annual Meeting, Business and Economic Statistics Section, American Statistical Association, 345-48.

Young, P. (1974), 'Recursive Approaches to Time Series Analysis', Bulletin of the Institute of Mathematics and its Applications, May-June, 209-24.

Zarley, C. (1975), 'Statistical Estimations in a Random Coefficient Errors in Variables Model', unpublished PhD thesis, University of Kansas.

Zellner, A. (1926a), 'An Efficient Method of Estimating Seemingly Unrelated Relations and Tests for Aggregation Bias', Journal of the American Statistical Association, 57, 348-67.

___________ (1962b), 'Estimation of Cross-Section Relations: Analysis of a Common Specification Error', Metroeconomica, 14, 111-17.

______ (1963), 'Estimators of Seemingly Unrelated Regressions: Some Exact Finite Sample Results', Journal of the American Statistical Association, 58, 977-92.

______ (1966), 'On the Aggregation Problem: A New Approach to a Troublesome Problem', report #6628, Center of Mathematical Studies in Business and Economics, University of Chicago, in K.A. Fox, et al. (eds.), Economic Models, Estimation and Risk Programming: Essays in Honour of Gerhard Tintner (Berlin-Heidelberg-New York: Springer-Verlag, 1969).

______ (1970), 'The Bayesian Approach and Alternatives to Econometrics - I', in M.D. Intriligator (ed.), Frontiers of Quantitative Economics (Amsterdam: North-Holland Publishing Co.).

______ (1971), An Introduction to Bayesian Inference in Econometrics (New York: John Wiley & Sons).

______ (1975), 'Time Series Analysis and Econometric Model Construction', in R.P. Gupta (ed.), Applied Statistics (New York: North-Holland Publishing Co.).

______ J. Kmenta and J. Dreze (1966), 'Specification and Estimation of Cobb-Douglas Production Models', Econometrica, 34, 784-95.

______ and F. Palm (1974), 'Time Series and Structural Analysis of Monetary Models of the U.S. Economy', unpublished manuscript, H.G.B. Alexander Research Foundation, Graduate School of Business, University of Chicago.

______ and H. Theil (1962), 'Three-Stage Least Squares: Simultaneous Estimation of Simultaneous Equations', Econometrica, 30, 54-78.

Authors Index